Birth Pattern Psychology

Birth Pattern Psychology

Personality Assessment Through the Birth Chart

Tamise Van Pelt

Para Research
Gloucester
Massachusetts

With love and respect
to the memory of
Joseph Van Pelt,
who encouraged me to think for myself;
and to Gayle Van Pelt,
who taught me to read
and to love books

Birth Pattern Psychology
by Tamise Van Pelt

The author gratefully acknowledges the following publishers and authors
for permission to cite copyrighted material:
    W.B. Saunders Company and Theodore Millon, editor for *Theories
of Psychopathology and Personality,* Second Edition, copyright © 1973.
    W.W. Norton and Co. and Erik Erikson, *Childhood and Society,*
Second Edition, copyright © 1963.
    Fleming H. Revell Company and Ray Hoekstra, *Will You Die For
Me?,* copyright © 1978.
    Anchor Books and June Singer, *Boundaries of the Soul,* copyright
© 1973.
    Julian Press, a division of Crown Publishers, Inc. and Frederick
Perls, Ralph F. Hefferline and Paul Goodman, *Gestalt Therapy,*
copyright © 1951, 1979.
    Science and Behavior Books and Virginia Satir, *Peoplemaking,*
copyright © 1972.

Library of Congress Card Number: 83-063066
International Standard Book Number: 0-914918-33-8

Typeset in 10 pt. English Times on Compugraphic MCS/8400
Printed by Alpine Press on
55-pound SRTII Paper
Edited by Marah Ren
Cover design by Ralph Poness and Todd Sweet
Graphics by Todd Sweet
Typeset by Camilla Ayers and Patrice LeBlanc

Published by Para Research, Inc.
85 Eastern Avenue
Gloucester, Massachusetts 01930

Manufactured in the United States of America

First Printing, March 1985, 5,000 copies

Contents

Preface

Birth Pattern Psychology presents personality measurements simply and clearly for those unfamiliar with personality theory or assessment. The book's informal, concrete style gives the reader a feeling for theoretical principles in action. This preface is for those readers specifically interested in the research methods and measurement theory on which Birth Pattern Psychology is based.

The basic research assumptions are:

1. Birth measurements measure core personality factors.

2. The most basic personality factor is the need.

3. The basic need, if it is to be considered a building block of personality, must be common to all people.

4. The theoretical framework of two dimensions yielding four distinct measurable factors, a popular psychological conceptual structure, suggests the possibility that the core needs might be four in number.

5. If four need themes do indeed exist, and if the birth pattern measures these needs, the measurement base requires a fourfold ground weighted by variables.

Sharon S. and Jack W. Brehm (*Psychological Reactance, A Theory of Freedom and Control,* New York: Academic Press, Inc., 1981) note that all theories begin with assumptions so that the game of empirical testing can begin. The truth or falsehood of the assumptions is far less significant than the outcome of the theoretical enterprise. Without the assumption, in this case, that birth measurements measure core personality factors, there can be no exploration of the remaining theories. The assumption that personality has its roots in human needs leads directly to those established personality theories based on fulfillment and actualization.

The actual research generated three distinct measurement factors: needs, traits characteristic of general life orientation, and behaviors. After establishing these factors, I found support for their theoretical existence in

Maddi's overview of personality theories and Millon's theoretical base for his assessment of personality disorders.

Salvatore R. Maddi (*Personality Theories, A Comparative Analysis,* Homewood, Illinois: The Dorsey Press, 1972 Revised Edition) presents the empirical analyses of existing core personality factors and peripheral factors as well. Maddi notes that empirical findings never contradict the actualization and perfection versions of the fulfillment model of personality and the activation version of the consistency model of personality. The latter model, too, is compatible with the concepts presented in *Birth Pattern Psychology.*

Theodore Millon's work concentrates primarily on disorders of personality. Millon suggests that the basic elements of personality are needs, attitudes and behaviors. The traits defined in this volume present differing individual orientations toward and perceptions of reality. They are compatible with the concept of a general attitude.

The remaining assumptions involve the universality of core personality factors, their number and measurement. These theories account for the actual research.

An extensive review of psychological theories defining core personality factors yields the following conclusion: some theorists are parsimonious and some are not. The former confine themselves to a few personality factors; the latter elaborate long lists of factors. Those theorists who favor the parsimonious approach to core theorizing tend to propose either three or four core factors. The theorists who offer threefold factors tend toward either a physiological/psychophysiological frame of reference (Kretschmer and Sheldon represent the former; psychological versions based on Paul MacLean's triune brain theory represent the latter) or a social psychological frame of reference (Freud, Horney). These two points of view are not so disparate as they seem for they come together in their underlying emphasis on the person/environment interaction. That is to say, they describe behaviors.

No single theorist provides a model for the fourfold conception of human needs. Theorists propose numerous needs but the core needs can be effectively captured in four need factors. These factors are distinct enough not to permit further reduction, yet are flexible enough to incorporate various theoretical elaborations. The four themes are the needs for growth, security, stimulus, and love.

How, then, might the birth pattern measure these four factors? The only possible variables are the planet factors. These variables could be viewed against two grounds—sign divisions or house sector divisions. Sign divisions are, however, divisions of the basic 360° circular measurement format. They establish the positions of and relationships between all birth pattern factors. Sign divisions are a measurement convenience. Sign references can be dispensed with entirely through the use of 360° notation without affecting the birth chart. This cannot be said of either the house sectors or the planet variables. Further, empirical testing so far fails to confirm the meaningfulness of sign references. (See Geoffrey Dean and Arthur Mather, *Recent Advances in Natal Astrology, A Critical Review 1900–1976,* Analogic, 1977.)

The twelve house sectors provide two possible fourfold division systems: triangular house patterns and quadrant divisions. Research by Metzner, R. Holcombe and J. Holcombe (*Journal of Geocosmic Research,* Monograph No. 1, 1980) fails to support hemisphere measures and, as the authors note, casts doubt on the quadrant measures since the logic of both hemisphere and quadrant measures is the same.

The quadrant is a biased measure because births are not randomly distributed throughout the day. Births, as researchers Michel and Françoise Gauquelin point out, show a definite diurnal pattern. This pattern biases quadrant measures in favor of the two midnight to noon quadrants and against the remaining two quadrants.

This leaves the triangular house sector patterns as the most logical fourfold measurement base. The planet variables give a ten-point scale by which to weight the four triangular sector patterns. Given a large sample of birth patterns (five hundred in the original sample) it is then possible to define those individuals whose birth measurements make them extreme examples of one measurement factor. I then paired biographical histories of those individuals with their birth patterns and examined them for common life themes. The result gave four distinct personality profiles reflective of the four extreme measurement groups. I then compared the profiles with the psychological needs to determine whether life in practice reflected life in theory. The methodology for determining the measurement of behavior factors was the same.

Biographical histories proved the only unbiased resource, particularly when viewed as a series of instances of behavior and a pattern of life choices indicative of underlying motives. Objective assessment of the latter is, of course, more difficult and here there is safety in acquiring numerous histories.

The third set of measurements presented in this book are the trait measurements. Max Lüscher's *The Four-Color Person* suggests that four single factors combine to yield six second-order factors. With a sample of five hundred birth patterns reduced to four-digit measures, it was quite simple to calculate the six combined measures for each individual. Not only did the extremes of each of the six new measurements yield temperamentally coherent groups, the measurements themselves produced three normal distributions. The importance of a normally distributed measurement in psychological research cannot be overestimated. Going on to reach a definition of the traits in concrete terms proved to be difficult. The only psychological author to propose this particular conceptual scheme is Malone in his book *Psychetypes.*

His traits are intriguing yet disparate enough to make one-on-one reconciliation impossible. Hence the traits, of all the material in this book, are most representative of my own theorizing based on empirical observation alone.

My research goal was to produce a system of personality measurement to enhance active listening. Since the theories in this book were designed with the intent to facilitate the counselling process, the only true test of their practical value was in application. Three years ago, Glenda Allen expressed the desire to use these theories in actual practice. Ms. Allen has now completed a graduate degree in marriage and family counselling. She was, at that time, a certified reality therapist, substance abuse counsellor and active in the Reno Committee to Aid Abused Women. Her use of Birth Pattern Psychology as an adjunct to counselling contributed to much of the material in the Analysis section of this work.

The material in this volume is as accurate and valid as theoretical soundness, empirical testing and practical verification can make it. It establishes a new avenue of research possibilities previously unavailable for examination and testing.

Tamise Van Pelt

Reno, Nevada
June 1983

Acknowledgments

I wish to acknowledge the valuable contributions of those people whose support made this book a reality:

My mother, my father and Mickey Roemer were the only taxpayers to fund this research. They made this work possible.

My parents made a much more fundamental contribution. From my preschool years through my high school years, every other week without fail, they made a twenty-mile round trip to a library. Our home was a place where issues were vigorously debated, the English language respected, and my ideas and opinions encouraged. They gave me a college education as well, but in sixteen years of formal education I never experienced the quality of thought nor the spirit of inquiry that existed in my own family.

My special thanks to Rosemary Thompson, whose friendship, emotional support and unflagging confidence in this project have sustained me through these last three years.

To Glenda Allen for her objectivity, perceptivity and critical application of these principles, thank you for helping me keep things in perspective. Linda Walker's willingness to read and reread the manuscript and her many helpful insights and suggestions provided an important resource.

To Noel Tyl who read and offered comments on the first manuscript and to Mike Munkasey who patiently and thoroughly explained the astronomy of house systems and to Neil Michelsen, who advised me of contemporary research resources, my gratitude.

Finally, to Shaun Levesque who shepherded me through turmoil and frustration and managed to maintain his sense of humor during it all, my respect and affection. Marah Ren pulled the project together. To Marah and Emily McKeigue, my appreciation.

And to all my friends who waited, thank you all for your patience, your encouragement and your generosity.

Introduction: The Birth Pattern Approach to Personality Measurement

You live in a world of measurement. Measurement is so much a natural part of your life that your environment is filled with measuring devices. Look around your home and you will see measuring cups and spoons in your kitchen, clocks and calendars on your walls. You might own a tape measure, scales, thermometer, barometer, ruler, yardstick. You drive a car equipped to measure its own speed, mileage and fuel supply. But you are unprepared to accurately and objectively measure the one thing in your life that affects you most: people.

Though we spend much of our lives meeting people, interacting with people and forming impressions of people, our impressions are not objective assessments. Imagine, for instance, casual, easy-going, informal Richard and conservative, restrained Allen attending a business luncheon. Barbara Brown, their hostess, is a potential client and both men's impressions of her will affect their future business dealings. Ms. Brown serves gourmet food. Her table is set with silver and china, flowers and finger bowls. She displays perfect manners. As they drive away from her home, Allen remarks, "Ms. Brown is really a tasteful, refined, elegant woman." "Refined!" Richard exclaims, "she's a stuffy, up-tight snob!"

Allen and Richard evaluated Barbara Brown in relation to their own self-concepts. "Even a highly trained judge will tend to take himself as the standard," writes Robert R. Holt, author of *Assessing Personality*. Holt lists moods, values, defenses, preferences and prejudices as subjective factors influencing both the way we see other people and the way we see ourselves.

People view one another subjectively. Consider the difference between the two following descriptions of Susie: "Susie seems cheerful and kind to me," versus "Susie is a kind, cheerful person." The first statement shows an awareness that Susie's cheerfulness may be in the eye of the beholder. It acknowledges its subjectivity. The second statement, however, *sounds* objective even though it is not. It is stated as a fact about Susie. When subjectivity masquerades as objective assessment, it leads to unrealistic expectations. If we *expect* Susie to be kind and she behaves cruelly, we might react to her cruelty with disbelief (how could she?) or denial (it is not like Susie to act that way) or outrage (what a terrible thing for Susie to do!). If Susie is our friend or relative or mate, we will in all likelihood react defensively to her cruelty. It is not our subjectivity, then, that is harmful to us. It is the associated unrealistic expectations which cause us to defend against rather than cope with the challenges of everyday life.

Objective insight into the structure and dynamics of our own personalities helps us appreciate our uniqueness. Realistic self-assessment counters the unrealistic expectations we have of ourselves, making us less apt to defend and more able to live effective, productive, creative lives.

The ability to objectively assess other people's personalities is crucial to the helping professional, but it is essential for all of us if we are to avoid the subjectivity, unrealistic expectations, and defensive exchanges that undermine personal relationships.

What is Personality?

Theodore Millon, editor of *Theories of Psychopathology and Personality*, defines a personality pattern: "When we speak of a personality pattern, then, we are referring to those intrinsic and pervasive modes of functioning which emerge from the entire matrix of the individual's developmental history, and which now characterize his perceptions and ways of dealing with his environment. We have chosen the term pattern for two reasons: first, to focus on the fact that these behaviors and attitudes derive from the constant and pervasive interaction of both biological dispositions and learned experience; and second, to denote the fact that these personality characteristics are not just a potpourri of unrelated behavior tendencies, but a tightly knit organization of needs, attitudes and behaviors."[1] Millon makes the following important points:

1. **Personality is intrinsic.** The inborn personality structure is the person's nature. Therefore, people do not adopt personalities as a framework for understanding themselves and their lives; they *are* their frames of reference. An individual's core personality is the self that person is, always has been and will continue to be. Hence, core personality is expressed automatically and tends to be invisible to the person expressing it.

2. **Personality is the individual's way of functioning in and dealing with the environment.** Personality involves the dynamic interaction between the person and his or her world. This interaction can be successful and satisfying or unsuccessful and self-defeating because any personality factor has both a constructive/coping and a destructive/defensive expression.

3. **Innate personality (nature) is shaped by development and life experience (nurture).** The environment that supports, appreciates and encourages the individual's natural self-expression leads to satisfaction and coping. The environment that frustrates the individual's nature, making him or her feel guilty and ashamed, breeds defense and dissatisfaction. Assessment reveals the structure of the individual's personality. The individual's behavior reveals the degree of coping and satisfaction versus the degree of frustration and defense.

4. **Personality is an organized whole composed of needs, attitudes, and behaviors.** Personality is not a random collection of independent factors but rather an internal organization or structure. Because people have needs, they act to satisfy those needs in ways that they perceive to be effective.

We cannot achieve an objective assessment of personality by simply willing ourselves to be objective. The impressions we form of others reflect us, the impression formers.

To assess a given individual's intrinsic personality structure objectively, we must have some means to measure that individual's needs, attitudes and behavior. In *Birth Pattern Psychology,* the birth pattern measures the motive force of fundamental human needs, the presence of general attitudes, the capacity for expressing distinct behaviors and the organization of these factors into a personality structure characteristic of the individual.

The Birth Pattern Approach

A birth chart maps the positions of the Sun, Moon, and planets at a specific moment as seen from a specific terrestrial longitude and latitude. The individual's date, place, and time of birth determine his or her distinctive birth chart. The chart itself is nothing more than a collection of objective astronomical data.

Data alone is useless without some context in which to make the data meaningful. Birth Pattern Psychology provides that context.

The following illustration depicts an individual's birth pattern with those astronomical measurements necessary for birth pattern assessments: a segmented ground with ten planet variables (markers). Birth Pattern Psychology groups these segments to form a patterned measurement base.

Birth Pattern Psychology reflects a holistic measurement philosophy, a philosophy characteristic of biology and cited earlier in Millon's definition of personality. Gestalt psychologist Max Wertheimer explains holism: "There are wholes, the behavior of which is not determined by that of their individual elements, but where the part-processes are themselves determined by the intrinsic nature of the whole." Hence, the whole defines its parts and no examination of parts alone, however detailed, can describe the nature of the whole.

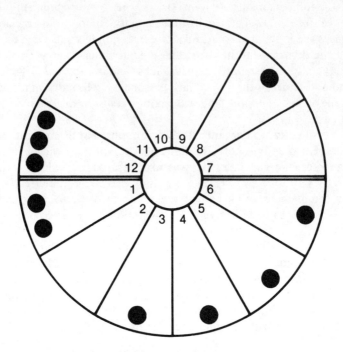

Birth Pattern Psychology, following holistic principles, sacrifices detailed measurement of many part factors in favor of in-depth measurement of core personality components: four fundamental human needs, three behavior modes and six basic traits. Each measurement in Birth Pattern Psychology uses all part factors to give a holistic result.

Need, attitude, and behavior factors are the building blocks of personality assessment. These factors require quantitative measurement because they imply quantitative questions: How much does Robert need security? How likely is Beth to behave aggressively? To what extent does Terry's general attitude reflect practicality? Birth Pattern Psychology uses birth data as ordinal or quantitative statistics. Its quantitative measurements answer the quantitative questions essential to personality assessment.

Human needs, attitudes and behaviors themselves define Birth Pattern Psychology's content. The basic psychological concepts presented in this book represent a synthesis of major personality theories. This synthesis was achieved by pairing biographical profiles of individuals with their birth patterns. The statistics presented in this volume are derived from a sample of five hundred such patterns.

The product of Birth Pattern Psychology is a personality assessment that provides an objective context in which to understand all that a person communicates through his or her words and actions. Birth Pattern Psychology is receptive in practice.

We have already noted that people are not very objective assessors of other people. We use ourselves as standards. The birth pattern provides an objective external standard to replace our subjective standards. We understand people best when we are able to see what their words and actions mean to them. We more accurately interpret their experiences when we see the events in their lives through their eyes rather than our own. Receptive, objective listening encourages clear communication between mates, between friends, between parent and child. It is valuable in any relationship but essential for the therapist as a powerful helping tool.

A Tool for the Helping Professional

Since personality theory, psychology and therapy have evolved over the past century without benefit of birth patterns, it is fair to ask what the psychologist or counselor gains from Birth Pattern Psychology's assessment techniques. The birth pattern is a significant helping tool for three reasons:

First, Birth Pattern Psychology allows each individual to be a unique psychological norm while retaining a general measurement context. Gordon Allport, America's pioneer personality theorist, was the foremost proponent of the individual approach. Allport's critics argue that individual orientation makes psychology itself impossible since psychologists cannot generalize from one case to another nor find the basic, uniform principles essential to theory formation. Birth Pattern Psychology's unique approach to individual assessment makes it possible to both employ general psychological principles while fully appreciating each individual.

Allowing each individual to be his or her own psychological norm has a deep human importance. Many personality theories present theoretical norms for psychological health and personal adjustment in lieu of the individual norm. This led gestalt psychologist Frederick Perls to lament that a patient is cured when the patient achieves the norm of the therapist's theory. Birth Pattern Psychology rests on the belief that any individual can express his or her distinct personality pattern in self-enhancing, satisfying ways, hence personal adjustment and self-actualization are synonymous.

Birth Pattern Psychology's second advantage is its practicality. In many counselling situations, personality testing is either impractical or intrusive. In such situations, the birth pattern provides an alternative to testing.

The third advantage of Birth Pattern Psychology is its use of objective ordinal measurements. The reliability and validity of its measurements and concepts can be easily tested. The individual birth pattern assessment yields a pattern of four need/motive measures, three behavioral measures and three trait continuum measures. This quantitative measurement of core factors simplifies testing.

Part One: Synthesis, presents the concepts and measurement techniques basic to Birth Pattern Psychology. It includes numerous birth patterns and provides all the materials essential for learning birth pattern assessment. Part Two: Analysis, explores the strengths and vulnerabilities of specific patterns. It is designed to stimulate self-analysis. You may want to explore your own birth pattern at this point. Appendix B tells you where and how to obtain your birth chart.

Birth Pattern Psychology presents measurements which, to be acceptable, must prove objective, valid (they must measure what they purport to measure), and reliable (they must measure consistently). An individual's date, place, and time of birth always yield the same birth pattern regardless of who or what performs the calculation. Given this objective set of measurements, the pure scientist would settle any further doubts by applying birth pattern theory to a large sample of birth patterns to check for validity, and examining individual birth pattern cases biographically to check for reliability. Others would simply accept the birth measurements. Most of us are incapable of either pure scientific detachment or blind faith. The birth pattern concept makes us pause to ask "Why?"

This "why" asks for a "because" answer; however, there is no answer since the question places psychological measurement in the irrelevant context of cause and effect. A depression scale is a psychological measure of an individual's emotional state. Though a high score on a depression scale correlates with the individual's depressed state, it does not cause the depression. The relationship of all psychological measurements to the factors measured is synchronous, not causal. Birth pattern measures synchronize with personality factors.

To study the birth pattern we must think holistically. We must set aside our Western, reductionist common sense and employ an Eastern, holistic intuition that we are not in the habit of using.

Contemporary physics reveals a common-sense-defying cosmos in the very heart of matter. The sub-atomic universe exists as a holistic pattern of ever-shifting relationships. This new physics literally brings form out of the formless. How do physicists make their magic? They take a measurement!

The universe that applies to our exploration of human personality also exists as a holistic pattern of ever-shifting cosmic relationships, a web of universal probabilities. The individual birth begins the human experiment that is life. Birth gives time to the timelessness of the universe. Birth takes a measurement.

An individual's birth moment reflects the pattern that transforms probability into actuality. The universe does not stamp its meaning on the individual; the individual stamps a private meaning onto the universe. According to Eastern wisdom, the *Tao* does not increase human life; a human life increases the Tao.

Part One: Synthesis

1 Measuring Basic Needs

Human beings have traded instinct for intelligence. People no longer survive automatically in an environment; people live consciously in a world. Living equals conscious process. This conscious human life process involves four significant part-processes. These part-processes define the four universal human needs for growth, security, stimulus and love.

If the keywords we use to label the concepts of Birth Pattern Psychology are to prove useful, we must remind ourselves at the outset that our labels can mislead us and frustrate our holistic thinking. The Security Need sounds as if it is an actual concrete building block of an actual concrete thing called personality. However, the personality and the personality factors composing it are all processes. It is simply less awkward to talk about the Security Need than to talk about the processes of securing, of maintaining, of using. To think holistically, we must use keywords to unlock the doors of our process perception.

Measurement sets the stage for assessment. To measure the basic Growth, Security, Stimulus and Love Needs, we must both qualify them and quantify them. The birth pattern provides sectors that qualify the basic needs and planet markers that quantify the basic needs.

The birth pattern sectors divide the measurement ground into twelve units numbered in counterclockwise order. The sector numbers name the individual sectors and nothing more. The sequential concepts of before and after are irrelevant in terms of holistic measurement. Holistic measurement demands pattern. The illustration on page 13 shows the association between the Growth, Security, Stimulus and Love Needs and the birth pattern sectors that qualify them. Note the geometry of the four triangular sub-patterns within the birth pattern as a whole.

Measurement sectors one, five, and nine qualify the Growth Need, the process of inventing, of using insight, of making personally meaningful. Sectors two, six and ten qualify the Security Need, the process of preserving, of nurturing, of maintaining. Sectors three, seven and eleven qualify the Stimulus Need, the process of identifying, of discovering, of exciting. Sectors four, eight and twelve qualify the Love Need, the process of committing, of making intimate, of caring.

The birth pattern's sector triangles form a universal mandala. Every individual birth pattern has the same ground as every other birth pattern. From the point of view of their needs alone, all people are alike. People differ from each other not in what they need but in how much they need it.

The birth pattern's ground exists on three distinct levels. The lowest level is a reductionist level of twelve units: sector one, sector two, sector three, etc. It does not interest us. The median level is a basic need level of four units: the Growth Need Triangle (sector one–five–nine), the Security Need Triangle (sector two–six–ten), the Stimulus Need Triangle (sector three–seven–eleven), and the Love Need Triangle (sector four–eight–twelve). Birth pattern assessment happens at this level and at this level only. At the highest level, the pattern becomes the whole, the single unit about which nothing can be known directly.

Quantifying each basic need translates the universal human pattern into a specific individual pattern. The ten planets provide a set of quantifiers. Planets is a general term that includes the Sun and Moon together with Mercury, Venus, Mars, Jupiter, Saturn, Uranus, Neptune, and Pluto. The table lists the planets, their symbols and abbreviations.

Each planet is a marker that indicates one unit of quantity. Since the planet is a unit of quantity, it possesses no quality and therefore no symbolic meaning. As units of quantity, all planets are equal. The planet positions in the birth patterns will be indicated by dots rather than symbols to reinforce their marker value.

The weight of the Growth Need in an individual's birth pattern equals the sum of the markers in the Growth Need Triangle (sector one–five–nine). The weight of the Security Need equals the sum of the markers in the Security Need Triangle (sector two–six–ten). The Stimulus Need and the Love Need are weighted in the same manner. The individual has ten units of awareness (planet markers) to spend within the economy of the personality (the four basic needs) and assessment means seeing how he or she spends this awareness. By adding the markers in a need triangle, we give the need a number value. The weighted value of the four basic needs gives the personality pattern called the Need Gestalt.

THE NEED TRIANGLES:
THE BIRTH PATTERN'S MEASUREMENT GROUND

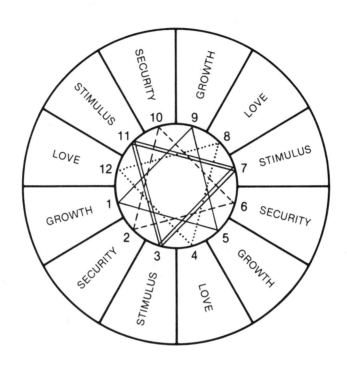

THE PLANET MARKERS:
THE BIRTH PATTERN'S MEASUREMENT VARIABLES

	Planet	Symbol	Abbreviation
●	Sun	☉	SU
●	Moon	☽	MO
●	Mercury	☿	ME
●	Venus	♀	VE
●	Mars	♂	MA
●	Jupiter	♃	JU
●	Saturn	♄	SA
●	Uranus	♅	UR
●	Neptune	♆	NE
●	Pluto	♇ (♀)	PL

Birth Pattern #1 illustrates the pattern belonging to actor Alan Alda. (Birth data for Birth Patterns used throughout can be found in Appendix A.) The illustration shows the addition of markers that weights each basic need and yields the Need Gestalt:

Alan Alda: Need Gestalt

Growth Need:	1
Security Need:	3
Stimulus Need:	2
Love Need:	4

Alan Alda's Need Gestalt weights his basic needs for love, security, stimulus and growth in this order. Interviewers frequently ask Alda how he has maintained a twenty-four-year marriage and a stable family life in the face of Hollywood's pressures and his fame. They note his cross-country commutes in order to spend time with his family. Alda's Need Gestalt indicates that the intimacy of marriage and the stability of family life fulfill his personal priorities and provide the necessary anchors for his public image and his private creativity.

Note well what has just been discussed because it is a personality assessment in miniature. Given certain facts about Alan Alda's life choices, facts that on the surface might seem puzzling, the Need Gestalt allows us to understand the facts by putting them in the context of Alda's own personality. Assessment allows us to receptively appreciate the individual's life choices; assessment does not allow us to second-guess the individual's life experiences.

Birth Pattern #1: Alan Alda

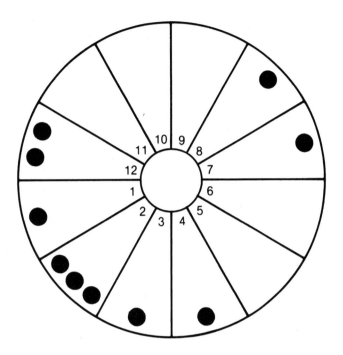

GROWTH NEED: First Sector   Fifth Sector   Ninth Sector
                  Planets   Planets   Planets
                    1   +   0   +   0   = 1

SECURITY NEED: Second Sector   Sixth Sector   Tenth Sector
                  Planets   Planets   Planets
                    3   +   0   +   0   = 3

STIMULUS NEED: Third Sector   Seventh Sector   Eleventh Sector
                  Planets   Planets   Planets
                    1   +   1   +   0   = 2

LOVE NEED: Fourth Sector   Eighth Sector   Twelfth Sector
                  Planets   Planets   Planets
                    1   +   1   +   2   = 4

Birth Pattern #2 is gangster John Dillinger's pattern. It yields the Need Gestalt:

John Dillinger: Need Gestalt	
Growth Need:	3
Security Need:	1
Stimulus Need:	6
Love Need:	0

Given Dillinger's Need Gestalt, we immediately observe that the Stimulus Need completely overpowers the remaining needs. Giving minimal importance to his personal safety or his intimate ties, John Dillinger would seek excitement above all else. His death came at an unguarded moment as the direct result of betrayal by the notorious Lady in Red. Though individuals often disregard their lesser needs and insist these needs are unimportant, needs so ignored do not go away. John Dillinger's disregard for loyalty led him to take an association for granted. Disregarding needs generally is not fatal but disregarding needs does, ultimately, diminish the quality of life experience by confining the personality within the bounds of the familiar and the easy.

BIRTH PATTERN #2: John Dillinger

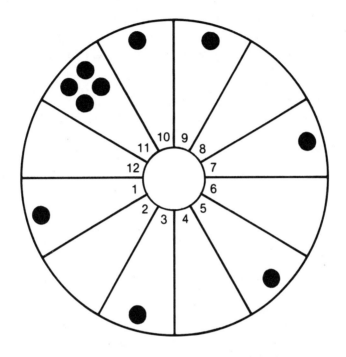

GROWTH NEED:	First Sector Planets	Fifth Sector Planets	Ninth Sector Planets	
	1 +	1 +	1	= 3
SECURITY NEED:	Second Sector Planets	Sixth Sector Planets	Tenth Sector Planets	
	0 +	0 +	1	= 1
STIMULUS NEED:	Third Sector Planets	Seventh Sector Planets	Eleventh Sector Planets	
	1 +	1 +	4	= 6
LOVE NEED:	Fourth Sector Planets	Eighth Sector Planets	Twelfth Sector Planets	
	0 +	0 +	0	= 0

The Jungian differentiation concept (see References, Chapter 6) best expresses the meaning of a weighted need. A need emphasized by four planets is more differentiated than a need emphasized by two planets. The greater the degree of differentiation, the more developed, modified and specialized the function. A highly weighted need seeks very specific need satisfiers. From the biological and evolutionary points of view, specialization increases the vulnerability of the whole.

The table of the distribution of weighted need triangles helps us judge the range of differences between individuals. A survey of five hundred birth patterns, each birth pattern accounting for four need triangles, yields two thousand weighted need factors. Need triangles containing no planet markers are relatively rare and account for 7.1 percent of all need triangles in the sample. An unweighted need still exists since the need is both a human universal and present in the ground of the personality pattern. An unweighted need is merely undifferentiated.

Most needs fall somewhere between the one-to-four range of psychological weight. Needs weighted beyond the four level become increasingly rare. Though it is possible in theory for all ten planet markers to appear in the sectors of a single need triangle, this would demand a highly improbable astronomical pattern. Need triangles weighted by eight planet markers occur only once in every thousand birth patterns. Though we know that people with extremely one-pointed personality patterns are not the norm, only they can tell us whether they feel frustrated and misunderstood or whether they feel deeply fulfilled in some distinctive, private way.

THE DISTRIBUTION OF PLANET MARKERS
IN 2,000 NEED TRIANGLES

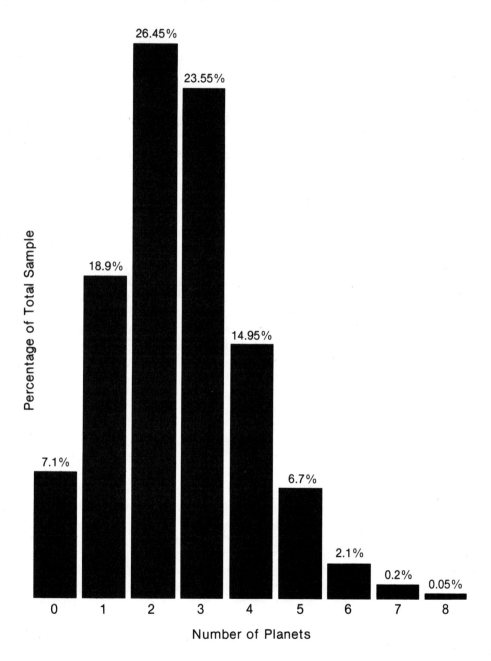

Percentage of Total Sample

26.45%

23.55%

18.9%

14.95%

7.1%

6.7%

2.1%

0.2%

0.05%

0   1   2   3   4   5   6   7   8

Number of Planets

Part Two: Analysis, presents the specific challenges, vulnerabilities and defenses related to each personality factor. Analysis reveals the way in which individuals use personality strengths to compensate for personality weaknesses. Practical counselling application of Birth Pattern Psychology has shown that the number of markers, the quantity measure in and of itself, is meaningful, a fact not anticipated by birth pattern theory. Bearing in mind that no single measurement ever exists apart from the whole and that analysis, too, depends on the whole, we will explore the quantity measures using the Stimulus Need as an example. The Stimulus Need involves all encounters but it is particularly relevant to social interaction and it is particularly visible in the individual's approach to first meetings.

No planet markers in a need triangle: The need processes occur spontaneously and automatically but are triggered by the situation. Generally, the need is not a conscious concern. When circumstances evoke this need, the individual adapts naturally. Various psychological disciplines offer differing explanations for such automatic adaptation. Some say it is instinctive; some say it is unconscious; some say it is the result of conditioning. An individual who lacks awareness of the Stimulus Need adapts automatically to the social circumstances of the occasion allowing himself or herself to be guided by the immediate social situation.

One planet marker in a need triangle: This need and its satisfactions seem unimportant and life choices tend to reflect this lack of overt concern. Needs weighted by only one marker (or singleton) are usually a source of great covert discomfort, causing the individual to avoid seeking necessary satisfactions. One has sufficient awareness to know that a need exists but insufficient awareness to adapt confidently to its demands. One stimulus marker is common to people who are not particularly social by temperament yet who experience social anxiety. These individuals would be very uncomfortable asking a stranger for directions.

Two planet markers in a need triangle: Two is impossible to assess without reference to a specific individual. In many cases, the Two suffers the same difficulties as the One.

Three planet markers in a need triangle: Three is effective and self-confident. Three is as automatic as One but it is an aware, active, directed naturalness rather than a simple response to circumstances. Three makes its own satisfactions. Three can maximize its gains and minimize its losses, thus Three represents a natural tendency for optimal satisfaction. Three expresses the Oriental ideals of the Golden Mean. An individual with three markers in a Stimulus Need possesses natural social poise, is at ease meeting new people and is able to put others at their ease as well.

More than three planet markers in a need triangle: Needs weighted by more than three markers tend increasingly to dominate the whole personality, making one satisfaction so important that it overshadows all others. People with very strong needs often behave as if they are addicted to the situations and people outside themselves which offer satisfaction. When the inner demand is very intense, the individual finds it difficult to see any potential satisfier in perspective. People with very strong stimulus needs risk getting "hooked" on their social involvements. High stimulus personalities frequently correspond with social self-consciousness and shyness because meeting new people is just too intense.

Those individual people who have either a strong Growth Need, a strong Security Need, a strong Stimulus Need or a strong Love Need live lives that best illustrate the search for a specific satisfaction. As we turn our attention to the four basic universal human needs, we will allow those people to act as our guides.

The Security Need

The Security Need includes safety, self-protection and the desire for order. Abraham Maslow sees security in terms of keeping things within limits to insure effectiveness and coping. Maslow, known for his theory of self-actualization, states that security creates feelings of trust, worth and competence. Erich Fromm writes of the basic human desire for rootedness, the need to draw upon something solid, substantial, and sustaining.

Nurturance and security go hand in hand. So long as our culture remains centered on the mother as the primary care-giver, the quality of mothering the individual has received will be reflected in his or her sense of security. Harry Stack Sullivan proposes the term "mothering one" to indicate that the actual mother may not be the only source of nurturing, but for practical assessment purposes, the high emphasis on security sensitizes us to the importance of the individual's relationship with the mother. Hans Sebald suggests that mothers are important power figures who shape their childrens' attitudes toward power, authority and control. Security problems may stem from erratic, abusive, neglectful mothering or from over-nurturant mothering or from what Sebald terms "Momism" in which the mothering appears perfect by all social standards but the child has been turned out like a corporate product.

Most major personality theorists discuss the consequences of unsatisfied security needs. Karen Horney emphasizes the resulting helplessness, hostility and guilt. Sullivan writes of the striving for power and the sense of incompetence that mark the insecure. Maslow equates lack of security with avoidance of the new and preference for rigid routine. Erik Erikson depicts childhood insecurity as basic mistrust with the experience of "total rage, with fantasies of the total domination or even destruction of the sources of pleasure and provision."

People whose security needs are satisfied on a regular basis are people confident of their ability to secure, to decide, to be consistent, to be productive. They show concern for the welfare of others, particularly those others who are helpless. Secure people are competent and self-maintaining; they easily cope with life's pressures and necessities.

Birth Pattern #3 is the personality pattern of consumer advocate Ralph Nader. Nader's occupation defines the security focus that we see in his personality and his nurturant attitude reminds us that there is nothing exclusively feminine about nurturance. Nader has made it his career to speak for those who lack the power to speak for themselves; it is his business to question big business, corporate power and executive authority.

Ralph Nader's family influences were studied by Victor, Mildred, and Ted George Goertzel as part of their research into the roots of eminent achievers.[2] The Goertzels describe Nader's mother Rose as the "steadying influence" in the Nader family, a sturdy and amiable woman who encouraged and supported her son's personal goals and abilities. Such support for the child's concerns breeds competence, in contrast to the self-doubt bred by a dominating parent whose own goals usurp the child's goals.

Other biographers characterize Ralph Nader as a driven workaholic and workaholic behavior is most common among people with high security need birth patterns. The insecure, driven individual generally tends to have an

Birth Pattern #3: Ralph Nader

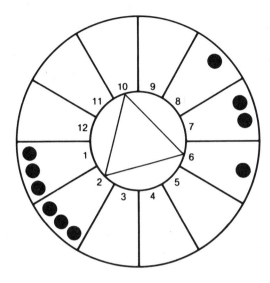

Need Gestalt

Growth Need:	3
Security Need:	4
Stimulus Need:	2
Love Need:	1

Birth Pattern #4: J. Edgar Hoover

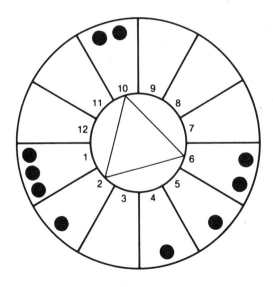

Need Gestalt

Growth Need:	4
Security Need:	5
Stimulus Need:	0
Love Need:	1

excessive interest in maintaining a specific position by out-producing others who may appear to be competing for that same spot. Most high security people are devoted to a career. Nader's sense of duty and his interest in the well-being of the consumer reflect his security orientation. A high degree of security is essential as a basis from which to question long-standing social practices and the "powers that be."

Birth Pattern #4 is that of former FBI director J. Edgar Hoover. The Need Gestalt shows a security emphasis that accounts for half the psychological economy of Hoover's personality. Like Ralph Nader, J. Edgar Hoover was a serious-minded honor student. The similarity ends here, however, and it is interesting to compare the forces that nurtured these different personality expressions. Hoover's life is a classic study in the power urges that form when a highly security-oriented male child is nurtured by an overprotective and smothering mother. The Goertzels note that smothering mothers often form such exclusive emotional ties with their sons that the sons never marry.

The Goertzels note that mother-smothering of the sort that shaped Hoover's personality is a rarity in this century. J. Edgar Hoover lived with his mother well into his adult life. It is often suggested that Hoover disliked women although he once wrote an article entitled "Mothers...Our Only Hope."

Though Hoover was an extremely secretive man and little is known about his personal life, a great deal is revealed by his career. He felt crime could be alleviated if only the American people would become more suspicious. One biographer describes Hoover as an "all-encompassing authority" who "wielded awesome and terrifying power," a "harsh and uncompromising man" with a tendency to view change as a "threat to his authority." Again and again, the dual themes of power and authority emerge with dramatic force from the fabric of Hoover's public life.

Birth Pattern #5 maps the personality of nutritionist Adelle Davis. Davis made nurturance and human welfare her life's work. Like Ralph Nader, she was often at odds with corporate powers. Adelle Davis openly criticized food industry policies. She was a prolific writer who could translate the difficult subject of nutrition into terms the general reader could easily understand.

When Adelle Davis was two, her mother died. She was raised within a supportive family circle, however, where the emphasis was on hard work and rural values. Davis was an enthusiastic student who took odd jobs to put herself through college. Her professional work was termed authoritative. The security bent, well used and well presented, is expressed authoritatively by self-confident individuals like Davis. This contrasts sharply with the authoritarian power tactics characteristic of the security-frustrated who attempt to impose their personal opinions on others through force.

Birth Pattern #5: Adelle Davis

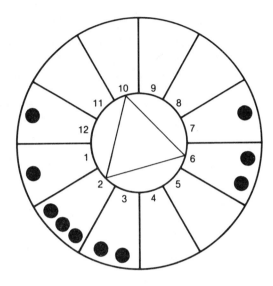

Need Gestalt

Growth Need: 1
Security Need: 5
Stimulus Need: 3
Love Need: 1

Birth Pattern #6: Angela Davis

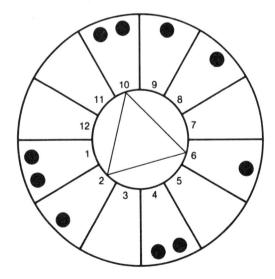

Need Gestalt

Growth Need: 3
Security Need: 4
Stimulus Need: 0
Love Need: 3

Adelle Davis supported nutritional research and opposed food faddists who oversimplified the complex subject of nutrition. She expressed the feelings of competence, productiveness and nurturance in her introduction to *Let's Eat Right to Keep Fit:* "When you have the ability to help your fellow-man, that ability ceases to be merely an ability and becomes a responsibility."

Birth Pattern #6 illustrates the personality of activist Angela Davis. Like the previous three security-oriented persons, she was a serious, studious and conforming youngster. Both parents were teachers though her father later opened a filling station to better support the family. The Davis family emphasized achievement and Angela Davis was attuned to their message. Her mother took the Davis children with her to New York while she completed her masters degree.

Angela Davis travelled to Germany to do her own graduate study. She was alone and outside the context of her secure, familiar world at home. She experienced a sudden, dramatic loss of security with severe consequences. Uprooted yet pressed to study and to achieve, she began to study compulsively. She experienced guilt over her privileged position in comparison to poor American blacks who were at the time rioting in frustration over their economic plight. As her workload increased and her insecurities became more pronounced, Davis became unable to cope with the simple, practical aspects of life. She forgot to buy food. Finally, she attempted suicide.

Angela Davis's experience is not unique. The sudden loss of the life circumstances that satisfy a dominant need paired with the increased demand for performance and coping can be a devastating experience leading to acute psychological crisis.

Angela Davis is best known for her Marxist philosophy. Marx, too, had a dominant Security Need. Many prominent female activists both liberal and conservative have dominant Security Needs, among them are Jane Fonda, Joan Baez, Judy Collins, Anita Bryant and Phyllis Schaffley, women who do not fear a power struggle.

The Love Need

The Love Need includes empathy, pleasure, affection and intimacy. Loving that fulfills must be *unconditional;* loving affirms what is, it never seeks what cannot be. Loving exchanges, establishes mutuality, brings close.

Anthropologist Ashley Montagu lists love's qualities as firmness, support, involvement, tenderness, joy and fearlessness. Love, Montagu says, is crucial to accepting life and adapting to the world. Maslow notes the atmosphere of honesty, generosity, and free self-expression that loving creates. Rollo May adds that love affirms value and expresses interest.

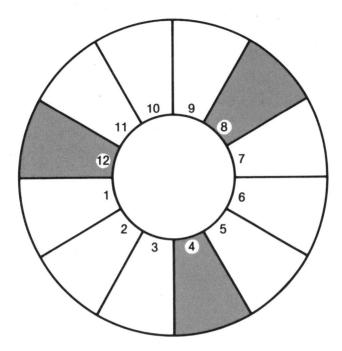

Good fathering is as important to loving as good mothering is to securing. Fathering provides the emotional satisfactions that parallel nurture. In practical assessment, personality patterns with strong Love Need emphases cue us to the possible impact of father influences.

Father-child interaction involves play and sharing, companionship and pleasure, warmth and joy. According to psychological studies, the father influences the child's sexual identity and supportive fathers tend to have more feminine daughters and more masculine sons in the traditional sense of femininity and masculinity. Pleasure, warmth and sexuality are all facets of intimacy as signified by the Love Need.

Love Need frustration has sad consequences. Ashley Montagu notes the fear and depression associated with lack of love. Carl Rogers says that unloved people experience life as a threat. Carl Menninger links too little love with dread and inhibition. Other personality theorists cite further symptoms: demand for proof, inhibited life progress, suspicion, self-isolation. Attitudes of indifference and laziness are common to the unloved who feel that it just is not worth it to try. Hopelessness dead-ends the life process. The lack of

Birth Pattern #7: Farrah Fawcett

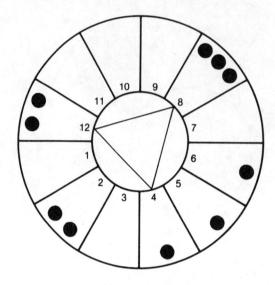

Need Gestalt

Growth Need: 1
Security Need: 3
Stimulus Need: 0
Love Need: 6

Birth Pattern #8: Colette

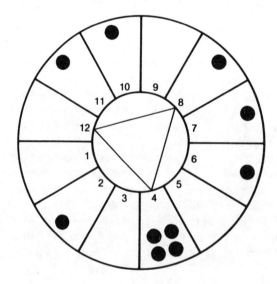

Need Gestalt

Growth Need: 0
Security Need: 3
Stimulus Need: 2
Love Need: 5

love may emerge in anti-social behavior and the unloved are often hyper-critical. Their endless wrangles and conflicts are misdirected attempts to get some kind of feelingful interaction because some interaction is preferable to none. In the Oriental wisdom of the *I Ching*, conflict means "not to love."

People whose love needs are satisfied on a regular basis feel confident in living life to the full. They don't need up-front guarantees to become involved. Loving people include, support and create because they feel accepting, aspiring and hopeful.

Birth Pattern #7 maps the personality pattern of actress-model Farrah Fawcett. When asked about the popularity of her television series *Charlie's Angels,* Fawcett commented, "I think people want to see some glamour, some clothes, some hair styles..." Fawcett later lent her image to a line of beauty products. An older sister also chose a career in the business of beauty. In interviews, Farrah Fawcett exemplifies the conventional feminine image shaped by the traditional family values of her Texas upbringing.

Given Fawcett's personality pattern, as assessors we see a personality that needs family support to develop and thrive. Farrah Fawcett grew up in a close, protective family atmosphere that complimented her needs. Those who knew her in her childhood and adolescence described her as cooperative, never rebellious, quiet and reserved.

Though she did local modeling jobs, Farrah Fawcett refused Hollywood offers until her father gave his permission for her to drop out of college and pursue a career. She states that she feels grateful for her adolescent experience which centered around family activities and kept her from becoming "too wise too soon."

Birth Pattern #8 is the pattern of Sidonie Gabrielle Colette, the famous French romantic writer. The dominant Love Need and secondary Security Need are quite similar to those of Farrah Fawcett's pattern but the two women provide a study in contrasts that reminds us of the fact that the personality evolves in and ultimately reflects its environmental input. While Fawcett and Colette had similar personalities, they had radically differing childhood experiences and family dynamics.

Colette's mother married Colette's biological father for money. He died while the mother was pregnant with Colette and the mother, within a few months' time, remarried. The only father Colette was to know was a charismatic good-for-nothing who squandered her mother's inheritance. The Goertzels studied Colette's childhood and remarked on the lack of affection that marked her early life. The mother often told the young girl that she looked like a boy. The Goertzels attribute Colette's bisexuality to this and yet more to her identification with her father. What a child cannot satisfy through interaction, a child may try to compensate through identification.

Colette's biographer, Margaret Crosland, titled her work *Colette: The Difficulty of Loving*. A first husband locked Colette in her room and forced her to write books which he published under his own name. All told, she had three marriages and numerous affairs. Loving means accepting what is as it is and finding pleasure in that. The difficulty in Colette's loving was even more obvious in her sentimental and nostalgic reinterpretation of her idealized past than in her affairs and marriages.

Birth Pattern #9 is the natal chart of director Sam Peckinpah. Again the love need is strong and the potential to be influenced by the father is very great. Peckinpah's father was a judge who sent the young Sam to military school where it was hoped he would learn moral discipline.

Children's love needs are best fulfilled when the father both takes an active interest in the child and regards the child with affection. The dominating parent often takes great pains to mold a child's character while omitting the equally essential warmth. Such was the case with Sam Peckinpah, whose father forced him to sit through a rape trial as a moral lesson.

While warmth encourages the child to identify with paternal values, strict discipline often creates just the reverse. Sam Peckinpah began to question all that his father had told him. Peckinpah's explicitly violent films have led his critics to comment that he glorifies brutality. Peckinpah himself insists that people must recognize the animal part of human nature.

As an artist, Peckinpah is known for his intensity and his temperament. Friends describe him as a man born in the wrong century who identifies with the "desert rat" character portrayed in many of his films. Peckinpah's film images of frontier justice echo the influence of his father. He wears a ring that was a childhood paternal gift and keeps his father's picture in his office.

Birth Pattern #10 is the personality pattern of former president John F. Kennedy. Though the American presidency represents a role in and of itself, it always bears the stamp of the man who holds the office. The Kennedy presidency was a time to dream, to aspire toward the conquest of space and to give new hope to those minorities whose lives seemed most hopeless. The Kennedy assassination was all the more dreadful because the death of the man was also the death of the dream.

Some biographers speculate that the bookish, literate, intellectual John F. Kennedy would have been far more fulfilled in an academic career. But Kennedy's personal achievements and aspirations bore the distinct imprint of his father. Joseph Kennedy Sr. was fascinated with politics and with political power. Politics was the central topic in family discussions. The most powerful politicians of the day were frequent guests in the Kennedy home. All the Kennedy children were encouraged to excel because, to Joseph Kennedy, there was no such thing as second place. Though John F. Kennedy's life was a short life, it was a creative life. His military, literary and political

Birth Pattern #9: Sam Peckinpah

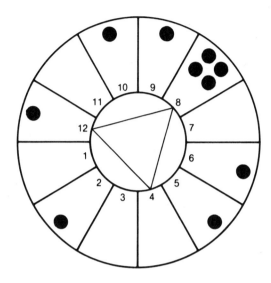

Need Gestalt

Growth Need: 2
Security Need: 3
Stimulus Need: 0
Love Need: 5

Birth Pattern #10: John F. Kennedy

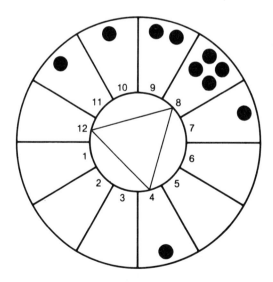

Need Gestalt

Growth Need: 2
Security Need: 1
Stimulus Need: 2
Love Need: 5

achievements reflect the fullness, the involvement and the freedom from inhibition characteristic of the adult who was loved and appreciated as a child.

The Growth Need

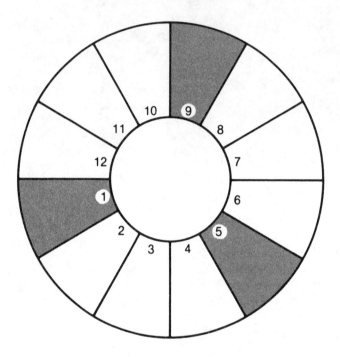

The Growth Need is the need to cope unassisted with life challenges in order to become, to test, and to define a private identity. Growth is enthusiastic, imaginative and self-reliant. Growth learns through trial and error.

C. R. Snyder and Howard L. Fromkin contend, in their theory of uniqueness, that people need to experience distinctive identities and that identity loss is frustrating. Both Horney and Maslow concur on the importance of the experience of individuality. Erich Fromm writes of the need to feel "the freedom to create the self."

Every child, notes Arthur Janov, needs to grow at its own pace in its own way. At the turn of the century, Karl Groos wrote of the child's delight "in being a cause." Contemporary researchers describe the child's capacity to find out what it can do in its environment (Piaget), the ability to explore specifically and to bring new and uncertain conditions under personal control (Berlyne), and seek out and conquer inconsistent situations in order to make maximum use of personal potential (Mischel).

Growth questions what is to prompt the discovery of what can be; growth poses and solves its own problems. Growth continually invents itself from the raw material of private life experience.

All external pressures to conform frustrate the Growth Need. Children who are not allowed to solve their own problems cease to trust their own abilities. Children who are pressed to perform beyond their abilities in age-inappropriate ways are destined to fail. Failure due to outside pressure involves humiliation and repeated humiliations leave a child discouraged, cautious and submissive, fearful of mistakes, avoidant of risks. There is, by contrast, no humiliation in the failure that inevitably occurs when a child attempts to push beyond its own limits. Where the Growth Need thrives, there will always be another day.

Growth frustrations leave the ego hungry for praise and attention. The secure identity, by contrast, is immune to flattery. Erik Erikson writes: "a weak ego does not gain substantial strength from being persistently bolstered. A strong ego, secured in its identity by a strong society, does not need and in fact is immune to any deliberate attempt at artificial inflation. Its tendency is toward the testing of what feels real, the mastery of that which proves necessary, the enjoyment of the vital, and the overcoming of the morbid."[3] Growth always accompanies a vital enthusiasm for living out one's distinct destiny.

Birth Pattern #11 maps the personality pattern of diarist-writer Anaïs Nin. Rarely does one life revolve so totally around a single need gratification or reflect so clearly the independence, freedom and uniqueness of growth's self-determination. Anaïs Nin courted the unconventional. She preferred being a mistress to being a wife. Women, Nin felt, were inherently more creative than men and were consequently responsible for nurturing masculine creativity.

When publishers rejected her books, she published them herself. One husband divorced her because she placed her personal creativity above her concern for society. She was a popular lecturer to feminist organizations though she herself argued against social causes of any kind. If change was to occur at all, Nin believed, it could only happen when individuals began to treat other individuals differently.

Anaïs Nin's life revolved around two important themes say the biographical researchers Mildred and Victor Goertzel: her pleasure in being a mistress to creative men and her emphasis on the "sacredness of the inner journey." She saw in psychoanalysis the means to liberate herself from her suffocating mother and her adored but unaffectionate father. Analyst Otto Rank attempted to use Anaïs as a lay therapist but her personality was simply too dominant.

Birth Pattern #11: Anaïs Nin

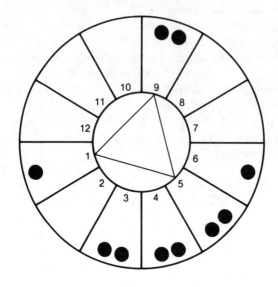

Need Gestalt

Growth Need: 5
Security Need: 1
Stimulus Need: 2
Love Need: 2

Birth Pattern #12: Ethel Kennedy

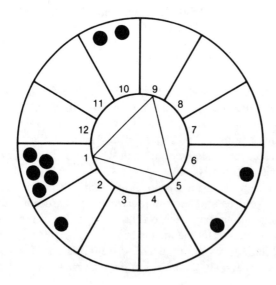

Need Gestalt

Growth Need: 6
Security Need: 4
Stimulus Need: 0
Love Need: 0

Very few individuals, male or female, script their lives as distinctively as Anaïs Nin. Nin wrote her own role. More commonly, high growth people seek demanding circumstances that challenge their capabilities.

Birth Pattern #12 is the personality pattern of Ethel Skakel Kennedy. Like Jacqueline Kennedy Onassis and Joan Kennedy, Ethel Kennedy has a strong Growth Need orientation. Her life typifies the usual growth experience of most women who expect to grow in conventional ways but, instead, find themselves in extraordinary circumstances.

Ethel Skakel's father, a self-made millionaire, provided a role model of growth. Her mother was a warm and devoutly religious person. Ethel Skakel spent her childhood in an atmosphere of freedom and play. The Skakel children were active children; they ran wild; they often took risks. The common assumption that childhood freedom encourages irresponsibility is well-countered in the life and personality of Ethel Skakel Kennedy. Freedom is essential to growth fulfillment.

The Goertzels describe the wealthy Skakel's home as a place where "dogs wet on the floor and children ran and wrestled." If the children were indulged, they were also encouraged to be generous.

Ethel Skakel's marriage to Robert Kennedy reflects her growth-oriented personality. She adopted his goals and supported his ambition. She actively involved herself in the role of political wife, studying issues and entertaining with the same open-door policy that marked her childhood environment. She grew as a wife, as a mother and as a social activist. She grew not by daring to be unconventional, but by an extraordinary capacity to survive.

Birth Pattern #13 is the personality pattern of John Anderson. From the standpoint of personal growth, there is no difference between the woman who grows through being a wife and the man who grows through casting his lot with a political party or a corporation. Growth-oriented people often borrow established roles in order to outgrow them, though it is rarely a conscious choice at the outset. John Anderson may be a unique example of a politician who outgrew the political system. Given Anderson's extreme growth focus, his 1980 independent bid for the American presidency may have been inevitable.

A political and Christian conservative during his first years in office, Anderson received a 95 rating from the conservative Americans for Constitutional Action. By the end of the sixties, he vocally opposed the Vietnam War. A few scant years later, he was the first Republican congressman to publicly suggest that Richard Nixon should leave office.

Too independent for political back-slapping and whiskey tipping, Anderson had few intimates among fellow congressmen. He was a political loner just as he had been a loner in college. His congressional forte was his striking personality projection and his skill in argument and debate.

Birth Pattern #13: John Anderson

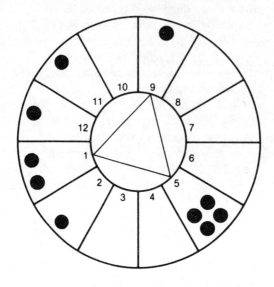

Need Gestalt

Growth Need: 7
Security Need: 1
Stimulus Need: 1
Love Need: 1

Birth Pattern #14: George Herman "Babe" Ruth

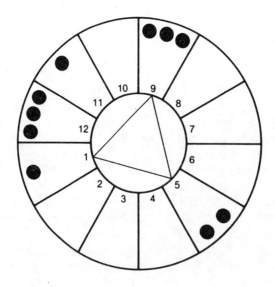

Need Gestalt

Growth Need: 6
Security Need: 0
Stimulus Need: 1
Love Need: 3

The small incidents in life reveal personality as clearly as life's crises and turning points. A *Newsweek* story reported a political rally at which Anderson was having trouble with a microphone. His wife and an aide prompted him to move the microphone aside. He looked down from the podium and said, "I'm getting all kinds of advice up here. I think I'll tell them to let me do it the way I want to."

Birth Pattern #14 maps the personality of baseball idol George Herman "Babe" Ruth. To people all over the world he was a symbol of American culture, so much so that Japanese soldiers in World War II used the battle cry "To hell with Babe Ruth!"

Babe Ruth's childhood experience might have devastated a personality oriented more strongly toward security and love satisfactions. He was severely rejected by both parents and as a delinquent seven-year-old he went to a Catholic boys' correctional institution. There he discovered his growth medium: baseball.

Babe Ruth was the unrivalled king of baseball. He accumulated records, fame and public acclaim. One sportswriter called Babe Ruth a one-man union because Ruth was the first baseball player to draw a large salary based on his personal image and his ability to pack the ballpark with enthusiastic fans.

The Stimulus Need

Human beings are social creatures. Psychology's pioneers each noted this fact. Freud stressed the compromise each person must make between the demands of personal satisfactions and the requirements and strictures of the culture. Jung saw in culture a deeply supportive force stemming from shared human symbols called archetypes. Adler stressed the significance of a child's relationship to its siblings and the family position the child occupies by virtue of its place in the birth order.

The family is the smallest social unit that shapes the child's social experience. Family dynamics and the presence of brothers and sisters create a shared experience in which a child learns that it is able to influence other people. The ability to participate in family interaction provides the first avenue of feeling that one belongs.

The Stimulus Need has the same expansive qualities as the Growth Need. Just as specific exploration expands the sense of control, Berlyne notes a second, diversive exploration designed to increase the experience of the environment through diversity, variety and information gain. Society is itself a collection of information and of established solutions to survival problems. Each individual discovers these solutions for himself or herself, however, and the stimulus of discovery is equally as motivating as the inventiveness of growth.

Just as children must grow in their own ways at their own paces, children have limits to their stimulus-handling abilities. Overstimulation causes confusion, chaos, and loss of meaning. The world intrudes when it informs too rapidly. Stimulus deprivation, if it is extreme, produces retardation; otherwise it leaves a sensory hunger that makes risky or dangerous situations seem appealing. Stimulus Need frustrations underlie boredom, depression, nervousness and irritability.

People whose stimulus needs are gratified on a regular basis are open to life, able to make effective choices from a variety of appealing alternatives, in contact with a general human essence that allows them to bridge the distance to others, and confident of their influence in shared situations.

Birth Pattern #15 maps the personality pattern of Senator Edward Kennedy. Kennedy was the youngest of the nine Kennedy children. Adler believed that the youngest child learns the fine art of social interaction early and is popular with peers because he or she has learned first to get along with siblings. Ted Kennedy spent his early school years in a variety of boarding schools where he was well liked.

Travel is an important stimulus to development as well and Kennedy travelled extensively before he entered public life. His broad-based background allows him to relate to a diverse number of minority groups whose social needs are reflected in his liberal voting record.

Birth Pattern #15: Edward Kennedy

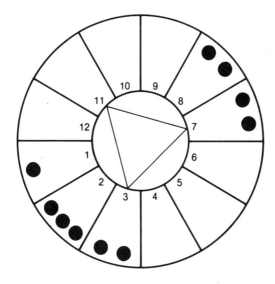

Need Gestalt

Growth Need: 1
Security Need: 3
Stimulus Need: 4
Love Need: 2

Birth Pattern #16: Billy Carter

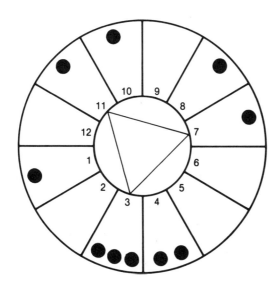

Need Gestalt

Growth Need: 1
Security Need: 1
Stimulus Need: 5
Love Need: 3

Ted Kennedy's first political experience came when he worked for his brother John's 1958 senatorial campaign. Adler's psychology stressed the significant pressures felt by younger family members when older siblings are extremely successful. Though the older child acts as a stimulus, the younger suffers both through comparison and through the pressure to catch up. A younger child rarely has the opportunity to be judged on the basis of his own merit alone. Billy Carter, another presidential brother, also suffered through comparison to an achieving older brother. Birth Pattern #16 maps Billy Carter's personality.

Billy Carter's early childhood years reflect the variety of human input essential to stimulus satisfaction. Like Ted Kennedy, Billy Carter was the youngest child of a large and competitive family. Carter's older sisters were both attentive and protective. His nanny and the family's handyman provided important adult influences in addition to his hard-working, achieving parents.

The high stimulus capacity to make other people feel at ease in his presence manifested early in Billy Carter's life and culminated in the press's "good old boy" image of him. His stimulus-related temperamental qualities, the intensity, the puckish humor, the mercurial image combined with his craving for excitement produced a media ideal. Billy Carter could be counted on to do or say something interesting or shocking or controversial.

People with high stimulus needs have abundant energy and the capacity to support multiple outlets for that energy. Billy Carter, his sister wrote, "can wear you out...it's impossible to stay up with him." Once Jimmy Carter became fully involved in politics, Billy took over the family peanut business. The business, once a source of tension and rivalry between them, fared well under Billy's management due to his easy, friendly openness with local peanut farmers. The famous Carter gas station, too, was an additional social stimulus satisfaction where the energetic, effusive Carter played host to friends, tourists and press alike.

Birth Pattern #17 is the natal chart of actress Barbara Stanwyck. Her life illustrates not only the stimulus themes of sibling influence and exciting travel but the stimulus challenges of overcoming timidity and developing social confidence. Orphaned at four, Barbara Stanwyck spent her childhood in a series of impersonal foster homes. Her sister Millie first arranged for the young Barbara's care but later took her travelling with road shows. The show business surroundings stimulated her interest and she taught herself to dance.

Friends and mentors shaped her early career and lent important social support. Stanwyck's social stimulus sensitivity became shyness, which made it difficult for her to interview for acting parts. She once fled director Frank Capra's office exclaiming that he "wouldn't want her anyway." Her husband persuaded the director to watch her screen test and she was hired.

Birth Pattern #17: Barbara Stanwyk

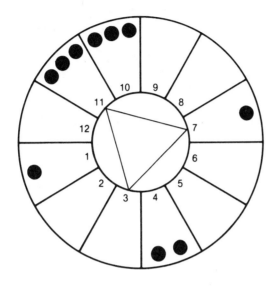

Need Gestalt

Growth Need: 1
Security Need: 3
Stimulus Need: 4
Love Need: 2

Birth Pattern #18: Eva Braun

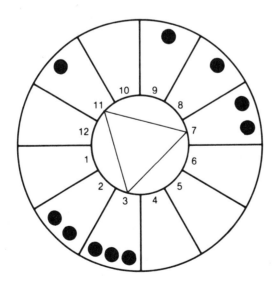

Need Gestalt

Growth Need: 1
Security Need: 2
Stimulus Need: 6
Love Need: 1

Capra went on to develop and shape Barbara Stanwyck's acting talent. He used special methods to cope with Stanwyck's spontaneous stimulus quality. Since she gave her all on a first take and had little reserve left for retakes, Capra rehearsed the rest of the cast and used Stanwyck's natural ability in one final filming.

When Barbara Stanwyck gained professional success, she became a particularly cooperative and hard-working actress. Director Capra commented that, "In a Hollywood popularity contest, she would win first prize hands down."

Birth Pattern #18 is the natal chart of Eva Braun, mistress of Adolph Hitler. The vivacious and impressionable young Eva experienced social and family forces that distorted her strong stimulus need and set the stage for her later stimulus-craving. Eva Braun's father was bitter over the German defeat in World War I. Her mother constantly stressed the importance of social standing and marriage to a man of prestige.

Eva went to a convent school though her mother felt her too "frivolous" to excel in studies. School was simply the place for Eva to develop the social poise necessary to attract the right man.

Eva's strong stimulus potential helped her assess situations quickly and come to socially expedient conclusions. She was at first shocked, but later influenced, by a friend who confided to Eva that she had begun to date wealthy, lonely men who bought her presents in return for her companionship. Shortly thereafter, Eva met the sullen Adolf Hitler. Though she did not like him, she did her best to put him at his ease and amuse him.

When Eva Braun discovered Hitler's celebrity status, he became the image suited to her stimulus needs. Her effort to win him over started in earnest. Competition with another mistress added more excitement but Eva won by default when Hitler's first mistress shot herself. Much later in the relationship when Eva heard rumors of other mistresses, she too attempted suicide. Her life was saved by a Jewish physician.

The difference between a very high concentration of markers in a single need versus a very minor one or no marker emphasis on that same need can be difficult to see in actual counselling practice. A Security Need problem is a Security Need problem, for instance, and the underlying feelings will always be related to the security theme. Jung notes that a well-differentiated factor operates actively and consistently as a facet of the will. A poorly differentiated factor operates erratically and reactively tending to find passive solutions to the demands posed by the need. The inability to adapt is always productive of some emotional response to the adjustment failure. This is the outstanding characteristic of the little-emphasized need as the person tends to experience it. By contrast, the frustrated dominant need is a frustration of some will-directed action. Often it comes as a surprise.

Holistic measurement is a powerful measurement because it directs our attention to the heart of the matter. Since holistic birth pattern measurement reduces measurement to a minimum, we never run the risk of becoming more interested in the measurements themselves than in the personality we are measuring.

Did you find yourself beginning to think holistically? Did you apply your knowledge of the Security Need when you got to John F. Kennedy's Need Gestalt with its single security marker? Since cultural conditioning cannot be relied on outside one's native culture, can you go back to Angela Davis's Need Gestalt now and apply what you know about the Stimulus Need to more fully understand the depth of her college-age crisis? Though both Ethel Kennedy and Anaïs Nin have powerful Growth Needs, what does the difference between these two women's Security Need emphases suggest? Learning assessment means learning to see the Need Gestalt as a whole.

Birth Pattern Psychology deals with universal human processes. Because we are human, we all experience the Security processes of utilizing and producing, the Love processes of bringing close and enjoying, the Growth processes of inventing and problem-solving and the Stimulus processes of discovering and making interesting. We do these things every day. We know how these processes feel. Simply by virtue of our human status, we are already experts. Birth patterns do not give us information but rather allow us a means to make full use of the human store of information we already possess. Birth patterns formalize and objectify our inherent knowledge of human nature.

2 The Hierarchy of Needs

Growth, security, stimulus and love are universal needs. We all seek identity, safety, belonging and intimacy. We differ from one another not in *what* we need but in *how much* we need it. We also differ in our priorities. You may value love and intimacy far more than growth, security or stimulus satisfactions. Your best friend may, instead, place security satisfactions over love, stimulus or growth. The study of individual differences is the study of personal priorities.

In Chapter 1, we explored each basic need individually. We cannot, in reality, separate these primary motivations since they do not truly exist as isolated units. The needs for growth, security, stimulus and love are a gestalt. Imagine that your basic needs are inner voices. Because they function as a gestalt or unified whole, they are all speaking to you *at the same time.* You hear the need that speaks with the loudest voice first. It makes the strongest bid for your attention. Once you satisfy your strongest need, it ceases to speak so loudly and you now hear the next loudest voice of the next most pressing need. So it goes until each need gets your attention and gains its appropriate satisfactions.

The need triangle containing the most planets speaks with the loudest voice. The need triangle containing the fewest planets speaks most softly. The Need Gestalt shows us the strengths of the various inner voices at a glance. It enables us to see the individual's personal priorities or hierarchy of needs.

Maslow's Hierarchy of Needs

Abraham Maslow, the father of humanistic psychology, popularized the concept of a need hierarchy. He believed that understanding personality meant understanding motivation as well. Maslow proposed a hierarchy of needs in the following order:

5. Self-actualization need
4. Esteem need
3. Belongingness and love needs
2. Safety need
1. Physiological needs

This hierarchy, Maslow believed, was common to most people. He ranked the needs from lowest or physiological needs to highest or self-actualization need.

Birth Pattern Psychology's need hierarchies differ from Maslow's hierarchy on two points. First, none of the primary needs for growth, security, stimulus or love is innately higher or lower than the others. Second, the order of these four motivations is distinctly personal. Maslow himself noted people whose priorities differed from his basic hierarchy.

Step one, the physiological needs, does not concern us. The basic survival drives for food, water, air, sleep or sex are completely physiological. These drives have specific biological satisfiers and measurable biological effects. We need not study personality to know how long the human being can exist without food or water or air. The sex drive alone can be considered a need as well as a drive. The physiological needs are understood; they are the foundation or "given" portion of human physical existence.

The second, third and fourth steps of Maslow's hierarchy correspond with Birth Pattern Psychology's four basic needs. Step two, safety needs, are security needs. Step three, belongingness and love needs, treats the interpersonal love and stimulus needs as a unit. Esteem needs, step four of Maslow's hierarchy, correspond to growth needs.

The highest rung of Maslow's motivational ladder is the need for self-actualization. It is, in Maslow's words, the need to "become everything that one is capable of becoming." The need for self-actualization is symbolized by the birth pattern as a whole.

A birth pattern's need hierarchy and Maslow's need hierarchy have much in common. Both hierarchies describe sets of priorities. Both hierarchies stretch from the greatest to the least pressing motivations. Most important, both hierarchies explore the process through which the person becomes a distinct individual.

Maslow's Views on Satisfaction

Need gratification is an ongoing process. First one basic need and then another demands our attention. Consequently, it is necessary to study a particular individual within a broad life context. The overall pattern of choice and development is far more significant than single events or isolated experiences. Individuals with minimal stimulus needs could be attending a group meeting on any given night. Group involvement is generally stimulus-satisfying but it would be wrong to conclude that everyone at one particular meeting has strong stimulus needs. It would require regular observation of a group to distinguish the high stimulus need members from the low stimulus need members.

Maslow points out another shortcoming inherent in studying specific events. An event or experience usually satisfies several needs simultaneously. Marriage is a prime source of intimacy and love need gratification but it would be a rare marriage indeed if elements of trust and safety, interest and stimulation, esteem and growth were totally lacking. Work establishes security but it also encourages growth and may lead to interesting new contacts that eventually become intimate friendships.

The Four-Digit Need Gestalt allows us to compare the pattern of personal needs with the pattern of personal experience. When need priorities clearly emerge in the pattern of life choices, the individual is basically satisfied. When the pattern of life diverges dramatically from the pattern of personal needs, a person is generally frustrated and unhappy.

The strongest need, indicated by the need triangle containing the most planets, speaks with the loudest inner voice. If it spoke constantly, the person would never hear the voices of the other needs nor climb the rungs of the distinctive inner need hierarchy. Something must obviously happen to quiet the voice of one need so that other needs emerge. That something is need satisfaction.

According to Maslow's theory, satisfaction changes our priorities and unfolds our hierarchy of needs. According to Birth Pattern Psychology, needs emerge in the order indicated by the Four-Digit Need Gestalt. The illustration shows Babe Ruth's birth pattern and his personal Four-Digit Need Gestalt. Ruth's individual need hierarchy would be:

5. Self-actualization
4. Security
3. Stimulus
2. Love
1. Growth

Exploring Ruth's life in depth will show us the satisfaction process in action.

The dominant Growth Need is the first step in Babe Ruth's need hierarchy. The Growth Need must be satisfied before other needs can emerge. Single, temporary growth satisfactions are not enough. Babe Ruth requires an overall life context that assures continual Growth Need gratification. From

Birth Pattern #14: "Babe" Ruth

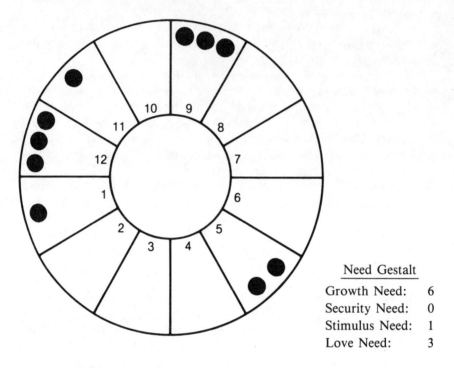

Need Gestalt

Growth Need:	6
Security Need:	0
Stimulus Need:	1
Love Need:	3

Chapter 1, we know that Babe Ruth's childhood love of baseball provides the essential identity, ego-gratification and self-expression his dominant Growth Need demands.

The year is 1914. The young Babe Ruth makes a confident professional debut with the minor league Baltimore Orioles. His talent commands attention, his salary escalates and the world champion Boston Red Sox buy his contract. In this first year alone, Babe Ruth lays the foundation of a baseball legend and establishes a life context of personal growth. Regardless of daily ups and downs or temporary fulfillments and frustration, Ruth can now satisfy his dominant Growth Need on an ongoing basis.

Maslow notes that satisfied needs recede into the background of our attention as long as they continue to be satisfied. Thus other, unsatisfied needs assume priority. From the Four-Digit Need Gestalt and the related need hierarchy, we anticipate a shift in Babe Ruth's attention from the satisfied Growth Need to the as yet unsatisfied Love Need.

At twenty, Babe Ruth has two years of professional success behind him. He marries Helen Woodford, a teenaged waitress from Texas.

Satisfaction changes our attitudes and values as well as our priorities. The satisfaction process is a very human process in which, Maslow points out, we tend to overrate the satisfiers of our ungratified needs while we underrate the satisfiers of our well-gratified needs. We feel the thrill of infatuation in that first taste of intimacy when the loved one is not yet ours. By contrast, we take the intimacy of a long-standing relationship for granted. Our first year on a new job is challenging and productive while later years become routine.

The youthful Babe Ruth, troubled and rejected, lives for baseball. Babe Ruth the successful athlete and baseball idol leads a life of extravagance. His drinking, gambling and fighting with people in authority jeopardize his career. Finally, he is suspended from baseball for a time. A plea from the New York Senator Jimmy Walker urges Babe Ruth to think of the impression he makes on countless children. Ruth must reevaluate his growth. He comes, once again, face to face with his own dominant need and tearfully vows to reform. It is a vow he will keep.

No planet markers emphasize the Security Triangle in Babe Ruth's birth pattern. The Four-Digit Need Gestalt shows us that security is Ruth's least significant need. According to Maslow, we underrate the satisfiers of our less important unsatisfied needs.

Ruth never feels that security is important. He is often in debt. Though he draws large salaries throughout his baseball career and makes additional money from endorsements and other business interests, he saves nothing. By 1924, Ruth's wife and his business manager persuade him to establish a trust fund. His biography labels this an "incredible feat."

Need satisfaction is the business of life. It can be a challenging, difficult business. Maslow believes that all of us, ultimately, need self-actualization. We need to be all that we can be; we want the proportions of our lives to match the proportions of our needs. Once we achieve such proportion, we become our most creative, productive, fulfilled selves.

Was Babe Ruth a self-actualizer? Maslow would undoubtedly say no. Though Maslow studied thousands of people, he could find but a handful who fit his criteria for self-actualization. If we take a broad view of self-actualization, however, and if we compare Babe Ruth's achievements with the pattern of his temperament, we see that his life priorities reflect his personal needs. To this extent, Babe Ruth fulfilled his distinct personality potential.

Dominant Needs

Any Need Triangle containing four or more planets signifies a dominant need. Dominant needs are strong motivators. All the birth patterns studied up to now have at least one dominant need; some have two. Where there is a dominant need, there is also a great demand for satisfaction. Lesser need satisfactions do not compensate for dominant need frustration. People who cannot satisfy a dominant need feel dissatisfied with life in general.

Chapter 1 explored the results of satisfaction and frustration in depth. Satisfaction strengthens the person from within. Growth satisfactions foster confidence and expressivity, security satisfactions foster productivity and stability, stimulus satisfactions lend informed objectivity and sense of belonging while love satisfactions promote self-acceptance and empathy.

Satisfied people are responsible people. Responsible people have an inner locus of control. Locus of control is an important psychological concept (see References, Chapter 2). It tells us whether the determining factors are within the person or outside the person and therefore outside his or her perceived control. Self-determining people have an inner locus of control; they make things happen; they do not expect the environment or other people to gratify their personal needs.

Frustration can put the locus of control in the environment. People see themselves as victims. Dominant need frustration gives tremendous power to potential dominant need satisfiers. When satisfiers possess the power to control, people feel they cannot actively achieve personal satisfaction.

Birth patterns have no signposts to indicate locus of control. People's attitudes express both their satisfactions and their frustrations, their self-determination or lack of it. Satisfied people would say, for instance, that Babe Ruth achieved greatness by playing baseball. This attitude emphasizes the *person*, Babe Ruth. Frustrated people would see the same situation in reverse. Baseball made Babe Ruth great. This attitude emphasizes the *satisfier,* baseball. It puts the person in a passive, receiving state.

Dominant need satisfiers control the frustrated person, they do not satisfy. The love-frustrated person, for instance, attempts to please the loved one at all costs. The potential satisfier's power grows with the increase in need frustration. Extreme frustration makes a potential dominant need satisfier look like the solution to all life's problems.

Birth pattern #19 is the personality pattern of former Manson family member Charles "Tex" Watson. The Four-Digit Need Gestalt indicates a dominant Love Need. Tex Watson met Charles Manson at the home of rock musician Brian Wilson. His description of their meeting testifies to both the power of a potential dominant need satisfier and the importance of unconditional love:

"Here I was, accepted in a world I'd never even dreamed about, mellow and at my ease. Charlie murmured in the background, something about love, finding love, letting yourself love. I suddenly realized that this was what I was looking for: love. Not that my parents and brother and sister hadn't loved me, but somehow, now, that didn't count. I wanted

Birth Pattern #19: Charles "Tex" Watson

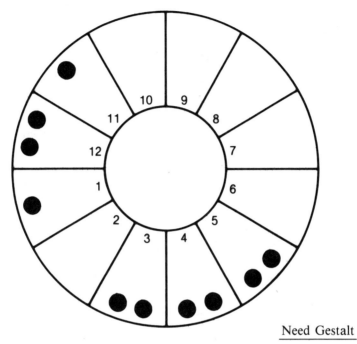

Need Gestalt

Growth Need:	3
Security Need:	0
Stimulus Need:	3
Love Need:	4

the kind of love they talked about in the songs—the kind of love that didn't ask you to be anything, didn't judge what you were, didn't set up any rules or regulations—the kind of love that just accepted you, let you be yourself...."[4]

Manson and his Family were such important sources of love and acceptance that when Manson asked, "Will you die for me?", Watson immediately answered, "Yes."

Note that Tex Watson's Growth and Stimulus Needs are equally motivating. Each need triangle contains three planet markers. Once Watson's dominant Love Need was satisfied, he would experience the next step of his personal need hierarchy. He would feel not one need but two. He would experience a conflict of priorities.

Conflicting Priorities

Need conflict is not only natural, it is desirable. Need conflict fuels development. These natural inner conflicts will be discussed at length in Part Two: Analysis. Like frustration, need conflicts are only difficult to master when the locus of control is in the satisfiers and not in the self.

Conflicting priorities immobilize the frustrated person. Two satisfiers have equal appeal. A step toward one is a step away from the other. Every potential gain is also a loss. The level of the conflict reflects the level of motivation inherent in the competing needs. Competing dominant needs thus indicate far greater conflict than weak competing needs.

People who accept the responsibility for their own satisfactions welcome choice, they do not fear it. For them, competing needs open alternative paths to satisfaction and self-expression. They emphasize the self as chooser rather than the satisfiers that are chosen. If people enjoy what they have, the satisfactions they achieve do not cancel the possibility of other potential satisfactions. Tomorrow they may choose what they did not choose today. Self-determining people resolve conflicting priorities by creating life contexts in which equally motivating needs are fulfilled equally.

Birth Pattern #20: Janis Joplin

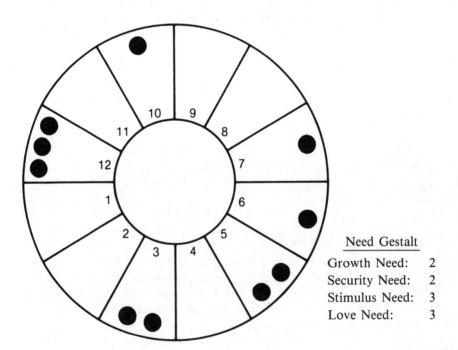

Need Gestalt

Growth Need:	2
Security Need:	2
Stimulus Need:	3
Love Need:	3

Birth Pattern #20 is the personality pattern of rock singer Janis Joplin. Joplin's Four-Digit Need Gestalt shows an average emphasis on each of the four basic needs. The 3-3-2-2 planetary distribution and its variations are doubly interesting. First, there is no dominant need. No one avenue of fulfillment can establish an overall life theme. Second, there are conflicting priorities. Since all four needs are average motivators, no one need can comfortably be set aside.

People who lack self-determination are particularly vulnerable in the face of multiple motivations. With no clear priorities, *everything* is important. They place heavy demands on life. They try to wring every ounce of satisfaction from every experience. Since they emphasize need satisfiers, any potential satisfier is appealing. They simply want it all. Because they want it all, something is always missing. Without inner self-definition, they try to be all things to all people. They also expect all things from other people and so disappoint themselves in relationships.

Janis Joplin was a gifted, multi-talented youngster. Her family supported and encouraged her talents. The local schools, unfortunately, provided neither support nor recognition. Janis, the versatile child, became Janis, the thoroughly rebellious adolescent. She moved to California where "all of a sudden someone threw (her) in this rock and roll band." She clearly felt that life was happening to her, not resulting from her personal choices. Janis's inner frustrations were fuel for her wants. She wanted, in her own words, "ten years of superhypermost." She did not get them.

Actresses Jean Harlow and Marilyn Monroe, actor Montgomery Clift, writer Ernest Hemingway, homosexual poets and lovers Paul Verlaine and Arthur Rimbaud, and rock star Jim Morrison all had some version of the 3-3-2-2 pattern of basic needs. All were depressed, frustrated people in spite of their personal successes. Several committed suicide. All were self-destructive.

Self-determining people make the most of any pattern of personal need and any hierarchy of personal motivation. Those with 3-3-2-2 patterns bring themselves fully and completely to all life situations. They meet challenges head-on and seek flexible solutions to life problems. Self-determining people emphasize what they do, not what they want. They can be as demanding, impatient and temperamental as their non-self-determining counterparts. The difference lies in the opposing viewpoints. The self-determining person brings all of the self to the moment. The non-self-determining person, conversely, takes all he or she can get from the moment.

The absence of a dominant need and the lack of a distinct need hierarchy are no barriers to achievement. Composers Verdi, Debussy, Mozart and Puccini all had equally weighted basic needs. The birth patterns of actors

Marlon Brando and William Holden indicate no one dominant need. Brando actively supports the American Indian movement. Holden struggled to save African wildlife on his Kenya game preserve for over thirty years. Scientists Kepler and Tesla, writers Hugo and DeMaupassant and contemporary philosopher Alan Watts all have some version of the 3-3-2-2 pattern of basic needs.

Women with 3-3-2-2 patterns of need are not well represented among high achievers. Society has dictated much narrower roles for women than for men. It may be that until recently a woman with one strong, dominant motivation could more easily break free from the stereotypical female role. Marriage and motherhood may, as well, offer the balance of satisfactions that appeal to women with balanced, multiple motivations.

Most personality patterns fall into two broad categories, patterns with dominant needs and patterns with balanced need distributions. The dominant need pattern (4-3-2-1 and others) contains three elements: a dominant need function capable of compensating weaker personality elements, a central level three function (i.e., one of the needs weighted by three markers) providing a point of stability, and weaker functions or potential anxiety sources. Anxiety sources *seem* less difficult because of the compensation. The separation into anxiety and compensation grows more pronounced and hence more obvious as the person matures. Life crises, often during the thirties and forties, lead to recognition and acceptance of personal weaknesses freeing the strength from its compensatory role.

The balanced 3-3-2-2 distribution has potential stabilizers and potential weaknesses but it lacks a compensation. Though compensations are basically illusions, they encourage the points of crisis that demand resolution through confronting inner weakness. Crisis points for the balanced psyche may be delayed since it is less obvious that the personality itself is the cause of difficulty. Crises, when they finally come, tend to be global rather than specific and involve the whole of the life rather than one life aspect.

Jung felt that a personality whose processes are not well differentiated remains uncertain, hesitating, vascillating and impressionable. Such individuals change constantly and restlessly or adopt rigid and conventional roles to protect against this tendency.

The 3-3-3-1 pattern, too, lacks a dominant need focus. This pattern also lacks the Peter Pan quality common to the 3-3-2-2 due to the greater emphasis of the solidity of the threes. The 3-3-3-1 can do almost anything with assurance and poise and is the pattern most likely to transcend any initial life drawbacks. The 3-3-3-1 is an Achilles heel personality whose single vulnerability can become its undoing. The weakness has an appeal bordering on outright fascination. The weakness is rarely seen as personal, however, since vulnerability seems unnatural in the context of the Achilles personality.

Richard Nixon typifies the Achilles heel pattern. His successes contrast with his father's failures. The family's extreme religious practices appear not to have unduly biased him, nor did the family's social status dampen his aspiration. For Nixon, the single stimulus factor was the heel of vulnerability in his otherwise highly capable pattern. It shows in his resentment over the social exclusion of his early career years, in his dislike of the press and most of all in the now-famous "enemies" list. Nixon's Watergate crisis depicts the Achilles pattern's capacity to delay major life crises to a stunning degree.

The personality pattern illustrated by the Need Gestalt represents the individual's own characteristic balance. The qualities of the whole, whatever its form, demand full actualization. The demand is inner, not outer. The demand is constant. To achieve a life whose proportions mirror the proportions of the psyche is an ongoing life task. It *is* life. Achieving the balance brings the experience of wholeness, the experience of meaning, the experience of Self.

3 Measuring Temperament Types

Personality types date back at least two thousand years. The ancient Greeks based their fourfold temperament typology on Empedocles's theory of the four elements. The element Fire signified a choleric temperament. The element Earth signified a melancholic temperament. The element Air indicated a sanguine temperament while the element Water indicated a phlegmatic temperament.

Johann Wolfgang von Goethe further divided these ancient temperament types into subtypes. The sanguine or cheerful types were poets, lovers and bonvivants. The choleric or quick-tempered types were adventurers, heroes and despots. The melancholic or sad types were monarchs, scholars and philosophers and the phlegmatic or calm types were teachers, historians and orators.

Theories using a fourfold division of personality types remain popular. Carl Jung's thinking, feeling, sensate and intuitive types are based on perception rather than temperament. The most popular contemporary temperament theory, that of Arnold Buss, measures emotionality, activity, sociability and impulsivity. Ivan Petrovitch Pavlov also believed that psychologists could not improve on the ancient fourfold scheme of personality typing. Birth Pattern Psychology's four temperament types are based on the growth, security, stimulus and love needs.

Gordon Allport defines temperament as "the characteristic phenomena of an individual's emotional nature, including his susceptibility to emotional stimulation, his customary strength and speed of response, the quality of his prevailing mood, and all peculiarities of fluctuation and intensity in mood, these phenomena being regarded as dependent upon constitutional make-up, and therefore largely hereditary in origin."[5]

Temperament is thus the overall tone of the personality. Since temperament exists at birth, it is clearly reflected in the birth pattern. Temperament is both mental and physical. The Four-Digit Need Gestalt indicates the individual's temperament as well as his or her needs and priorities.

Temperament types are broad, general descriptions of the whole personality. Types show us the person's overall life context. All typologies identify people by one strong characteristic. Not all people have a single, emphatic need as we have seen in the last chapter. Thus not all birth patterns fit a personality type. Three out of four need gestalts have one foremost need. For these birth patterns, the related personality type provides additional insight into the individual's temperament.

Birth Pattern Psychology's four temperament types based on the primary needs are:

    The Individualist . . . . .Growth Need Priority
    The Realist . . . . .Security Need Priority
    The Humanist . . . . .Stimulus Need Priority
    The Romanticist . . . . .Love Need Priority

To identify the temperament type, look to the strongest single need in the Four-Digit Need Gestalt. Here are four examples of need gestalts:

Barbra Streisand		Judy Garland	
Growth:	4	Growth:	1
Security:	3	Security:	4
Stimulus:	2	Stimulus:	0
Love:	1	Love:	5

Martin Luther		Johann Wolfgang von Goethe	
Growth:	0	Growth:	3
Security:	0	Security:	3
Stimulus:	5	Stimulus:	1
Love:	5	Love:	3

Barbra Streisand's first priority or strongest need is her Growth Need. She fits the Individualist temperament type. Judy Garland's need gestalt has two dominant needs, the need for security and the need for love. The Love Need is stronger; she fits the Romanticist personality type. It is the strongest need, the first priority that sets the overall theme of the life. Thus no one fits two types. Judy Garland has the Romanticist temperament. She is not a Realist even though she has a strong Security Need.

Martin Luther, leader of the Protestant Reformation, has two very powerful needs for stimulus and for love. He does not have one foremost priority. Therefore he does not fit a temperament type. Goethe's need gestalt indicates a relatively balanced set of motivations. He has no dominant need, thus he does not fit a temperament type.

The following descriptions explore each personality type in depth. Remember that types are generalities. As you read each type, concentrate more on the general mood and temperament tone than on specifics. Temperament type should indicate a broad, overall feeling for the whole personality.

The Individualist

The Individualist's typical moods, attitudes, actions, and responses reflect his or her prominent Growth Need. Individualists are independent, determined people bent on expressing themselves to the fullest. They often behave as if rules were made for other people, not for them. Since they easily ignore traditional values and ideas, Individualists tend to blaze the trails that other people follow. Their courage can border on foolhardiness but they insist on the freedom to make their own mistakes and learn from their own experience.

Individualists' personal experiences provide the raw material from which they construct their unique identities. They measure an experience or event by the amount of personal growth they gain. Thus they rarely shrink from potentially painful situations. Individualists interpret life events idiosyncratically. What appears quite trivial to another's eye may be fraught with personal meaning for an Individualist.

Individualists are self-made men and women. They would rather fail on their own than succeed through someone else's influence. Individualists prefer doing things the hard way to asking for help. They can be quite insulted by unsolicited help or advice.

Individualists are willful children and rebellious adolescents. Their adolescent growth spurt causes self-consciousness. Individualists are particularly sensitive about their appearance. Youthful Individualists may not know who they are, but they often sense who they are not. The early years usually involve a struggle against external pressures. Time helps the Individualist grow into his or her own distinct temperament. Maturity alone can form the self the Individualist wants so much to express.

Each temperament has its weaknesses as well as its strengths. Individualists can be egocentric and selfish. Some have a penchant for exaggeration because they want so much to be special and to have special experiences. An Individualist who has discovered *the* truth will spare no effort in convincing others, whether they want to listen or not. Individualists are demanding and bossy when their personal goals are involved. When Individualists' authority or ideas are questioned, they become self-righteous and superior.

[59]

If you ask for an Individualist's opinion, you must be prepared to suffer the consequences. They are always frank, sometimes brutally so. Individualists would rather speak their minds than spare your feelings.

Individualists take most things personally. They live in a highly personal world full of the people, thoughts and activities with which they particularly identify. Time is of the essence in this world. Things must happen when the Individualist is ready. Too much too soon unsettles them but too little too late saps their enthusiasm.

We see the Individualist's distinctive image. Individualists involve us in their uniqueness. We do not see the job that is done, we see the Individualist who is doing the job. We may be shocked and surprised by the Individualist's ideas but we are fascinated as well. Though others may have the same career or concepts, it is often the Individualist who emerges as a focal point.

The Individualists in the original birth pattern sample of five hundred show us Individualism in action. Individualism is Roy Rogers, the archetypal cowboy. It is Babe Ruth, the "Sultan of Swat" stamping his identity on Yankee Stadium, "The House that Ruth Built" and right field, "Ruthville."

Individualists are never shy about voicing their personal opinions, particularly when they have a strong sense of mission. Individualism is Gloria Steinem speaking out for women's rights and F. Lee Bailey criticising the American legal system. Individualism is the stamp of Henry Kissinger's style on the face of international diplomacy.

The Individualist's quest for personal identity is embodied in Alex Haley's search for his roots.

There is simply no replacement for the Individualist. Imagine the *Tonight Show* without Johnny Carson. Anyone singing Bob Dylan songs simply sounds like a Dylan imitation.

Individualists often break down long-standing social barriers. They open seemingly locked doors through sheer willpower. Individualist Marie Curie excelled in the "man's world" of science. Individualist Robyn Smith proved that a woman could be a successful jockey. Individualist Elizabeth Kubler-Ross brought the subject of death and dying out of the psychological closet.

Individualists project erotic sexual images. Individualist Brigitte Bardot symbolizes the come-hither physical allure of Individualism. Youthful Individualist Brooke Shields aroused public controversy with her provocative movies and her advertisements for designer jeans. Individualist publisher Larry Flynt walks a fine line between the erotic and the sensational. Individualist Anaïs Nin's *Delta of Venus* is a classic work of erotic fiction.

Individualists are free spirits. They pursue life with vitality and enthusiasm, exploring all possible alternatives in their quests for personal growth.

Here are more Individualists from the birth pattern sample. The number following each name indicates the total number of markers in the Growth Need Triangle.

Richard Alpert, guru (4)
John Anderson, politician (7)
Rudolph Bing, opera manager (6)
Lord Byron, poet (5)
Jimmy Carter, president (4)
Richard Chamberlain, actor (5)
Isadora Duncan, dancer (4)
Peggy Fleming, skater (5)
George Foreman, boxer (5)
Stephen Foster, composer (4)
Francisco Franco, dictator (4)
Dorothy Hamill, skater (4)
Lyndon Johnson, president (6)
Helen Keller, lecturer (4)
Grace Kelly, princess (6)
Ethel Kennedy, political wife (6)
Jacqueline Kennedy Onassis, first lady (4)
Joan Kennedy, political wife (5)
Janet Leigh, actress (5)
Nicolo Machiavelli, statesman (4)
Margaret Mead, anthropologist (4)
Walter Mondale, politician (5)
Aldo Moro, Italian Premier (5)

Pat Nixon, first lady (5)
Sidney Omarr, astrologer (5)
Vance Packard, writer (4)
Leontyne Price, opera singer (4)
Rafael, artist (5)
Jerry Reed, singer (6)
Mickey Rooney, actor (4)
Susan Saint James, actress (4)
Franz Schubert, composer (4)
Peter Sellers, actor (4)
Dinah Shore, singer (4)
Margaret Chase Smith, politician (4)
Ringo Starr, musician (6)
Barbra Streisand, entertainer (4)
Algernon Swinburne, writer (7)
Shirley Temple Black, actress (5)
Henri Toulouse-Lautrec, artist (4)
Margaret Trudeau, political wife (4)
Jon Voight, actor (4)
Diane Von Furstenberg, entrepreneur (5)
George Wallace, politician (4)
H.G. Welles, writer (4)
Orson Welles, actor (4)

The Realist

The Realist's typical moods, attitudes, actions and responses reflect his or her prominent Security Need. Realists want to have something concrete to show for their efforts. They like to see tangible results. Realists stress personal responsibility. They hold themselves accountable for their own actions and demand accountability from others as well.

Realists make things happen. They are the movers and the shakers of the world. Realists seize every opportunity, great or small. Their strength lies in their ability to turn ordinary events into extraordinary successes. The Realist's power base is a strong sense of day-to-day living. They budget their time, are perfectionists at heart, delight in a job well done and resent disorder and confusion.

Continuity is important to the Realist. The Realist sees life as a flow. Events do not simply happen, they happen for a reason. When Realists see an effect, they want to know the cause. They admire solid logic and enjoy figuring out complex problems to find workable solutions.

Realists are calm, self-sufficient people blessed with common sense and fortitude. They often succeed through sheer persistence. Realists stress the fundamentals and master the basics. They are adept at finding the best in the past and they have a strong sense of heritage.

Realist children are alternatively bold or shy, depending on their comfort in their surroundings. Parents rarely understand when their considerate Realist children become stubborn, resistant adolescents. Adolescent Realists begin to test the limits of their personal power and authority. Part of the testing process lies in questioning the authority of others, particularly their parents.

Realists, too, have their less than endearing qualities. The time to talk rationally with a Realist is *before* the Realist makes up his or her mind. Once a Realist makes a decision, the topic is closed. Question the authority of a Realist and he or she becomes parental, the voice of experience and wisdom.

Realists do not like losing. They believe in fairness and when they feel they have been treated unfairly, they go to great lengths to even the score. Realists dislike failure in any form. They find it difficult to let go, especially in jobs or relationships that seem unfinished.

Realists have a down-to-earth quality that makes them seem familiar, like one of the family. They are self-directed but they love the opportunity to prove what they can do. Realists prefer substance. Their senses are very acute and they surround themselves with objects that spell quality and value.

The Realists in the original birth pattern sample show us Realism in action. Realism is the practical advice of Ann Landers applied to the problems and crises of everyday life. Realism is the financial empire of J. Paul Getty as well as the financial theory of Karl Marx. The supreme genius of Realism, Albert Einstein, looked within the physical world and formulated its laws.

Realists excel in activities that demand physical mastery, endurance and stamina. We admire the athletic excellence of boxer Muhammad Ali, swimmer Mark Spitz or golfer Jack Nicklaus. We appreciate physical mastery raised to an art form by the choreography of Realist Anver Joffrey.

Realists often master their crafts so thoroughly that they have long, productive and durable careers. The persistence of Realism shows in the comedy of Lucille Ball, the acting of Helen Hayes and the dance of Gwen Verdon.

We feel a girl-next-door familiarity for Realists Doris Day and Sally Field. We identify with Henry Winkler's "Fonzie" because he depicts an easily identifiable type.

The Realist's relationship to his or her mother is an important life factor. The Goertzel studies (see Notes, Chapter 1) link maternal influence, sense of security and preference for military careers. Such was the case with Realist Dwight D. Eisenhower. National security was Realist J. Edgar Hoover's life work.

[62]

Realists are sensual rather than sexual. They project a solid, earthy quality that tends to inspire lust rather than passion. The forthright sensuality of Henry Miller's literature caused his books to be banned in more places than Boston. Realist Elvis Presley's physical presence aroused far more controversy than his music. Some of the screen's most sensual images stem from the performances of Realists Paul Newman, Robert Redford, and Valerie Perrine.

Realists stress the continuity of their personal drive for success. They live life head-on and find security in self-reliance.

Here are more Realists from the original birth pattern sample. The number following each name indicates the total number of planets in the Security Need Triangle.

Elizabeth Arden, entrepreneur (4)

Joan Baez, singer (4)

Harry Belafonte, singer (4)

William Blake, poet (4)

Jerry Brown, politician (5)

Anita Bryant, singer (4)

William F. Buckley, columnist (5)

Glen Campbell, singer (6)

Albert Camus, writer (4)

Steve Cauthen, jockey (5)

Judy Collins, singer (4)

Leonardo da Vinci, genius (4)

Adelle Davis, nutritionist (4)

Angela Davis, activist (5)

Amelia Earhart, aviator (4)

George Eliot, writer (5)

Mia Farrow, actress (4)

Jane Fonda, actress (4)

Betty Ford, first lady (4)

Joe Frazier, boxer (5)

Zsa Zsa Gabor, actress (5)

Merv Griffin, entertainer (5)

H.R. Haldeman, government official (7)

Jack Kerouac, writer (4)

Vivian Leigh, actress (4)

Ann Morrow Lindbergh, writer (8)

Dean Martin, singer (4)

Rollo May, psychologist (5)

Paul McCartney, musician (4)

Zubin Mehta, conductor (5)

Ralph Nader, consumer advocate (4)

Jack Nicholson, actor (6)

Sidney Poitier, actor (5)

Sylvia Porter, columnist (4)

Freddie Prinze, actor (5)

Ronald Reagan, president (4)

George Lincoln Rockwell, nazi (4)

August Rodin, sculptor (4)

Françoise Sagan, writer (4)

Arthur Schlesinger Jr., historian (5)

Max Schmeling, boxer (4)

Sally Struthers, actress (6)

Alfred Lord Tennyson, poet (4)

Gene Tierney, actress (4)

Abigail Van Buren, columnist (4)

Jules Verne, writer (6)

Oscar Wilde, writer (4)

Kaiser Wilhelm II, emperor

The Humanist

The Humanist's typical moods, attitudes, actions and responses reflect his or her prominent Stimulus Need. Humanists like to know everything about everything. They thrive on diversity and freedom of choice.

Humanists do not have acquaintances, they only have friends. They have an instinct for making other people feel good about themselves. The Humanist's openness and understanding make him or her a natural diplomat. Humanists work to bridge social differences and harmonize conflicting viewpoints; affiliation is important to them.

Humanist children are full of "whys," "whats," and "hows." The adolescent Humanist's peer-group relationships are particularly important. Young Humanists often attach themselves to an idealized teacher, mentor or hero whom they hope to emulate.

Humanists prefer to work within existing social institutions whenever possible. They are not beyond questioning things as they exist, but they would rather make improvements than start from scratch.

Humanists are not simply tolerant of human differences, they thrive on them. They seem to be born with the social graces that other types have to learn. Humanists are able to adapt rapidly to any social climate and they often have different sets of friends for each personal project or activity they pursue.

Humanists prefer movement to routine, relevant information to trivia and answers to philosophical speculation. Humanists want to see progress and change. The facts they gather must therefore lead to conclusions and the conclusions must lead to human applications.

Humanists can be curious to a fault. A Humanist in search of information will not take no for an answer. Humanists can be kind, courteous and charming to absolute strangers but critical and detached from their loved ones.

Humanists often take on more projects and commitments than their time allows because they hate to be left out of anything that is happening. The overbooked Humanist is the proverbial chicken with its head cut off, running in all directions, juggling schedules and giving each project short shrift.

Humanists want more than anything else to know what makes people tick. Humanists love to analyze people, people in groups, people in organizations or people in civilizations. The science of psychiatry was pioneered by Humanists Sigmund Freud, Carl Jung and Alfred Adler. In the media age, it is popularized by Humanist Joyce Brothers.

Humanists are often proud of their cultural backgrounds and knowledgeable of manners and mores. Humanist Bruce Lee stimulated public interest in the martial arts. Humanist Philip Roth's tongue-in-cheek novels communicate the essence of growing up Jewish.

Humanists are such keen observers of human nature that they rarely miss humanity's failures and foibles. They make this the basis of their humor. Humanism is the wit of George Bernard Shaw. It is the slapstick of Charlie Chaplin, the biting social satire of Lenny Bruce, and the multiple comedic personalities of Lily Tomlin.

The Humanist often relies on humor to soothe hurt feelings and bridge personal differences. Nothing is beyond the scope of Humanism's wit. Humanists love to poke fun at social sacred cows. Humanism's greatest virtue is its ability to laugh at itself.

Humanists often occupy positions of leadership. Sometimes they lead from necessity since they dislike group projects that get bogged down. Humanists want action, not chatter, so they take it on themselves to get people involved and motivated.

When Humanists go astray they rarely go alone. They have the ability to mislead as well as to lead. Humanists Adolph Hitler, Joseph Stalin, and Benito Mussolini used social divisiveness as a tool for their political ambitions. Jim Jones and Charles Manson did the same.

The Humanist's sexual image is exciting. Humanists fascinate us, arouse our curiosity, stimulate our interest. Humanism is the electric presence of Elizabeth Taylor and the madcap antics of Burt Reynolds. Some Humanists go to great lengths to provoke a public response. They do not mind resorting to extremes if their outrageous images and behavior prove attention-getting. Humanists Jayne Mansfield and Alice Cooper exploited the shock-value of their performances to their financial advantage.

Humanists stand at the crossroads where all paths meet. They develop broad public awareness and uncanny human insight through their diverse experience.

Here are some other Humanists in the original birth pattern sample. The number following each name indicates the number of planets in the Stimulus Need Triangle.

Spiro Agnew, politician (4)

Alice Bailey, occultist (4)

Honore de Balzac, writer (5)

Eva Braun, mistress (6)

Billy Carter, first family (5)

Dick Cavett, entertainer (4)

Paul Cézanne, artist (5)

Michael Crichton, writer (5)

Bette Davis, actress (4)

Edgar Degas, artist (5)

Robert DeNiro, actor (4)

Phyllis Diller, comedienne (4)

John Dillinger, criminal (6)

Bobby Fischer, chess master (4)

Zelda Fitzgerald, socialite (5)

Paul Gauguin, artist (4)

Marjoe Gortner, actor (4)

Merle Haggard, singer (6)

Jimi Hendrix, musician (4)

Doug Henning, magician (4)

Hermann Hesse, writer (5)

Katherine Hepburn, actress (5)

Jennifer Jones, actress (6)

Immanuel Kant, philosopher (4)

Diane Keaton, actress (4)

Evel Knieval, daredevil (4)

Charles Lindbergh, aviator (5)

James Lovell, astronaut (4)

Guglielmo Marconi, inventor (6)

Penny Marshall, comedienne (4)

Herman Melville, writer (4)

Grandma Moses, artist (5)

Joe Namath, athlete (4)

Madeline Murray O'Hair, atheist (5)

Jack Paar, TV host (5)

Louis Pasteur, scientist (7)

Gregory Peck, actor (5)

Della Reese, singer (5)

Christopher Reeve, actor (4)

Debbie Reynolds, entertainer (5)

Bertrand Russell, writer (6)

Jill Saint John, actress (6)

Omar Sharif, actor (4)

Robert Shields, mime (4)

O.J. Simpson, athlete (5)

Upton Sinclair, writer (5)

Brenda Vacarro, actress (4)

Barbara Walters, broadcaster (4)

Cindy Williams, comedienne (5)

Joanne Woodward, actress (4)

William Butler Yeats, poet (5)

The Romanticist

The Romanticist's typical moods, attitudes, actions and responses reflect his or her prominent Love Need. Romanticists live in a qualitative rather than a quantitative world. Objects and people must have emotional significance. Romanticists are empathetic, caring people who value loyalty, commitment and intimacy.

While the Humanist loves people for what they are, the Romanticist loves people in spite of what they are. Romanticism penetrates the surface of life and Romanticists look into people, not at them.

Romanticists live in the world as it should be, not as it necessarily is. They have high expectations, personal dreams and a visionary approach to living. Romanticism softens life's sharp edges. Romanticists are keenly attuned to human suffering, yet they have a boundless hope for progress and change.

Romanticists are sensitive, imaginative children. Adolescent Romanticists are moody and somewhat secretive. Their first love experiences run the gamut of emotion from exhilaration to despair. Adolescent Romanticists are acutely conscious of peer group acceptance.

Romanticists treasure objects that have some sentimental meaning. They save driftwood from their first trip to the ocean, a corsage from their first big date and every love letter they ever received. A Romanticist would get up in the middle of the night to retrieve a favorite but worn-out pair of slippers from the trash.

Romanticists have vivid imaginations. They are attracted to anything mysterious, mystical or surreal. Romanticists view life as an adventure. They believe that all things are possible no matter how improbable. Romanticists succeed in the most quixotic schemes through faith alone.

Romanticists' strengths are also their weaknesses. Romanticists are constantly disappointed because they hope for so much both from themselves and other people. They create nightmares as well as dreams and they can be childish, naive and gullible. Romanticists are often self-dramatizing. They are masters of the fine art of martyrdom and will let you know in no uncertain terms that *you* have broken their dreams and caused their suffering. Romanticists often read deep meanings into perfectly natural events and are capable of outlandish misinterpretations of reality.

It is hard to penetrate the Romanticist's image and he or she is rarely seen in perspective. Romanticists involve others in their dreams. They are the fairest of the fair and the bravest of the brave. The Romanticist who falls into public disfavor is vilified out of all proportion to his or her actual sins. Romanticism is an enigma and we are drawn to its magnetism and its mystery.

The original birth pattern sample contained more Romanticists than any other temperament type. We see Romanticism in action through the lives of the Romanticists in the sample. Romanticists have a larger-than-life, heroic quality. We see Romanticism in the epic journeys of astronauts John Glenn, Scott Carpenter and Buzz Aldrin, archetypal heroes of our scientific age. Romanticism is in the presidency of John F. Kennedy and the sacrifice of Tom Dooley. Romanticism is the legend of Judy Garland living on in Liza Minelli. It is Bob Hope's global popularity.

Romanticists inspire us. Romanticism is Yogananda's vision of peace through devotion. It is Albert Schweitzer's missionary effort. Romanticism is Mary Baker Eddy's refusal to accept the limits and ailments of the body. It is Maria Montessori's work with disadvantaged children.

A Romanticist with a dark vision weaves a web of suspicion. Romanticists can be cunning propagandists bent on self-glorification. Thus Joseph McCarthy's private nightmare generated public witch hunts. Adolf Eichmann's twisted vision of a perfect world demanded the sacrifice of millions of people.

We all love to dream and the Romanticist feeds our imagination. Romanticists let us escape from the confines of day-to-day reality through sharing in their personal fantasies. Romanticism is Farrah Fawcett, little girls with Farrah dolls and teenage girls with Farrah hairdos. Romanticism is John Travolta and young men in discotheques dressed in white Travolta suits.

Romanticists are often anti-heroes. They are targets for endless criticism. We magnify their faults as well as their virtues but we never see them clearly. How could anyone be so annoying (Romanticist Howard Cosell), so completely intimidating (Romanticist Jimmy Hoffa) or so thoroughly evil (Romanticist Aleister Crowley)?

The Romanticist's sexuality is as mysterious as his or her temperament. Romanticists are magnetic and alluring but we sense that something about them is hidden. We know we cannot take them at face value without missing their essence. The mystery of Romanticism draws us to Greta Garbo, to Lauren Bacall, to Ava Gardner or Liv Ullman. Romanticist men have a little-boy-lost quality typified by Dustin Hoffman's role in *The Graduate.*

Romanticists generate hope for the future through their optimism and acceptance. Their prominent love needs urge them toward life's subtleties and secrets.

Here are more Romanticists. The number following each name indicates the total number of markers in the Love Need Triangle.

Jack Anderson, columnist (6)
Arthur Ashe, tennis player (4)
Fred Astaire, entertainer (4)
Jim Bailey, female impersonator (6)
Pearl Bailey, entertainer (4)
Warren Beatty, actor (4)
Leonard Bernstein, composer (5)
Rosalynn Carter, first lady (5)
Johnny Cash, singer (4)
Catherine the Great, empress (4)
Coco Chanel, designer (4)
Cher, singer (4)
Gordon Cooper, astronaut (5)
Nicolaus Copernicus, astronomer (4)
Jacques Cousteau, oceanographer (5)
John Davidson, singer (5)
Simone de Beauvoir, writer (4)
John Denver, singer (5)
Werner Erhard, founder of est (4)
Chris Evert, tennis player (4)
Galileo Galilei, astronomer (5)
Indira Gandhi, prime minister (4)
Dave Garroway, TV personality (4)
Thor Heyerdahl, explorer (5)
Hubert Humphrey, politician (4)
Elton John, singer (5)

Tom Jones, singer (4)
Caroline Kennedy, first family (4)
Billie Jean King, tennis player (4)
Shirley MacLaine, entertainer (5)
Liberace, entertainer (4)
Paul Lynde, comedian (5)
Henry Mancini, composer (5)
Sir Lawrence Olivier, actor (5)
George Patton, general (5)
Erwin Rommel, general (4)
Jane Russell, actress (4)
Jean Paul Sartre, writer (5)
Jack Sheldon, musician (6)
Mary Shelley, writer (4)
Paul Simon, singer (4)
Tom Smothers, comedian (4)
Tom Snyder, TV personality (4)
Tokyo Rose, propagandist (4)
Gloria Vanderbilt, heiress (4)
Victoria, Queen of England (6)
Simon Wiesenthal, nazi hunter (5)
The Dutchess of Windsor (5)
 (The Duke of Windsor also had a dominant Love Need although he was not the Romanticist temperament type.)
Emile Zola, writer (6)

4 Measuring Temperament Traits

Types are the nouns of personality assessment. They stand for the whole person much as a name does. Traits, on the other hand, are like adjectives. They modify a general type description and make it more specific.

Allport notes that people *fit* a type while they *have* a trait. Types are categories. People either belong to a type or they do not. Temperament traits are dimensions. We can measure all people along a trait continuum just as we can apply the continuums of height or weight to all people.

Our daily conversation is full of type and trait descriptions. We often type people by the work they do. If you ask your friend, "Who is Mary?", your friend might reply, "Mary is a teacher." You then form a mental image of Mary the person based on her teacher-type. Your mental image of Mary would be quite different if Mary were a doctor. Birth Pattern Psychology's temperament types also answer the question "Who is Mary?" Your mental image of Mary the Individualist will be different than your image of Mary the Realist.

Temperament traits answer the question, "What is Mary like?" If Mary is a cheerful person, cheerfulness is her trait. She might be a cheerful teacher or a cheerful doctor, a cheerful Individualist or a cheerful Realist. We can put all people somewhere on the trait continuum cheerful–serious regardless of their types.

Our language contains thousands of words that describe people but not all of these descriptive words are trait names. Words like beautiful, interesting or important tell us the taste and opinion of the person who is doing the describing. Traits do not evaluate a person, they define his or her characteristic temperament.

Allport defines a trait as "a neuropsychic structure having the capacity to render many stimuli functionally equivalent, and to initiate and guide equivalent (meaningfully consistent) forms of adaptive and expressive behavior."[6]

If Ruth has the trait orderliness, she will see the world through this trait as though she were wearing glasses. She will innately look for the order in her life. Well-organized meetings that follow a format, buses that run on schedule, and clean, well-run stores would all appeal to Ruth's trait orderliness. Ruth would avoid unkempt people and she would be uncomfortable in messy surroundings. The many stimuli in Ruth's life, the buses, stores, meetings and people become "functionally equivalent," they attract or repel Ruth according to their inherent order.

Ruth's trait orderliness also "initiates and guides...meaningfully consistent behavior." Ruth may be filing her personal papers, tying a child's shoelaces or outlining a speech for her women's club. These actions are not the same but they share the same meaning to Ruth. She is expressing her trait orderliness by bringing order to life situations. Traits thus tell us both how the person interprets life events and how the person expresses himself or herself in a meaningful way.

We all have one or more core temperament traits. While all birth patterns do not indicate a type, *all* birth patterns reveal from one to three significant traits. The temperament traits, like the temperament types, are based on the primary needs for growth, security, stimulus and love. These need-based traits are personality constants. They are life themes that give us additional insight into the qualities of the whole person.

We begin to assess the personality when we calculate the Four-Digit Need Gestalt. This simple technique shows us the extent of the basic needs, the personal hierarchy of needs and the temperament type. The Four-Digit Need Gestalt shows us the temperament traits as well. Each basic need contains three trait factors:

Growth Need	Security Need
Trait Spontaneous	Trait Continuous
Trait Hypothetic	Trait Empiric
Trait Organic	Trait Organic

Stimulus Need	Love Need
Trait Spontaneous	Trait Continuous
Trait Empiric	Trait Hypothetic
Trait Panoramic	Trait Panoramic

Note that each basic need shares one trait factor with every other basic need. The Growth Need and the Stimulus Need contribute to Trait Spontaneous, the Growth Need and the Love Need contribute to Trait Hypothetic, the Growth Need and the Security Need contribute to Trait Organic, etc.

As we turn our attention from the needs themselves to their inherent trait factors, we begin to see a new level of meaning in the Four-Digit Need Gestalt. It is as though we were turning up a microscope to the next power of magnification.

To isolate a trait factor and measure its weight within the whole personality, we simply find the sum of the planet markers in the two needs which share that trait. We would calculate the first two traits as follows:

Growth Need planet markers + Stimulus Need planet markers = Trait Spontaneous
Security Need planet markers + Love Need planet markers   = Trait Continuous

Trait Spontaneous and Trait Continuous indicate two contrasting time perceptions. Spontaneous people live fully in the now. They give maximum weight to their current experience and involve themselves completely in the present. To Spontaneous people the past is over and done. By contrast, Continuous people live in the flow of experience. They are sensitive to their personal histories and feel that the past has a great bearing on the present.

The second trait pair indicates two contrasting perceptions of matter. They are calculated as follows:

Growth Need planet markers + Love Need planet markers   = Trait Hypothetic
Security Need planet markers + Stimulus Need planet markers = Trait Empiric

Trait Hypothetic people stress the content of material experience. They seek the inner meaning of life events and look for general principles. Hypothetic people are speculative so Trait Hypothetic is the "what if" trait. Conversely, Trait Empiric people want the facts. They stress the practical, quantitative forms of their experience. Empiric people like to apply principles to see what works. Trait Empiric is the "it is" trait.

The final pair of contrasting traits, Trait Organic and Trait Panoramic indicate two differing perceptions of space. They are calculated as follows:

Growth Need planet markers + Security Need planet markers = Trait Organic
Stimulus Need planet markers + Love Need planet markers   = Trait Panoramic

Trait Organic people see events and people in hierarchical terms and seek self-definition by carving out their own special place in the over-all life hierarchy. They stress autonomy and willpower. Trait Organic is the "I am" trait. Trait Panoramic people emphasize the interpersonal aspect of life and their closeness to or distance from others. They want sharing, togetherness, and good will. Trait Panoramic is the self-transcending "we are" trait.

We use the Four-Digit Need Gestalt to measure each of the six temperament traits. The measurements yield numbers from zero to ten. We will refer to the number value of a trait as its *level*. So that we can apply the same measurement scale to each trait, we will measure the six traits individually even though they are, in fact, three sets of opposing traits. Those traits having a value of six or more are the traits that shape a person's views and behavior. Trait behaviors that we display only occasionally or sporadically say little about our basic personality. Thus traits that measure five or less do not reflect the special qualities of the individual. Temperament traits must characterize the person, must mark the majority of his or her experience.

Here is the need gestalt of entertainer Barbra Streisand. Note how the temperament traits refine our first impression of the overall personality based on needs, priorities and temperament type.

Barbra Streisand

Growth Need:	4
Security Need:	3
Stimulus Need:	2
Love Need:	1

Trait Calculation

Growth	+	Stimulus	=	Trait Spontaneous
4	+	2	=	6
Security	+	Love	=	Trait Continuous
3	+	1	=	4
Growth	+	Love	=	Trait Hypothetic
4	+	1	=	5
Security	+	Stimulus	=	Trait Empiric
3	+	2	=	5
Growth	+	Security	=	Trait Organic
4	+	3	=	7
Stimulus	+	Love	=	Trait Panoramic
2	+	1	=	3

Personality assessment begins with the Four-Digit Need Gestalt. Streisand's need gestalt indicates a strong need for growth. Independent, explorative self-expression is the first priority. Barbra Streisand's personal creative talent expanded from her theatrical beginnings to television, recording, and film. The Security Need, second in importance, is reflected in her perfectionism and mastery in several art forms. Streisand is an Individualist, a unique performer with a distinctive style.

Streisand is a Trait Spontaneous person. This trait, at the six level (i.e., six planets total in the combined Growth and Stimulus Needs), shows in the intensity of her presence and in her willingness to transcend past successes to seek new and present challenges. The second set of traits, Trait Hypothetic and Trait Empiric, are equally weighted. She is equally as likely to consider the possibilities of a situation as the practicalities involved. Neither trait is therefore characteristic of her. Barbra Streisand's most marked trait is Trait Organic. She wants personal control, is uncompromising in her standards and sees creative projects as a vehicle for self-definition. The force and power of Trait Organic show in Barbra Streisand's vocal style.

Here is the need gestalt of entertainer Judy Garland. Her need gestalt brings its own distinctive traits to the fore.

Judy Garland: Need Gestalt

Growth Need:	1
Security Need:	4
Stimulus Need:	0
Love Need:	5

Trait Calculation

Growth	+	Stimulus	=	Trait Spontaneous
1	+	0	=	1
Security	+	Love	=	Trait Continuous
4	+	5	=	9
Growth	+	Love	=	Trait Hypothetic
1	+	5	=	6
Security	+	Stimulus	=	Trait Empiric
4	+	0	=	4
Growth	+	Security	=	Trait Organic
1	+	4	=	5
Stimulus	+	Love	=	Trait Panoramic
0	+	5	=	5

From Judy Garland's Four-Digit Need Gestalt, we immediately note the strong influence of both parents. Her show-business family shaped her entertainment career. The dominant Love Need paired with the low Growth Need reflects an identity vulnerable to the influence of others' hopes and desires. Garland's Romanticist personality type indicates her sensitivity. Her fans still remember her as the girl who hoped to find her dreams somewhere over the rainbow.

Judy Garland's Trait Continuous is extremely important. Continuous people demand continuity and can be disoriented and confused by sudden changes. They find it difficult to adapt and they must resolve their relationship with their parents, something that Judy Garland was unable to do. She has Trait Hypothetic at the six level. The possibilities invite her and the practical considerations can be set aside. Judy Garland's struggle to escape the pressures of her success led to drugs, alcohol and even attempted suicide. Her life and her behavior become more understandable in light of her personality. The hope that things might be better (seen in her Trait Hypothetic) coupled with an acute sensitivity to continuing difficulties surely added to her inner conflict. For Judy Garland, performance to gain love was woven deeply into the fiber of her experience.

The next two need gestalts do not indicate a personality type. The temperament traits thus provide an important key to the whole personality. Here is the need gestalt of religious leader Martin Luther.

Martin Luther: Need Gestalt

Growth Need:	0
Security Need:	0
Stimulus Need:	5
Love Need:	5

Trait Calculation

Growth	+	Stimulus	=	Trait Spontaneous
0	+	5	=	5

Security	+	Love	=	Trait Continuous
0	+	5	=	5

Growth	+	Love	=	Trait Hypothetic
0	+	5	=	5

Security	+	Stimulus	=	Trait Empiric
0	+	5	=	5

Growth	+	Security	=	Trait Organic
0	+	0	=	0

Stimulus	+	Love	=	Trait Panoramic
5	+	5	=	10

Martin Luther's need gestalt shows two strong dominant needs, the needs for stimulus and love. There is no personality type and the first four traits, all at the five level, cannot be said to be characteristic of him. Trait Panoramic at the maximum level of ten planet markers is the key to Martin Luther's temperament. Luther's imperative urge for self-transcendance led him to choose a religious career over the protest of his father. Hans Luther had high expectations. One of his greatest hopes was that his son Martin would succeed in law. Though Martin Luther did become a lawyer, he continued his studies and received a doctor's degree in theology.

Trait Panoramic people are influenced by other people's experiences as much as their own. Luther entered the monastery after a close friend was killed by a lightning bolt. While Trait Organic people accumulate and exercise personal power and authority, Trait Panoramic people draw power from a sense of unity with someone or something outside themselves. Martin Luther was not the only theologian to object to papal abuses of power. Others, too, condemned the sale of indulgences whereby people bought forgiveness with money. Martin Luther was unique in his Panoramic Christian concept. He believed that no human effort leads to salvation, rather that we are saved through God's grace alone.

Here is the Four-Digit Need Gestalt of Johann Wolfgang von Goethe. The even distribution of basic needs does not give us a clear picture of Goethe's personality. Goethe's temperament traits clarify his distinct life theme.

Goethe: Need Gestalt

Growth Need:	3
Security Need:	3
Stimulus Need:	1
Love Need:	3

Trait Calculation

Growth	+	Stimulus	=	Trait Spontaneous
3	+	1	=	4
Security	+	Love	=	Trait Continuous
3	+	3	=	6
Growth	+	Love	=	Trait Hypothetic
3	+	3	=	6
Security	+	Stimulus	=	Trait Empiric
3	+	1	=	4
Growth	+	Security	=	Trait Organic
3	+	3	=	6
Stimulus	+	Love	=	Trait Panoramic
1	+	3	=	4

Goethe's need gestalt indicates three temperament traits at the six level, Trait Continuous, Trait Hypothetic and Trait Organic. The celebrated German dramatist and poet's temperament is revealed in his writing. Goethe's *Faust* is a classic study of humankind's craving for personal power. Trait Organic and Trait Hypothetic mark Goethe's ability to present the will to power in an archetypal dramatic setting. Trait Continuous people persist in their efforts and can devote years to the shaping of personal projects. Goethe took sixty years to write *Faust*. Goethe's own motto, "Without haste, but without rest," eloquently expresses Trait Continuous.

The illustration depicts the "bell curve" or normal distribution. Many human qualities follow this statistical model. If we measured the heights of several hundred people, we would find that a few are very short, more people are short, still more are slightly less than average. Most of the people we measured would be average, slightly fewer would be above average, even fewer would be tall while a very few would be quite tall. We could diagram the heights of our sample placing the height values at the bottom of the diagram and plotting the number of people with each height along the vertical. Our diagram would look like the illustration.

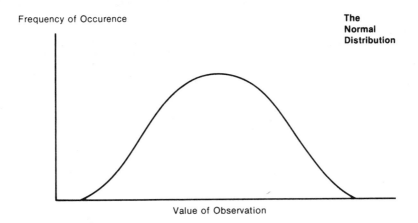

Frequency of Occurence   **The Normal Distribution**

Value of Observation

Gordon Allport notes that general traits also have a normal distribution. If we measure Trait Spontaneous in five hundred birth patterns, we would expect the greatest number of patterns to have Trait Spontaneous at level five, slightly fewer charts would have Trait Spontaneous at level six, fewer still at level seven and so on. The actual distribution of the six temperament traits in the original birth pattern sample appears in the following table. The traits are indicated by letter, Trait S is Trait Spontaneous, Trait C is Trait Continuous, Trait H is Trait Hypothetic, etc. Only traits Organic and Panoramic depart slightly and insignificantly from the normal distribution. The sample showed slightly fewer examples of Trait Organic and slightly more examples of Trait Panoramic than expected. Note that very few birth patterns have traits at the nine or ten level. Such a strong trait colors virtually all of the individual's life experience.

Trait Distribution in the Original Birth Pattern Sample

Planetary Markers	Trait S	Trait C	Trait H	Trait F	Trait C	Trait P	Total Trait Distribution
0	0	0	0	0	3	3	6
1	7	2	7	5	6	6	33
2	15	22	34	28	29	28	156
3	65	54	66	56	67	59	367
4	108	102	99	92	109	82	592
5	125	125	113	113	108	108	692
6	102	108	92	99	82	109	592
7	54	65	56	66	59	67	367
8	22	15	28	34	28	29	156
9	2	7	5	7	6	6	33
10	0	0	0	0	3	3	6
Sample Total	500	500	500	500	500	500	3000

The next illustration depicts the distribution of all three thousand traits in the sample. The curve is a perfect bell shape because the distribution of each trait is mirrored by its opposing trait. The frequency is expressed as a percentage of the three thousand traits. Thus one in every four traits will probably occur at level five. The traits in a hundred birth patterns could be calculated without finding a single trait at the ten level. The higher the numerical weight of a trait, the more intensely and frequently it is displayed. We display a six level trait more intensely and frequently than two-thirds of the general population. We display a seven level trait more intensely than 80 percent of the general population. At level eight, we display a trait more intensely than 95 percent of the general population. At levels nine and ten, any show of the behaviors and attitudes of the opposing trait is virtually nonexistent.

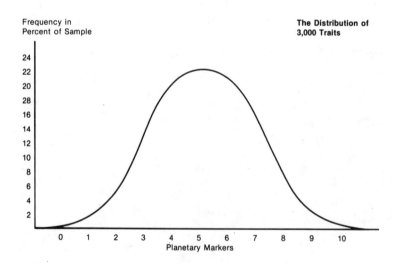

Frequency in Percent of Sample

The Distribution of 3,000 Traits

Planetary Markers

Some personality theorists describe traits as the basic building blocks of personality. Cattell, Eysenck and Guilford (see References, Chapter 4) each define a set of basic traits. Birth Pattern Psychology's temperament traits suggest tentative correlations with traits measured by the Guilford-Zimmerman Temperament Survey. The following trait descriptions include the related Guilford traits as well as the comments of individuals who have these traits.

Trait Spontaneous

Spontaneous people make vivid first impressions. They hold back nothing, therefore they express the full thrust of their personalities. The immediacy of Spontaneous people lends an air of excitement to what they do.

Trait Spontaneous people live fully in the moment. It is important for them, in the words of guru Baba Ram Dass, to "Be Here Now." They seem intent on wringing every ounce of meaning from an experience. They savor the present. Spontaneous people seem to expand the moment making even the most mundane events seem quite significant. Whatever Spontaneous people do, they do with a sense of adventure. They have flair and an eye for the dramatic in life.

Enthusiasm is crucial for Spontaneous people. They follow where their interest leads them and become totally absorbed in whatever excites them. Spontaneous people will work constantly and rapidly as long as their interest level remains high. When interest and enthusiasm wane, they feel that they have completed their project. With Trait Spontaneous, the vigor and intensity of mood measures the endurance of projects, relationships and experiences. They sense finality with the falling off of emotional intensity. Literal completion, tying up loose ends or reaching firm agreement is not necessary to them.

Spontaneous people are impatient. They dislike waiting and when they want something, they want it now. Barriers and delays that seem minor to others can halt the Spontaneous person's effort altogether. Spontaneous people rely on constant feedback and stimulation to maintain their momentum. When they cease to progress, they are apt to drop the subject and turn to something new. What they lack in patience and endurance, they compensate through diversity. Spontaneous people are most successful when they start several projects and follow through on the most promising option.

Since Spontaneous people live fully in the now, they are influenced primarily by current relationships. Their personalities are shaped more by social influences and peer interaction than by parental models. Trait Spontaneous people are deeply affected by social prejudice or peer rejection that inhibits their free range of experience. They do not want to miss anything, so social exclusion is particularly painful.

Spontaneous people put the past behind them and progress without looking back. Churchill expressed this attitude when he stated, "If we open a quarrel between the past and the present, we shall find that we have lost the future." What is done is done and it is far more important to forge ahead. Trait Spontaneous people particularly dislike being reminded of past mistakes. You cannot change the past, they will tell you, so it is a waste of time to look back. Since time is always of the essence in the Spontaneous person's life, he or she has something much better to do right this minute than reminisce.

Spontaneous people rarely relax and do nothing. They cannot tolerate boredom. Any project or activity is better than no activity at all and, since they tend not to evaluate the relative importance of things, they do lots of "busy work."

Trait Spontaneous people shift life direction suddenly and with amazing ease. They are distractible and often go off on tangents. Sometimes they turn a tangent into a paying proposition. Thus they appear lucky when it is not luck but rather the ability to respond immediately to opportunity which underlies their success.

Spontaneous people do best in careers that give them freedom and flexibility. They avoid repetitive work. Fashion designer Bill Blass notes that in his business, "You're only as good as your last collection." While others interpret such circumstances as high-pressure situations, the Spontaneous person sees only the excitement. Challenge must be constant. The safe approach is for other people. Spontaneous people take risks, if not of life and limb then at least of money and reputation and talent.

Anger a Spontaneous person and he or she is completely upset with you. The fact that you may have been intimate friends for the past ten years is irrelevant. The Spontaneous person's anger evokes only the memory of those times in the past when he or she was mad at you. Once the anger subsides, the Spontaneous person will be hard pressed to understand why you are offended. A Spontaneous person's current feelings set the tone of relationships. They are detached from their personal histories and feel as if someone else did those things, spoke those words or made those promises.

Trait Spontaneous compares with a low score on the Guilford trait Emotional Stability. Stability here means only *consistency* and the low end of this trait continuum measures changeability of mood.

Self-determining people who have Trait Spontaneous are delightful companions. They are courageous individuals who live comfortably and completely in the present. In those people who lack an inner locus of control, Trait Spontaneous is often a psychological "last straw" as it adds instability to the whole personality.

Guilford describes the problematic aspects of this trait as "depression, inferiority feelings and nervousness." The defenses are poor and the individual lacks self-protection. There is "a greater response to the stimuli that arouse fear and depression."

The Trait Spontaneous person who lacks a sense of self-determination is truly at the mercy of the environment. There is no emotional reserve and since he or she is fully immersed in the moment, there is vulnerability to feelings of being overwhelmed. The Spontaneous person is easily pushed to extremes when an inner locus of control is lacking.

No single psychological trait and certainly no single birth factor is in itself problematic. Birth pattern measurements give us a personality portrait but the pattern does not tell us whether the individual has or does not have an inner locus of control. The individual's behavior alone conveys his or her psychological adjustment to the trained observer.

We live in a culture that esteems some of the temperament traits more than others. While no trait is inherently better or worse than any other, some traits are more difficult to fully actualize in this society. In this sense, Trait Spontaneous can be considered the most difficult trait because we tend to label those people who live fully in the moment as irresponsible or shallow.

In every trait sample drawn from the original birth pattern study, there are people of high achievement and there are deeply troubled individuals. Guilford considers this trait (low Emotional Stability) to be a measure of neuroticism. Of the famous men in the sample who have Trait Spontaneous 10 percent were psychologically troubled. Of the famous women, the figure jumps to 20 percent. Nearly a third of those having Trait Spontaneous at the eight and nine levels were significantly troubled. There are instances of alcoholism, nervous breakdown and suicide among those troubled individuals who have Trait Spontaneous. Again, it is not appropriate to designate this trait problematic in and of itself; it is fair to conclude only that Trait Spontaneous tends to magnify problems *if* problems do exist.

Trait Spontaneous in non-self-determining people is displayed as exploitation. They will do or say whatever they must to turn a present situation to their advantage. Promises are easily made because there is no intention of follow-through. They use the emotions and resources of others for a quick thrill or a moment of glory. Then they move on.

The following adjectives describe Trait Spontaneous as it is constructively displayed: adaptable, adventurous, changeable, enthusiastic, excitable, high-strung, impatient, impulsive, quick, restless, and versatile.

Here are some well-known individuals who have Trait Spontaneous. The numbers indicate the level at which the trait is displayed and reflect the total number of planet markers in the Growth and Stimulus Need Triangles.

9

John Dillinger, criminal

8

Diana Barrymore, actress
Polly Bergen, actress
Bill Blass, fashion designer
Richard Chamberlain, actor
Zelda Fitzgerald, socialite
Merle Haggard, singer
Mick Jagger, singer
Lyndon Johnson, president
Amadeo Modigliani, artist

Madelyn Murray O'Hair, atheist
Korla Pandit, musician
Louis Pasteur, scientist
Jerry Reed, entertainer
Bertrand Russell, writer
Jill Saint John, actress
Margaret Sullivan, actress
Algernon Swinburne, writer
William Butler Yeats, poet

7

Richard Alpert (Baba Ram Dass), guru
F. Lee Bailey, lawyer
Brigitte Bardot, actress
Bernadette, Saint of Lourdes
Rudolph Bing, opera executive
Eva Braun, mistress
Dick Cavett, entertainer
Alice Cooper, singer
Peggy Fleming, skater
Paul Gauguin, artist
Marjoe Gortner, actor
Alex Haley, writer
Katherine Hepburn, actress
Herman Hesse, writer
Washington Irving, writer
Immanuel Kant, philosopher
Joan Kennedy, political wife
Charles Lindbergh, pilot
Don Loper, fashion designer
Nicolo Machiavelli, politician
Jayne Mansfield, actress

Margaret Mead, anthropologist
Walter Mondale, politician
Aldo Moro, politician
Benito Mussolini, dictator
Joe Namath, athlete
Anaïs Nin, writer
Rafael, artist
Della Reese, singer
Burt Reynolds, actor
Philip Roth, writer
"Babe" Ruth, athlete
Peter Sellers, actor
Upton Sinclair, writer
Margaret Chase Smith, politician
Richard Speck, murderer
Elizabeth Taylor, actress
Shirley Temple, actress
Rip Torn, actor
Henri Toulouse-Lautrec, artist
Johnny Weismuller, actor
Edward White, Jr., astronaut

Trait Continuous

The strength of Trait Continuous measures the extent of family influence. The stronger this trait, the more powerful are the internalized parents. Early family experiences shape the personality and in this sense, family is destiny for the Trait Continuous person. Career choice, adult relationships and personal attitudes tend to reflect parental goals and values.

It is vital for Continuous people to get off to a good start in life since they are historical creatures. They take their pasts with them through life in a very real way. Continuous people constantly compare the present to the past and use this extended perspective when adapting to change. They take time to make adjustments and dislike feeling rushed. Experiences must be reviewed and digested before fresh experiences are sought.

Trait Continuous people will continue to discuss and assess an unresolved event long after the event itself is over. They must have the *feeling* of finality that is measured not in calendar days and years but in some inner awareness that every alternative has been fully explored. Once an event feels complete, Continuous people move on without looking back. They will not appreciate any additional information that forces them to review the decisions they struggled so long to make.

Like the Boy Scouts, Continuous people feel that it is best to "Be Prepared." Anything radically new, different or surprising that is unrelated to their past experience puts them on the defensive. Continuous people rarely accept or fully understand events that cannot be explained in terms of life's flow. Events must come from somewhere and lead to something, they cannot simply appear full-blown in the present for no good reason. Since everything must have a reason, Continuous people see events or decisions not based on the past as arbitrary and puzzling.

Continuous people are time travellers. They often diffuse the present moment through memory or through anticipation. If they impress others as removed or distant, they may indeed be mentally far away. Such detachment from the moment gives the Continuous person time to ease into events, to achieve a feeling of familiarity and comfort by noting the similarities between present and past.

Continuous people deal with difficult situations by projecting themselves into the future, into a time when they will have solved the current difficulty and realized the benefit of the experience. They are thus capable of facing distasteful chores and tedious work because they look beyond the task to the ultimate benefit.

Because Continuous people have an extended perspective, they are not easily impressed. They appreciate whatever stands the test of time and look for the enduring value in ideas, relationships and achievements. They rarely form opinions of people on first impression since they like to know a person's past.

Risks are for others. Continuous people prefer the tried and true. They are planners rather than gamblers, strategists rather than speculators. If it is really important, it will keep until tomorrow when they have had time to think things through carefully. Continuous people often set aside immediate gratifications in favor of long-term gains. They have patience and endurance and believe with Disraeli that "Everything comes if a man will only wait."

Familiarity and comfort are one and the same to the Continuous person. They like their favorite chair, their old slippers and their cherished friends. They are the preservers of objects, memories and relationships, the defenders of culture, tradition and custom. John Galsworthy notes the central difficulty of this trait when he writes, "How to save the old that's worth saving is one of our greatest problems."

Once the Continuous person commits to a project or a partner, he or she persists in that commitment in spite of difficulty or opposition. Hubert Humphrey expressed this persistence: "Some people look upon any setback as the end. They're always looking for the benediction rather than the invocation. But you can't quit." Continuous people see daily ups and downs as part of the larger, overall scheme of things. Large projects and enduring relationships are attractive to them since they want a sense of ongoing involvement.

Trait Continuous resembles a high score on the Guilford trait Emotional Stability. People with this trait maintain a high mood consistency regardless of outer circumstances. A complainer with Trait Continuous would complain in most situations, even if he or she were having a good time. A cheerful person would be cheerful at a party, at the office or in the dentist's chair. Guilford notes that this trait indicates low flexibility coupled with the ability to remain calm in stressful situations.

Trait Continuous people handle stress well because a part of their personality is not fully engaged in the difficult circumstance. They have a reserve of self and they draw on this reserve when things get tough. Mentally, they retreat to a familiar past or project ahead to a calmer future thus minimizing the current stress.

Continuous people who lack an inner locus of control are rigid and dogmatic. The past holds them prisoner and serves as a convenient excuse for their problems. They blame their backgrounds, parents or childhoods for their own inability to progress.

The internalized parental images in self-determining Continuous people are supportive, helpful models. In the Continuous person lacking self-determination, these inner models nag, criticize and complain. Such negative inner images are frequently projected onto a current partner giving the Trait Continuous person someone to blame for his or her own difficulties.

When self-determination is lacking, Continuous people cling to their problems. They repeat the same mistakes over and over again. The familiar problem seems more desirable than its unfamilar solution.

The following adjectives describe Trait Continuous as it is constructively displayed: calm, cautious, deliberate, dependable, loyal, patient, persistent, serious, steady, thorough, and unexcitable.

Here are some well-known individuals who have Trait Continuous. The numbers indicate the level at which the trait is displayed and reflect the total number of planet markers in the Security and Love Need Triangles.

9

Gregg Allman, musician
Jim Bailey, female impersonator
Alexandre Dumas, writer

Farrah Fawcett, actress
Judy Garland, singer
Anne Morrow Lindbergh, writer

8

Glenn Campbell, singer
Colette, writer
Joe Frazier, boxer
Greta Garbo, actress
Ava Gardner, actress
H.R. Haldeman, government official
Glenda Jackson, actress

Henry Jackson, politician
Sam Peckinpah, director
Arthur Schlesinger, Jr., historian
Mark Spitz, swimmer
Gwen Verdon, entertainer
Simon Wiesenthal, nazi hunter
Paramahansa Yogananda, mystic

7

Buzz Aldrin, astronaut
Muhammad Ali, boxer
Jack Anderson, columnist
Lauren Bacall, actress
Joan Baez, singer
Kay Ballard, comedienne
Warren Beatty, actor
Jerry Brown, politician
Anita Bryant, singer
William F. Buckley, writer
Steve Cauthen, jockey
Jacques Cousteau, oceanographer
Leonardo da Vinci, genius
Angela Davis, activist
Simone de Beauvoir, writer
John Denver, singer
Dwight D. Eisenhower, president
Werner Erhard, est founder
Sally Field, actress
Indira Gandhi, politician
Dave Garroway, TV personality

Arlo Guthrie, musician
Helen Hayes, actress
Dustin Hoffman, actor
Tom Jones, singer
Liberace, entertainer
Paul Lynde, comedian
Shirley MacLaine, entertainer
Rollo May, psychologist
Jack Nicholson, actor
Sir Lawrence Olivier, actor
George Patton, general
Sylvia Porter, columnist
Freddie Prinze, actor
Robert Redford, actor
Erwin Rommel, general
Wallis Simpson, Dutchess of Windsor
Pierre Teilhard de Chardin,
   philosopher-priest
John Travolta, actor
Jules Verne, writer
Victoria, Queen of England

Trait Hypothetic

The absent-minded professor, that genius in mismatched socks who cannot find his briefcase or remember his appointments, is a classic stereotype of Trait Hypothetic. Hypothetics look to essence rather than substance and seem out of place in a world of solid objects and real people. Though the Hypothetic may not *be* different, he or she often *feels* different. Try as they might, they seldom fit the patterns of cultural roles and expectations.

Intrinsic values and intangible content shape the Hypothetic's experience. They take pleasure in the meaning of what they do so money or status does not motivate them. Hypothetics want a calling, not a career. If they are successful in the conventional sense, it is by accident and not by design. Making a living, paying bills, doing housework and the other necessities that most people take for granted strike the Hypothetic as distinctly burdensome. These simple tasks may well be more difficult for the Hypothetic whose detachment from physical reality makes it hard to negotiate in a world full of solid objects taking up real space. Hypothetics frequently lose things or get lost because they fail to notice tangible landmarks in their surroundings.

Hypothetics agree with Disraeli that "little things affect little minds," so they put off little things as long as possible. You might well find your Trait Hypothetic friend with his or her nose in a book and a sink full of dirty dishes. The book, your friend will explain, is significant; the dishes are not.

The search for significance is constant. Hypothetics dream, imagine, and question. These themes permeate the work of Trait Hypothetic writers from Anaïs Nin ("Dreams are necessary to life") to poet Carl Sandberg ("Nothing happens unless first a dream") to Anatole France ("To know is nothing at all; to imagine is everything"). No idea is so sacred, socially accepted or intellectually entrenched that it escapes the Hypothetic's probing mind. Hypothetics live with doubt. This allows them to go beyond the obvious to the truly inspired. Nowhere are the Hypothetic's questions and doubts more beautifully expressed than in Ernest Renan's Skeptic's Prayer: "O Lord, if there is a Lord, save my soul, if I have a soul."

Let others deal in facts, statistics and probabilities. Hypothetics live in a world full of possibilities. Whatever they see suggests new possibilities; whatever they hear or read fuels their imagination. They are rarely content just to let things be. Everything that exists can be changed or improved. Hypothetics seek the freedom to explore many alternatives. They avoid anything that confines their sense of freedom and limits them to a single possibility, be it a schedule, an appointment, or a social institution.

Since Hypothetics ignore the constraints of social expectation and feel free to question anything and everything, they sometimes solve the very problems that appear to have no solution. Franklin Roosevelt led the United

States through the Depression years with a philosophy of "bold, persistent experimentation." Hypothetics see the world as it ought to be, not as it necessarily is, and through sheer persistence sometimes bring the real closer to the ideal.

Hypothetics seem to court trouble. They cannot do or say the easy thing simply because it is easy, personally profitable, or socially acceptable. Trait Hypothetics are the whistle-blowers who call attention to injustice even at their personal expense. It is the *principle* of the thing and Hypothetics stand by their principles, even when they must stand alone.

Hypothetics live according to their personal standards, standards that differ from yet often exceed social demands. Though they recognize accepted norms and rules, they feel as if the rules do not apply to them. Rules are made to be bent, if not actually broken, and nothing is more boring than normality. Hypothetics simply do not want to swim in the mainstream of society.

Since our culture does not esteem Trait Hypothetic, it is a challenging temperament trait to fully actualize. People who display this trait are frequently labeled odd, foolish or eccentric. We do, however, admire those Hypothetics whose personal vision provides the solution to widespread problems. When we positively interpret a Hypothetic's differentness, we think of him or her as daring and courageous.

Trait Hypothetic compares to a high score on the Guilford trait Thoughtfulness. This trait marks the person who "wants to know, who *has* to know and who will spend all kinds of time trying to find out—why?" Guilford notes that people with this trait make excellent researchers. This trait in the extreme becomes compulsive and inflexible. This marks those individuals who become so immersed in a problem that they lose perspective and the ability to try a different approach.

Trait Hypothetic people who lack an inner locus of control are extremely gullible. Their unrealistic and outlandish attitudes stem not from personal inspiration but from sheer willingness to believe anything. They prefer fantasy to reality because fantasy affords them the chance to feel special without effort or accomplishment. Collectively, such people make up what is generally called the "lunatic fringe."

When Trait Hypothetic individuals are unable to satisfy their basic needs and adjust effectively to their environments, they adopt what Theodore Millon describes as passive-independent coping strategies. Passive independence involves "narcissism and self-involvement" and fantasies of superiority. These people feel that others should validate their self-worth yet they maintain a distant and aloof air toward their "inferiors."

The self-determining Hypothetic's creative interpretation of life offers new and better solutions to problems. The creative misinterpretation of reality by the non-self-determining Hypothetic is an attempt to evade responsibility and glorify the self. It solves nothing and it contributes nothing.

The following adjectives describe Trait Hypothetic as it is constructively displayed: dreamy, idealistic, imaginative, ingenious, insightful, inventive, original, resourceful, and unconventional.

Here are some well-known individuals who have Trait Hypothetic. The numbers indicate the level at which the trait is displayed and reflect the total number of planet markers in the Growth and Love Need Triangles.

9

Rudolph Bing, opera executive
Janet Leigh, actress

Dick Martin, comedian
"Babe" Ruth, athlete
Algernon Swinburne, writer

8

Jack Anderson, columnist
Rosalyn Carter, first lady
Julia Child, chef
John Derek, actor
F. Scott Fitzgerald, writer
Peggy Fleming, skater
Susan Ford, president's daughter
George Foreman, boxer
Galileo, astronomer
Pancho Gonzalez, athlete
Alex Haley, writer

Susan Hayward, actress
Lyndon Johnson, president
Grace Kelly, princess
O. Henry, writer
Marcel Proust, writer
Robyn Smith, jockey
Shirley Temple, actress
Morris Udall, politician
Liv Ullman, actress
Walt Whitman, writer
The Duke and Dutchess of Windsor

7

Edie Adams, singer
Buzz Aldrin, astronaut
Desi Arnaz, Jr., actor
Brigitte Bardot, actress
Alexander G. Bell, inventor
Lord Byron, poet
Johnny Cash, singer
Coco Chanel, designer
Prince Charles of England
Jacques Cousteau, oceanographer
John Denver, musician
Isadora Duncan, dancer
Chris Evert, athlete
Farrah Fawcett, actress
Larry Flynt, publisher
Greta Garbo, actress
Ava Gardner, actress
Jimmy Hoffa, labor leader

Helen Keller, lecturer
Joan Kennedy, political wife
Elizabeth Kubler-Ross, psychologist
Paul Lynde, comedian
Shirley MacLaine, entertainer
Robert McNamara, cabinet official
Margaret Mead, anthropologist
Anaïs Nin, writer
Vance Packard, writer
Sam Peckinpah, director
Roy Rogers, actor
Mary Shelley, writer
Brooke Shields, model
Phoebe Snow, singer
Tom Snyder, TV personality
John Travolta, actor
Tex Watson, cultist
Emile Zola, writer

Trait Empiric

"Education is the instruction of the intellect in the laws of Nature, under which name I include not merely things and their forces but men and their ways..." wrote scientist T.H. Huxley. Huxley's definition captures the essence of Empiric experience: the world of natural and social forms subject to natural and social laws. Empirics feel at one with the earth, the times, existing social institutions and established systems of thought.

On the personal level, Empirics want concrete rewards for their individual efforts. On the social level, they seek the greatest good for the greatest number of people. Empirics admire efficiency, technology, productivity and progress. Hard work and determination help the Empiric achieve these goals but, more than anything else, the Empiric must have information.

Facts, proven methods, standard procedures and cultural mores all provide essential information that relieves the burden of countless trivial decisions. The Empiric uses information to predict the logical outcome of his or her actions. Empirics prefer to know what to expect in a given situation and to know what is expected of them as well. Information affords them the opportunity to make productive personal choices. The more information they have, the more confidently they choose.

Empirics work within a system because a system helps them achieve their goals. They change the system only when it ceases to be efficient, effective or beneficial. Normally, Empirics have better things to do than quibble over rules or question established practices or authority.

Empirics avoid uncertain situations lacking clear-cut guidelines. Unlimited choice threatens the Empiric's desire for system and order. As the possibilities increase, the probability of benefit decreases. Open alternatives present too much room for error or loss. Empirics want to make the best use of their time and effort; they do not want to be chasing down a blind alley while opportunity knocks somewhere else.

Because Trait Empiric reflects the natural and social environments, we see Empirics as genuine, unsophisticated, honest people. Superstar Elvis Presley's fans saw him as "just plain folks" in spite of his tremendous success. The public cherished Empiric genius Albert Einstein and ignored his personal idiosyncracies. Since Empirics innately sense the socially appropriate behavior, they strike us as natural and relaxed whatever their surroundings.

Empirics are keen observers. They appreciate detail and their perceptiveness makes them natural analysts of people and events. Trait Empiric writers make scenes and personalities come alive through verbal recreation of reality.

Empirics rely on their common sense. Einstein himself felt that science was just "a refinement of everyday thinking." Common sense stems from an instinct for the actual rather than the visionary. Empirics seek real rather than ideal ends and generally agree with Karl Marx that value and utility are one and the same. The Empiric's career success rests in an ability to give the public what it wants, needs, and can use. Empirics prefer to work within the bounds of popular taste and opinion in order to reach, effect, and communicate with as many people as possible.

Empirics appreciate the ordinary things in life and through their appreciation they often elevate the ordinary to the extraordinary. There is nothing dull or trivial in the world when seen through an Empiric's eyes. Empiric novelist George Eliot writes: "If we had a keen vision of all that is ordinary in human life, it would be like hearing the grass grow or the squirrel's heart beat..." Empirics draw strength and comfort from this attunement to everyday life.

Empirics want the facts. They believe what they see, touch, smell or taste. Rarely do they believe what they hear unless it comes from someone with credentials or practical experience. This show-me attitude reflects the Empiric's desire to invest personal resources wisely. To gain the Empiric's trust, you must prove that your idea or product works. Until they see proof, Empirics follow T.H. Huxley's motto: "Skepticism is the highest of duties, blind faith the one unpardonable sin."

Trait Empiric is similar to a low score on the Guilford trait Thoughtfulness. This indicates the person who wants action, not talk. People with this trait dislike theories. Instead, they want only relevant information sufficient to the practical task at hand.

The generally accepted theory of cognitive styles outlined by Bruner et al. in the 1950s distinguishes two basic cognitive modes, focusing and scanning. Focusers resemble Trait Empiric individuals; they pay attention to attributes. Scanners equate with Trait Hypothetics; they are hypothesis testers. Those remaining individuals who fall in the middle of the Trait Empiric/Trait Hypothetic trait-continuum appear to be "tacticians," a later cognitive mode defined by Johnson (1971) to describe people who typically find quick solutions to cognitive problems by deliberate yet unsystematic means.

Empirics who lack an inner locus of control sheepishly comply with established social institutions. They are quick to criticize those who question authority or society. Non-self-determining Empirics wear their conformity like merit badges. They are prim, proper and incapable of original thought.

Frustrated Trait Empirics who fail to adjust adequately in their environments exhibit the qualities Theodore Millon describes as passive-dependence. They "search for relationships in which (they) can lean upon others for affection, security and leadership." They seem content to accept what comes their way from others, are submissive, and "lack both initiative and autonomy."

The Empiric without an inner locus of control is all form and no content. He or she is apt to think that people are religious if they attend church regularly or patriotic if they vote in every election. This is often the sign of a marketplace mentality that measures all things in dollars and cents. Success means money and money, in turn, means social superiority. Social superiority means consumption of goods, the more conspicuous, the better.

The following adjectives describe Trait Empiric as it is constructively displayed: capable, conventional, discreet, efficient, enterprising, helpful, natural, organized, perceptive, practical, realistic, and sincere.

Here are some well-known individuals who have Trait Empiric. The numbers indicate the level at which the trait is displayed and reflect the total number of planet markers in the Security and Stimulus Need Triangles.

9

Dwight D. Eisenhower, president
Anne Morrow Lindbergh, writer
Lily Tomlin, comedienne
Arturo Toscanini, conductor

8

Muhammad Ali, boxer
Honoré de Balzac, writer
Hugo Black, jurist
Eva Braun, mistress
Helen Gurley Brown, publisher
Ellen Burstyn, actress
Adelle Davis, nutritionist
H.R. Haldeman, government official
Patricia Hearst, heiress
Hugh Hefner, publisher
Ann Landers, columnist
Charles Lindbergh, aviator
Don Loper, designer
Guglielmo Marconi, scientist

Zubin Mehta, conductor
Michaelangelo, genius
Gregory Peck, actor
Valerie Perrine, actress
Bertrand Russell, writer
Jill Saint John, actress
Upton Sinclair, writer
Suzanne Somers, actress
Mark Spitz, swimmer
Peter Ustinov, actor
Jules Verne, writer
Duke of Wellington, general
Kaiser Wilhelm, emperor
Cindy Williams, actress

7

Gregg Allman, musician	Diane Keaton, actress
Elizabeth Arden, entrepreneur	Jack Kerouac, writer
Alice Bailey, occultist	Evel Knieval, daredevil
Harry Belafonte, entertainer	Vivian Leigh, actress
Dr. Joyce Brothers, psychologist	James Lovell, astronaut
William F. Buckley, writer	Karl Marx, philosopher
Glen Campbell, singer	Rollo May, psychologist
Paul Cézanne, artist	Henry Miller, writer
Doris Day, actress	George Moscone, politician
Edgar Degas, artist	Jack Nicholson, actor
Robert DeNiro, actor	Jack Paar, TV personality
Phyllis Diller, comedienne	Louis Pasteur, scientist
John Dillinger, criminal	Elvis Presley, entertainer
Adolf Eichmann, nazi	Christopher Reeve, actor
Zelda Fitzgerald, socialite	Debbie Reynolds, entertainer
Peter Fonda, actor	Albert Schweitzer, humanitarian
Betty Ford, first lady	Omar Sharif, actor
David Frost, TV personality	George Bernard Shaw, writer
Marjoe Gortner, actor	O.J. Simpson, athlete
Merv Griffin, TV personality	Sally Struthers, actress
Merle Haggard, singer	Alfred Lord Tennyson, poet
Doug Henning, magician	Brenda Vaccaro, actress
Henry Jackson, politician	Johnny Weismuller, actor
Anver Joffrey, choreographer	Oscar Wilde, writer

Trait Organic

Trait Organic is the personal power trait. Organics are passionate, intense people whose forceful presence turns heads and commands attention. It may well be true, as Henry Kissinger suggests, that "power is the great aphrodesiac" because part of the Organic's forceful personal style is undeniably physical. Willpower and self-assurance complete the Organic's power base.

Because Organics are attuned to power and to power differences, they see the world as a hierarchy. Organics are aware of class differences, the distribution of wealth, political forces and individual status. Though they defer to those with greater authority, they also protect others who seem powerless and vulnerable. Organics thus adapt their personal behavior to fit the power structure of each life situation.

Upward striving marks the Organic's experience. Organics raise their standard of living, climb the ladder of success, become their best selves, and even perfect their spirits. Everything the Organic does reflects this bottom-to-top life perception. Organics set priorities, aspire to lofty goals, and seek improvement.

Organics do not mind blowing their own horns. When they feel they have dome something important, they will tell the world. Organic boxer Muhammad Ali lets us know that he is "the greatest." Only by promoting themselves and their causes can Organics acquire enough power to make changes and improvements.

Organics are often involved in power struggles. They refuse to back down from a fair fight simply because the going gets tough. Both politicians and politicians' wives tend to have this trait as do social activists on the political left as well as the right. Their causes run the gamut from environmental preservation (Robert Redford), to consumer protection (Ralph Nader), to human rights (Jimmy Carter) to economic reform (Ronald Reagan). Whatever the cause, Organics strive to do the right, the fair, the just thing.

Organics are self-contained people. They must experience things for themselves. Look beneath an Organic's cause and you will find something that has touched the Organic's life and made a deep, lasting impression. What happens to the Organic affects the Organic; all else is irrelevant. Their lives take on a sharp, distinctive focus made possible by this concentration on highly personal objectives.

Organics must know where they fit in the overall scheme of things. They want to know where others fit in as well. Who am I? What is my purpose? Why am I here and why are you there? These are the questions the Organic must answer. Organics are rarely happy until they find their special mission in life. Once they define this role, however, they play it with tremendous enthusiasm. They are here to do something significant and if anything is going to happen, they know they must make it happen.

Organics often feel that people are all basically alone; thus the experience of self is the height of Organic living. All else radiates from this personal, central life core. As Sir Richard Burton noted: "He noblest lives and noblest dies who makes and keeps his self-made laws." Above all else, Organics remain true to themselves. Honor, integrity and self-respect are crucial. Trait Organic people prefer the risk of losing altogether to the dishonor of compromising their personal standards.

Trait Organic writers examine themes of purpose and selfhood. The path to others is through the self or, as Proust contends: "Man is the creature that cannot emerge from himself, that knows his fellows only in himself;

when he asserts the contrary, he is lying." Anne Morrow Lindbergh states the same theme: "When one is a stranger to oneself then one is estranged from others too."

Organics are persuasive people who want others to share their personal passions. "Try it, you'll like it," they insist, often over your protest. Robert Redford's friends have commented on the injuries they sustained when he induced them to try his favorite sport, skiing.

Organics make good directors, administrators or office holders since they enjoy running things and do not mind the responsibility involved. Organics have broad shoulders and a good sense of direction that evokes admiration and respect.

More than anything else, Organics insist on the right to chart their own life-course. In the end, they do as they please and let the chips fall where they may.

Trait Organic compares to a low score on the Guilford trait Personal Relations. This indicates strong personal attitudes and an "unshakeable belief in one's self." At the extreme, this trait may indicate the person who lacks tolerance because he or she insists that the self is right; others are wrong.

Self-determining Organics emphasize the power to achieve goals. Non-self-determining Organics simply want power over others and they do not care how they get it. They are the dictators who rule others in a particularly authoritarian manner.

When Organics lack an inner locus of control, they use a cause, religion, or ethical stance to gain a feeling of superiority. They expect everyone else to applaud their smug morality and are forcefully intolerant of the opinions and rights of others. A non-self-determining Organic who has found *the* truth spares no effort in imposing that truth on others. Organics without inner control often demand oppressive external systems. They are egocentric yet are not centered in themselves, thus they resent the position or authority of others and are jealous of the success of others as well.

Failure to adjust to the environment in Trait Organic terms results in what personality theorist Theodore Millon describes as the active-independent coping strategy. This indicates an individual who does not trust others and thus feels justified in striving for power and rejection of people. The active-independent strategy is tinged with suspicion and people using its tactics assume others intend to betray them, thus autonomy and initiative appear to prevent such betrayals.

The following adjectives describe Trait Organic as it is constructively displayed: ambitious, autonomous, confident, determined, forceful, head-strong, powerful, responsible, self-made, self-sufficient, self-willed, and tough.

Here are some well-known individuals who have Trait Organic. The numbers indicate the level at which the trait is displayed and reflect the total number of planet markers in the Growth and Security Need Triangles.

10

Ethel Kennedy, political wife
Leopold Stokowski, musician
Edward White, astronaut

9

Sally Field, actress
Zelda Fitzgerald, socialite
J. Edgar Hoover, FBI chief
Robert Redford, actor
Sally Struthers, actress

8

Brigitte Bardot, actress
Carol Burnett, comedienne
Van Cliburn, musician
Bob Dylan, musician
George Eliot, writer
Elizabeth II of England
David Frost, TV host
Zsa Zsa Gabor, actress
Merv Griffin, TV host
H.R. Haldeman, government official

Grace Kelly, princess
Anne Morrow Lindbergh, writer
Jack Nicholson, actor
Sidney Omarr, astrologer
Valerie Perrine, actress
Sidney Poitier, actor
Jerry Reed, entertainer
Auguste Renoir, artist
P.B. Shelley, poet
Robyn Smith, jockey
Ringo Starr, musician

7

Joan Baez, singer
William Blake, poet
Jerry Brown, politician
Lord Byron, poet
Glen Campbell, musician
Albert Camus, writer
Steve Cauthen, jockey
Richard Chamberlain, actor
Judy Collins, singer
Angela Davis, activist
Mia Farrow, actress
Jane Fonda, actress
George Foreman, boxer
Stephen Foster, musician
Joe Frazier, boxer
Dorothy Hamill, skater
Jacqueline Kennedy Onassis, first lady
Vivian Leigh, actress
Mahara Ji, guru
Thomas Mann, writer

Karl Marx, philosopher
Paul McCartney, musician
Zubin Mehta, conductor
Walter Mondale, politician
Paul Newman, actor
Jack Nicklaus, golfer
Leontyne Price, singer
Freddie Prinze, actor
Rafael, artist
George Lincoln Rockwell, nazi
August Rodin, sculptor
Mickey Rooney, actor
Susan Saint James, actress
Brooke Shields, model
Dinah Shore, entertainer
Margaret Chase Smith, politician
Barbra Streisand, entertainer
Algernon Swinburne, poet
Jules Verne, writer
George Wallace, politician
Raquel Welch, actress

Trait Panoramic

Trait Panoramic is the only temperament trait based entirely on inter-personal needs. Thus, to the Panoramic, all space is shared space. "You don't live in a world all alone," states the Trait Panoramic humanitarian Albert Schweitzer whose life illustrates how seriously Panoramics take their interpersonal relationships. Panoramics have a keen sense that they are part of a larger scheme of things. They know that their individual actions have a ripple effect; what they do eventually reaches out to touch many other people. Panoramics see the full sweep of life and the complex web of human interaction.

The Panoramic life process constantly increases the scope of the personal world. Panoramics reach beyond themselves; they grow by inclusion. Their life structures are based on proximity versus distance. Some people, ideas or activities feel close to them while others seem very far away. From this perspective, however, all things are on the same plane of importance and all people are on the same level.

Panoramics treat others as equals. They would display the same behavior in the presence of a beggar or a king, the garbage collector or the President. Their democratic attitude can offend people who expect special treatment or deference due to their status, authority or prestige.

Unity means strength to the Panoramic. As Robert Burton notes, "A dwarf standing on the shoulders of a giant may see farther than a giant himself." Because unity is important, Panoramics develop the fine art of compromise and do not feel diminished by it. They prefer reaching a common understanding to alienating others by insisting on their own way. Their innate flexibility helps them adapt to the demands of shared situations.

Peacemaking Panoramics strive to find the common ground between people. While they are fully aware of the many human differences, Panoramics see the differences as superficial. Beneath the surface variations lies an inner level of commonality. "Though the leaves are many, the root is one," writes the poet Yeats.

The urge to unite with someone or something beyond the self can have mystical significance. Some Panoramics are deeply spiritual people for whom self-transcendence means union with one supreme being. Leaders of major religions tend to have this trait as do cult leaders. The objective is completion through mystical union, a process that the priest Pierre Teilhard de Chardin describes as "the magic feat of 'personalizing' by totalizing."

Since they see themselves as part of the larger whole, Panoramics make personal decisions that take into account the influence of their decisions on all concerned. They will forego an opportunity if it means they can profit at another's loss. Panoramics go out of their way to help strangers, do for others what they would not do for themselves, and make time for those who need them.

Panoramics are open, friendly, self-disclosing people. There is nothing secretive about them. Trait Panoramic friends are apt to invade your private space without realizing what they are doing. They simply do not think in terms of barriers and boundaries. Panoramics may ask very personal questions of absolute strangers. They are not looking for any dark, hidden secrets; they are simply trying to establish a rapport and forge a common bond.

Panoramics resist roles, definitions and categories. They see such things as basically alienating. Every self-definition stands as a category that includes some but excludes others and ultimately breaks down the unity the Panoramic strives to achieve.

These Renaissance people with diverse interests and enthusiasms rarely chart a single course toward a single objective. Teilhard de Chardin was priest, paleontologist, professor of geology, mystic and archeologist. He wrote several books attempting to reconcile the theory of evolution with religious concepts. No matter how diverse the Panoramic appears to others, he or she maintains a distinct and unified synthesis blending many experiences into one philosophy.

Trait Panoramic people's greatest difficulties stem from their greatest strength: the ability to think holistically. Their lives are a series of whole states, open, all-inclusive and unsegmented. When they are happy, they are completely happy. When they have a problem, however, they can be completely miserable. Finding the source of the problem is particularly hard because when one thing goes wrong, everything seems wrong.

Trait Panoramic compares to a high score on the Guilford trait Personal Relations. This indicates acceptance of others as they are and tolerance toward those who are different from the self. Guilford notes that an extremely high score on this trait can mean that the person is "too much of an observer and not enough of a participant in life."

Though Trait Panoramic people are concerned for the welfare of others and often put others before themselves, this is not in itself indicative of an external locus of control. Panoramics have strong interpersonal needs which this trait prepares them to fulfill. Their concern for others allows them to actualize their personal potential.

Panoramics who lack an inner locus of control become adept at avoiding all responsibilities. They make countless excuses for themselves by insisting their own actions are just responses to other people. This is the classic case of "Look what you made me do."

Without an inner locus of control, Trait Panoramic is more libertine than liberal. Non-self-determining Panoramics are usually aimless wanderers.

The all-important unifying life-concept evades them so they easily fall into relationships that seem to give them answers. Like chameleons, they take on the attitudes and behavior of a mate or a group.

Trait Panoramic individuals who do not adequately adjust to their environments display what Theodore Millon terms the active-dependent coping strategy. They show "an insatiable and indiscriminate search for stimulation and affection" and though they seem to be independent because they are friendly and "capricious," they demand acceptance, approval and affection from all human encounters.

The following adjectives describe Trait Panoramic as it is constructively displayed: considerate, cooperative, easy-going, generous, kind, peaceable, sympathetic, tolerant, understanding, and unselfish.

Here are some well-known individuals who have Trait Panoramic. The numbers indicate the level at which the trait is displayed and reflect the total number of planet markers in the Stimulus and Love Need Triangles.

10

Charles Baudelaire, poet
Jennifer Jones, actress
Martin Luther, reformationist

9

Pierre Teilhard de Chardin,
  philosopher-priest
Paul Goebbels, nazi

Jim Jones, cult leader
Louis Pasteur, scientist
Jack Sheldon, musician
Victoria, Queen of England

8

Buzz Aldrin, astronaut
Leonard Bernstein, musician
Phillip Berrigan, pacifist
Billy Carter, first family
Paul Cézanne, artist
Wilt Chamberlain, athlete
Sean Connery, actor
Gordon Cooper, astronaut
Howard Cosell, sportscaster
John Davidson, singer
Sandy Duncan, entertainer
Peter Fonda, actor

Jackie Gleason, entertainer
Jimmy Hoffa, labor leader
Washington Irving, writer
Elton John, musician
Carole King, musician
Sybil Leek, witch
Guglielmo Marconi, scientist
Grandma Moses, artist
Lance Rentzel, athlete
Carl Sandburg, writer
O.J. Simpson, athlete
Lee Trevino, athlete
Emile Zola, writer

7

Jack Anderson, columnist
Fred Astaire, dancer
Susan Atkins, cultist
Jim Bailey, female impersonator
Warren Beatty, actor
Scott Carpenter, astronaut
Rosalyn Carter, first lady
Dick Cavett, entertainer
Cher, singer
Colette, writer
Nicolaus Copernicus, astronomer
Bette Davis, actress
Rennie Davis, activist
Edgar Degas, artist
Adolf Eichmann, nazi
Sigmund Freud, psychiatrist
Ava Gardner, actress
Galileo Galilei, scientist
Merle Haggard, singer
Katherine Hepburn, actress

Herman Hesse, writer
Mario Lanza, singer
Liberace, entertainer
Don Loper, fashion designer
James Lovell, astronaut
Henry Mancini, musician
Jayne Mansfield, actress
Herman Melville, writer
Liza Minelli, entertainer
Elizabeth Montgomery, actress
Benito Mussolini, dictator
Della Reese, singer
Christopher Reeve, actor
Jean Paul Sartre, writer
Robert Shields, mime
Tom Snyder, TV personality
Tokyo Rose, propagandist
Gloria Vanderbilt, heiress
Charles Tex Watson, cultist

The six temperament traits form three trait continuums. When each trait is paired with its opposite, the measurement continuums appear as follows:

Trait Spontaneous									Trait Continuous
10	9	8	7	6	5	6	7	8	9	10

The Time Continuum

Trait Hypothetic									Trait Empiric
10	9	8	7	6	5	6	7	8	9	10

The Matter-Energy Continuum

Trait Organic									Trait Panoramic
10	9	8	7	6	5	6	7	8	9	10

The Space Continuum

Whenever you calculate the traits shown by a birth pattern, you place the individual somewhere on each of these three continuums. This gives you the ability to see life from his or her distinct perspective. Time, space, and matter-energy are the three core components of physical experience. They are so fundamental that we rarely stop to question or examine them yet they are the basis for all we perceive. Each of us sees the world in our own distinctive way. Our personal life-perspective insures that we see the world in the very terms that make it possible for us to fulfill our unique pattern of basic needs and our innate potential.

Those people who fall at the center of a trait continuum face unique challenges. They, too, have the perspective that best allows them to fulfill their pattern of needs but they often must cope with contradictory feedback from other people. Those at the center of the time-trait continuum, for instance, appear to have Trait Continuous to their Trait Spontaneous friends. This group treats and responds to them as if they had Trait Continuous. By contrast, Trait Continuous friends see these individuals at the center as having Trait Spontaneous and respond to them as such. The people caught in the middle cannot help but wonder why half the people they meet see them as careful, cautious and consistent while the other half treats them as adventurous, impulsive free spirits!

The center of each trait continuum forces individuals with a bit of each distinct perspective to forge a special blend of two opposing qualities. At the center of the time-trait continuum we find guarded optimism, planned adaptation and deliberate response. The center of the matter-energy continuum combines practical inventiveness, imaginative enterprise and well-disciplined artistry. The center of the space-trait continuum marks the loosely-worn identity, broad principles and the capacity to convey personal ideals to a wide variety of people.

Psychologists have sometimes presented these six themes as types. Early in this century, Spranger proposed six basic value systems. His *Types of Men*[7] describes the theoretical, economic, esthetic, social, political and religious ideal types. Lüscher, an expert on color and personality, postulates six ego norms: serene, serious, self-assured, carefree, self-reliant and content.[8] Michael Malone's *Psychetypes*[9] presents these six themes in the Jungian context. Malone describes both the Continuous and Discontinuous perceptions of time and four space-perception types: the Volcanic, the Territorial, the Aetherial and the Oceanic.

Birth Pattern Psychology's six temperament traits provide important measurement tools for both synthesis and personality analysis. Temperament traits define the world in which the individual needs and behaves.

Trait Spontaneous reflects the combined influence of the Growth and Stimulus Need Triangles.

Trait Continuous reflects the combined influence of the Security and Love Need Triangles.

Trait Spontaneous and Trait Continuous form the Time Trait Continuum.

Trait Hypothetic reflects the combined influence of the Growth and Love Need Triangles.

Trait Empiric reflects the combined influence of the Security and Stimulus Need Triangles.

Trait Hypothetic and Trait Empiric form the Matter-Energy Trait Continuum.

Trait Organic reflects the combined influence of the Security and Growth Need Triangles.

Trait Panoramic reflects the combined influence of the Stimulus and Love Need Triangles.

Trait Organic and Trait Panoramic form the Space Trait Continuum.

5 Measuring Behavior

Gordon Allport describes motivation as the "Go of personality." The Need Gestalt and trait qualities show what moves an individual. Yet it is not enough to need and to have a point of view. Needs and traits demand outward expression through action. Behavior enacts the personality pattern; behavior provides the Do that compliments the Go.

Karen Horney's social-psychological theory identifies three behavior trends which she labels moving toward, moving against and moving away. These are the three directions action may take, directions characterized by general attitudes of friendliness, ascendance, and restraint, respectively.

While needs and traits emerge and differentiate over the course of development, behavior, by contrast, is shaped at distinct developmental stages. Measuring behavior puts the personality gestalt within a time frame. This time frame is a useful indicator of the developmental point at which the experiences of success and failure have the greatest impact on the forming personality.

Traditional Freudian psychoanalysis says that either too much satisfaction or too much frustration at some developmental stage can be equally harmful. According to Freud, people may remain psychologically fixated at the developmental stage they experienced as ideal or as difficult and therefore incomplete.

Measuring behavior requires us to see the birth pattern in a new perspective. The measurement triangles provide the Need Gestalt and the trait measures. We have used these patterns both singly and in combination, exhausting their measurement possibilities. The fourfold pattern of triangles must give way to a different pattern capable of expressing the threefold nature of behavior.

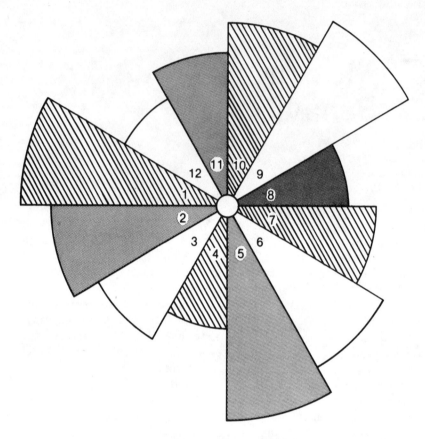

Figure and Ground in the Birth Pattern:
The Triangles and the Quadrangles

The illustration shows two distinct sets of patterns within the overall birth pattern. All sectors of the same *size* belong to the same measurement triangle. All sectors of the same *color* belong to the same measurement quadrangle. These three new quadrangular patterns provide a new measurement base that allows us to both assess the behavioral style and explore the course of development characteristic of the individual.

Karen Horney is not alone in suggesting that behavior has a threefold nature. Behavior's threefold quality may spring from the organization of the human brain into three levels of function. The triune brain theory developed in recent years by Paul D. MacLean and expanded by Arthur Janov as the basis of Primal Therapy suggests that brain growth and organization underlies the maturation process. Theodore Millon's biosocial-learning theory of personality also suggests three distinct levels of development. Measuring behavior means weighting each behavior mode to achieve a Behavior Gestalt, a pattern of behavior and a developmental time guide.

The Behavior Gestalt

The behavior quadrangles are wholes just as the need triangles are wholes. Neither quadrangles nor triangles can be reduced to a lower level of measurement. The pattern and not the sectors involved contains the meaning. Thus there are really *three* behavior patterns within the personality gestalt.

Sensitive Behavior moves toward the environment with friendly, open expectation. Sector pattern two–five–eight–eleven qualifies Sensitive Behavior.

Strong Behavior moves against the environment with an ascendant attitude. Sector pattern one–four–seven–ten qualifies Strong Behavior.

Strategic Behavior moves away from the environment with a detached, restrained attitude. Sector pattern three–six–nine–twelve qualifies Strategic Behavior.

Every birth pattern yields a distinct balance of these three behavior trends characteristic of the individual's abilities to seek, to compete and to plan. Defensive behaviors, too, involve either flight to a harbor of protection, standing ground to fight, or rising above the threat through detachment.

Birth Pattern #21 maps the personality of cult leader Jim Jones. Each behavior is weighted by the sum of the planet markers in its measurement quadrangle. The illustration shows this simple calculation. Here is the resulting Behavior Gestalt:

Jim Jones:
Behavior Gestalt

Sensitivity:	2
Strength:	5
Strategy:	3

Birth Pattern #21: Jim Jones

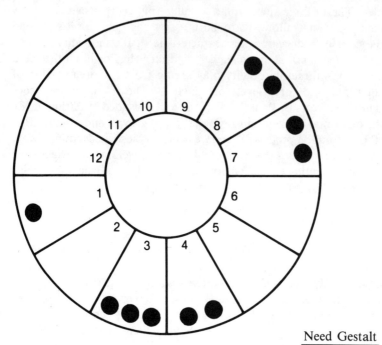

Need Gestalt

Growth Need: 1
Security Need: 0
Stimulus Need: 5
Love Need: 4
Temperament Type: Humanist
Trait Panoramic: 9
Trait Spontaneous: 6

THREE-DIGIT BEHAVIOR GESTALT CALCULATION

SENSITIVITY:	Second Sector Planets		Fifth Sector Planets		Eighth Sector Planets		Eleventh Sector Planets		
	0	+	0	+	2	+	0	=	2
STRENGTH:	First Sector Planets		Fourth Sector Planets		Seventh Sector Planets		Tenth Sector Planets		
	1	+	2	+	2	+	0	=	5
STRATEGY:	Third Sector Planets		Sixth Sector Planets		Ninth Sector Planets		Twelfth Sector Planets		
	3	+	0	+	0	+	0	=	3

The Strength emphasis suggests take-charge behavior that expresses forcefully with an ascendant, powerful self-projection. Competition outweighs either cooperative Sensitivity or communicative Strategy. Souls are to be won over, not merely charmed or convinced.

The Need Gestalt and temperament traits emphasize the interpersonal with both the excitement of the larger group and the intimacy of close association overriding the more private growth or security concerns. As a Humanist temperament type, Jones's interpersonal interests sought the established social channel of religion and of social reform. The Panoramic message of equality and tolerance and peace and the religious aura of mystical transcendence contributed to Jones's charisma. The force and eventual domination come, however, from the combination of these temperamental qualities with a conquering, dynamic behavior pattern. The introduction of a more competitive action pattern helps us see the in-group, out-group trend where the followers banded together and outsiders posed a threat. Given Jones's Behavior Gestalt, the Guyana move was probably never a move to a new paradise but rather a move to insure easier control through domination and authoritarian tactics.

Each behavior mode has its place and its function. No matter how awkward or vulnerable a behavior mode may make the person feel, the individual survives best when cooperation, competition, and detachment are all viable behaviors. Low Sensitivity makes the identification of appropriate need satisfiers more difficult. Low Strength makes the ability to actively struggle with the environment weaker. Low Strategy undermines the objective assessment of experience.

The following table assesses the display of each behavior according to its marker emphasis:

Number of Planet Markers in Behavior Quadrangle	Attitude Toward the Related Behavior Mode
0	Will not, by choice, display this behavior. Can display this behavior when the situation calls for it but feels somewhat forced and unnatural. In non-self-determining people, this behavior is unavailable and situations calling for this behavior are feared.
1	Little display of this behavior. Tends to confine this behavior to familiar situations and display this behavior in the presence of those he or she knows well. In non-self-determining people this behavior may not be recognized as a valid part of the self.
2-3	Average display of this behavior. Feels comfortable with this behavior though it is not preferred and occasionally seeks situations that demand this behavior. Less display of this behavior with strangers. In non-self-determining people this behavior may be a front or tool to serve the preferred behavior mode.
4	Feels comfortable and confident with this behavior mode. If it is the preferred behavior, considers this his or her personal style and problem-solving mode. Actively seeks and thoroughly enjoys situations that call for this behavior. Non-self-determining people rely on this behavior if it is the preferred behavior mode.
5	This is the most frequent emphasis indicating a preferred behavior mode. Sees self as highly competent in situations calling for this behavior. Capable of superior performance in tasks that emphasize this mode. In non-self-determining people, this behavior is displayed regardless of its appropriateness.
6 or more	Great demand for situations in which the self can excel through this behavior. Prominent enough to challenge the flexibility of self-determining people. Rigid, indiscriminate display in non-self-determining people.

Behavior, like motivation, is a gestalt. Every person's behavior is a distinctive blend of sensitivity, strength, and strategy. We interpret behavior most accurately when we see it as a pattern. Consider these three Behavior Gestalts:

Person A		Person B		Person C	
Sensitivity:	2	Sensitivity:	2	Sensitivity:	2
Strength:	1	Strength:	3	Strength:	2
Strategy:	7	Strategy:	5	Strategy:	6

For Person A, sensitivity is secondary to strategy. By contrast, sensitivity is person B's least preferred behavior mode. Person C views sensitivity and strength as equally available personal qualities. Clearly these three individuals will express their sensitivity differently. Though each person's sensitivity carries equal weight, each person's evaluation of his or her sensitivity springs from a distinct context. Each person has different behavior priorities. Person A might say, "When planning fails, I ask a friend for help." Person B might express a very different attitude, "I don't ask for help unless all else fails." Person C has another attitude, "Since I can't solve this problem through planning, I can either adopt stronger methods or ask for help." If we want to understand behavior, we must remember that the Behavior Gestalt determines how the sensitivity, strength and strategy will be displayed.

Cultural expectations influence behavior and powerfully shape behavior display. Our culture still equates strength with masculinity and sensitivity with femininity. The sensitive man and the strong woman must overcome cultural stereotypes to use their full behavior potential. The birth patterns of American presidents indicate that we prefer a strong, competitive leader. We will, however, accept a friendly team player who urges cooperation and tells us that government cares. We do not accept detached, ivory-tower intellectuals. Such cultural bias affects our behavior in a wide variety of social, employment, and relationship situations.

We express ourselves most naturally and effectively through our preferred behavior mode. This behavior comes to the fore when we are faced with problems and when we have the freedom to choose our own activities. We simply like to do what we do best. We feel natural, comfortable and at ease with our preferred behavior mode. Eighty-four percent of the sample birth patterns have a preferred behavior. The remaining 16 percent have two equally weighted behavior modes. In self-determining people, the preferred behavior mode shapes the self-presentation and attitude toward the environment. In non-self-determining people, the preferred behavior dominates the personality and can become an end in itself.

Every behavior mode has three important characteristics. First, behavior has a source. Behaviors are shaped at specific stages in the ongoing developmental experience from infancy to adulthood. The source of a behavior mode defines its roots, roots planted in the human biological make-up. Second, every behavior mode has an external target since behavior links the person to the environment. Behavior targets are the other people and the objects in the person's world. Finally, behavior has function. It makes contact with the world, expresses inner states, motives and traits and actively copes with or defends against the challenges of everyday experience.

Sensitive Behavior

Birth Pattern Sectors Two, Five, Eight, and Eleven

The first life stage, termed the *sensory-attachment* developmental phase by Theodore Millon, extends from birth to age eighteen months. Infants cannot independently get the fulfillments they require, therefore successful behavior at this first activity stage elicits a helping response from adult caregivers. The infant's only behavior task is to signal its sensations of need so that the caregiver will bring the desired stimulation, attention, nurturance, or affection.

Because of their helplessness and their physical appearance, infants invite caretaking. The fact that babies physically appeal to their helpers insures their survival. The capacity to court favor through "playing cute" and through physical appeal remains a part of the general complex of sensitive behavior, behavior designed to satisfy need by appealing to some other's willingness to provide.

The mother is the behavior partner almost exclusively. She is both protector and provider and the Sensitivity Quadrangle's birth pattern emphasis indicates her significance as a shaper of the person's behavior. Behaviors expressive of this life stage put others in the mother role.

Harry Stack Sullivan's social psychological theory defines personality in terms of the "relatively enduring pattern of recurrent interpersonal situations. . . ." The preferred behavior actively recreates the most meaningful developmental stage and casts the other toward whom it is directed in a stage-related role. Sullivan noted that the infant forms two mother concepts, the Good Mother and the Bad Mother. These concepts stay within the behavior network to the degree that sensitive behavior characterizes the behavior gestalt.

Friendly, sensitive behavior appeals to the Good Mother, the source of satisfaction. The Good Mother will provide whatever the person desires. In return, the person offers the Good Mother affection, attachment and bonding. The Bad Mother, by contrast, withholds satisfaction and frustrates the person's wishes. In the adult with preferred sensitive behavior, both acting to elicit Good Mother/Bad Mother responses and adopting the Good Mother/Bad Mother conduct are alternatives. The contact, expressive, coping and defensive qualities of the sensitive behavior mode all retain the element of seeking the Good Mother and avoiding the Bad Mother via friendliness and amiability.

Karen Horney explores the tendency to "move toward" others, a tendency she terms a neurotic trend. She stresses the manipulative objective in moving toward that exploits the other toward whom the behavior is directed. The moving toward behavior sees these actions as love and is apt to have the illusion that love solves all problems. Intimacy is not the goal, however. Moving toward behavior attempts through affectionate acts to unite with a source of provision, attention, protection, and support.

Horney points out that the desire to depend on others and to evoke their good will through cooperative friendliness is not neurotic but natural. When the behavior becomes a rigid trend, the individual *must* behave endearingly, *must* charm, *must* rely on some other person to feel important and capable. The compulsive behavior trend is both rigid and automatic.

Every behavior has a dark aspect, a hidden side that only emerges when the behavior does not achieve the desired satisfaction. The sensitive, vulnerable person who is easily hurt has a dark and hostile shadow side. Hostility reacts to the foe or Bad Mother aspect in the other. The hostility emerges in tantrums, in moody accusation, in the manipulative or punitive use of sex or in depression.

Sensitive contact, self-expression, and friendliness actively manage everyday life events to provide required satisfactions. Even the self-defeating moving toward behavior trend attempts to actively satisfy needs. Both coping and self-defeating sensitive behaviors represent adult expressions of behavior potentials biologically rooted and developmentally shaped in infancy. These biological and environmental roots emerge in sensitive behavior's defensive manifestation: flight behavior.

While coping behavior actively approaches some need satisfier, defensive behavior actively protects the person. Preferred sensitive behavior makes flight the preferred defensive behavior. How does Horney's "moving toward" behavior spring from the same roots as flight behavior when flight commonly means getting away from difficulty? Flight, Freud notes, is most understandable as a move toward a position of safety, comfort or protection. Flight seeks the Good Mother who will make the bad things in life go away; flight runs to some place that is free of demands or danger.

Flight behavior, in everyday language, seeks the easy way out and takes the path of least resistance. Flight is escapist but flight escapes into some protective other or pleasurable activity. Freud writes of flight into illness in which the person uses illness to escape pressures and demands. People commonly escape into alcohol, drugs, relationships, indulgence or stimulus-seeking and the alcohol, the lover, the pleasure all act as Good Mothers providing comfort, ease and freedom from external pressures and problems.

When neither friendliness nor flight, neither coping nor defensive behavior is possible, the person feels trapped. The long-term consequences affect the body and undermine the health of the behavior system. Since sensitive behavior is biologically based in infancy, the symptoms of failure to cope or defend are visceral. The infant lives primarily through sensation and the organs that are fully developed at birth: the heart, respiratory organs, bladder and bowel, stomach, glands and blood-forming organs. Symptoms related to this first developmental stage are heart palpitation, colitis, asthma, bowel dysfunction, ulcer and migrane. The body's sensation processing function also includes the genitals and sexual dysfunctions often signal failure to cope through the sensitivity behavior mode.

The preferred behavior gives multiple assessment alternatives. It enriches observation since the behavior mode, unlike the motives and traits which must be inferred, is so visible. Contacting, expressing, coping and defending give clues to the life stage most important in development and to the physical results of long-term coping failures.

Strong Behavior

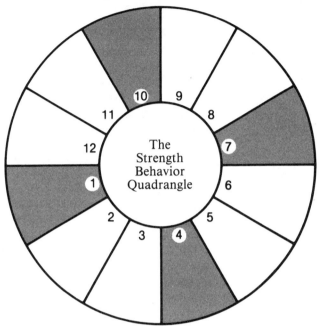

Birth Pattern Sectors One, Four, Seven, and Ten

The second developmental phase, Millon's *sensorimotor-autonomy* stage, begins after the first year and peaks at age six. While infants live mainly through their internal sensations, toddlers live through their muscles. The new phase of maturation involves movement, active play and active assertion of the child's wishes.

These are the discipline years when children run headlong into power struggles and adult authority. The child can now assess the parents' real feelings and attitudes and perceives whether the parents are truly loving and concerned or are, instead, disinterested and uncaring. Since the child begins to assert its wishes, those wishes may well conflict with the wishes of other people. In this developmental phase, the child learns to compete.

The father now participates more actively in the child's life. The strength behavior mode's connection with father as a behavior partner is similar to the sensitivity behavior mode's connection with the mother. The young child is no longer a helpless infant and this allows the parents the opportunity to resume their relationship. Father now competes for mother's attention in ways the infant did not experience.

Though Sullivan did not propose a Good Father/Bad Father behavior archetype, it is entirely possible that such role images emerge during this life phase. The world is still very big and the child is very small. The toddler struggling to confirm new abilities and succeed in an environment that constantly challenges the budding self-esteem can use a Good Father, a trusted ally whose strength supports and encourages and models self-assertion. The Bad Father, by contrast, would compete with the child and thwart the child's wishes. He would be the Freudian image of father as competitor, as the winner of mother's affection.

The strong behavior mode's contact, self-expressive and coping versus defending functions all express the underlying theme of the second developmental phase: the assertion of personal wishes and autonomy in a world filled with others who also have wishes and autonomy.

Karen Horney's social-psychological theory proposes a second neurotic trend, moving against people, in which driving ambition and will to win at all costs emerge and take over the Behavior Gestalt. This rigid behavior orientation centers on fantasies of success for success brings the solution to all life difficulties.

The moving against behavior trend marks the person to whom all life is a Darwinian struggle for survival. The fittest rule; others fall by the wayside. Conquest is imperative. Might makes right. In the grip of rigid moving against behavior, the person *must* prevail, *must* get respect, *must* feel sought after, significant, and admired.

Horney points out that there is nothing neurotic about wanting to succeed. It is having to succeed rather than wanting to that makes rigid moving against behavior compulsively ascendant.

Gordon Allport wrote that in every human encounter there is a subtle contest for control. One person will eventually lead the flow of conversation or shape the course of action and the other will follow. The ascendant person determines to take the lead.

Just as sensitivity shows a hostile shadow side, strength shows a dark and submissive side. The rigid success-at-all-costs winner has a loser standing in his or her shadow self and the behavior stems more from fear of weakness and loss than from enthusiasm for winning. The weak, submissive loser also sees life as a battleground and the loser's defeatist attitude is the flip side of the winner's never-say-die position.

Compulsively strong people must prove themselves. Since others are Bad Father symbols, they are out to get the strong person so it only makes sense for the strong person to move first. The attitude toward people in general is one of scorn. Since people are bad, they do not deserve consideration; since people are stupid, they deserve to be used. Work, play, sex, relationships all provide competitive arenas in which to excel, to find status and prestige.

Assertive contact, self-expression and strength cope forcefully with the person-environment interaction. Both self-assertion and the self-defeating moving against behavior trends attempt to achieve satisfaction. The defensive or protective parallel to assertiveness is the fight response. The fight reaction confronts and attempts to overpower difficulty.

The fight defense need not entail actual physical combat. The fight mechanism appears in any confrontation and the confrontation may be with a situation or obstacle as well as with a person. The fight defense underlies acts that obstruct or hinder and conversations that move from simple discussions to heated debates.

Fight behavior is rooted in the active, aggressive years of childhood when new territories of life experience are both claimed and defended. The muscular growth during this phase brings a new physical system to developmental precedence. Psychologist Arthur Janov, creator of Primal Therapy, suggests that the symptoms related to frustration and failure at this second developmental stage include muscular tics, eye blinking, slumped posture, low-back muscle pain and tension headaches. All these symptoms involve muscle tension and all spring from attempts to suppress movement.

Strategic Behavior

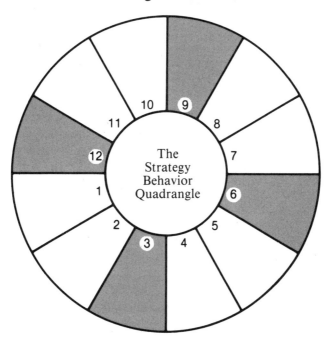

Birth Pattern Sectors Three, Six, Nine and Twelve

The final developmental stage covers the educational phase from the earliest school years through college age. Millon terms this the *intracortical-initiative* stage. The brain now leads the viscera and muscles and the nervous system gains complexity and organization. The child is increasingly more head than body, a fact that makes this enduring phase more subtle and complicated.

The child adds rational coping and planning abilities in preparation for independent adult life in the broader social environment beyond the home. The sense of identity and personal integrity emerge along with greater adaptability and flexibility.

The behavior partners are now others outside the family circle, the teachers and peers who make up the greater social world. There are goals to define, purposes to discover, fantasies to transform into concrete aspiration. The school years mean learning to coordinate and direct a life plan.

The behavior partners are important not for willingness to provide or protect or ally, but rather for their willingness to inform. The archetypal other at this stage is a Good Mentor, a teacher or friend whose advice is both honest and wise and who can be counted on to tell the behaver how he or she is doing. The opposite, the Bad Mentor, lies and deceives, withholds important information and undermines the behaver's integrity through appealing to fantasies and wishes.

The qualities of planning, restraint, and intellectual coping formed in the final developmental stage color the contact, self-expressive, and adjustment behaviors that are strategy.

Strategy is, in a sense, the civilized alternative but it is also the weakest behavior mode because of it. It centers on detachment, on putting up with a situation until the choices in the situation become clear. All too often strategy adapts to situations that could be changed by more forceful behavior or should be left for more appealing alternatives. Strategy deteriorates in the face of the irrational and the unreasonable with resulting anxiety and fear of falling apart.

Because strategy leads with the head rather than the heart or the chin, strategy demands time to think clearly. When troubled, people with this behavior need time to be alone in a private place of their own free from intrusions and distractions.

Strategy, like sensitivity and strength, can become rigid and compulsive. Karen Horney describes a third neurotic trend, moving away from people. Here, the goal is to promote a feeling of superiority, perfection and unassailability through detachment. The person, because of the sense of superiority, has nothing to prove. Others are simply supposed to bow before a superior presence, to accept a greater knowledge. Compulsive strategy rarely stoops to display the virtues it feels it possesses. If others cannot see, they are ignorant, foolish, or unaware.

Just as the compulsively sensitive person grasps for love and the compulsively strong person chases success, the compulsively strategic person seeks perfection through independence. He or she never asks for anything. That would be humiliating. Strategy's goals, writes Horney, are wholly negative: it seeks "not to be involved, not to need anybody, not to allow others to intrude...or influence...."

The shadow side of strategy's superiority is inferiority. Strategy splits itself into objective and subjective. This split alone is characteristic but not problematic. The fear of exposure and the anxiety and strain of remaining above it all contribute to the shadow. The vascillation between objective, detached assessment and subjective willingness to believe fails to integrate the two. Strain constantly threatens the veneer of cool indifference.

To fulfill needs, strategic contact, self-expression and restraint cope cautiously and methodically with the demands of other people and the environment. Both planning and self-defeating moving away behavior attempt to gain satisfaction. The defensive or protective parallel to strategic behavior is, in the words of stress specialist Hans Selye, "putting up with it." This freeze reaction neither runs from difficulty nor struggles against it; it ignores the difficulty and goes about the business of life in spite of it.

The primary quality Horney associates with moving away behavior is detachment and putting up with difficulty is, in effect, behavioral detachment. It resembles animal camouflage in which the animal changes its appearance to continue to live and function in a threatening environment. Perls, Hefferline and Goodman suggest that putting up with frustration is the only alternative when a need satisfier contains both appealing and unappealing qualities. Thus a woman might, for instance, love her husband and so adjust to the travel his job requires even though she feels frustrated by the amount of time she spends alone.

Selye believes that of the three biological defense behaviors, putting up with things may cause the greatest physical strain. This defensive behavior mode relates to stress disorders such as fatigue or insomnia.

None of us persistently displays our best behavior. Whatever our preferred behavior mode, we generally show characteristics of the related neurotic trend. The neurotic trends arise in response to extreme difficulty in some stage of development and oppose some overwhelming environmental frustration. Who has not wanted to cling to a loved one for support when times get hard? Who has not flaunted a success to soothe a wounded ego? Who has not wished that a difficult problem would simply go away? None of these behaviors is inherently neurotic; they are part of human nature.

Reasonably self-assured, capable people do not, however, sacrifice basic satisfactions to compulsive behavior. Rigid, compulsive behavior is a psychological last resort. The truly inflexible behavior pattern arises to protect the injured psyche from any further damage.

All people have the potential to perform all basic behaviors. All people experience hostile feelings, fear of loss, anxiety over potential inferiorities. If one of these patterns dominates the personality, if the related behavior serves as an end in itself rather than a means to gratification, if the person is unable to set some behavior aside when it becomes inappropriate, these are indications of potential developmental problems. Something in the person's nurture fixated the person's behavioral nature.

Six Lives: Studies in Nature and Nurture

The Behavior Gestalt is a pattern of possibilities, not a predictor of experience. The following studies are extreme examples of individual temperament shaped by actual experience. Developmental psychologists often point out that children, by virtue of their own distinct temperaments, contribute to their own actual experience. The child's behavior determines the parent's child-rearing tactics. Whether, for instance, a sensitive, warm infant elicits a more indulgent parent response while a willful, strong child demands greater discipline is impossible to say. The parent, too, has an innate personality pattern. The meeting of circumstance, environment and personality in the following six brief studies is striking however, and the studies illustrate the shaping of behavior by actual life events.

Birth Pattern #22 and the accompanying Behavior Gestalt illustrate the behavior pattern of Zelda Sayre Fitzgerald. The preferred sensitive behavior mode with its related tendencies to crave attention and affection may be indulged in the first child born to a mother, particularly if the child is a boy. But it is the baby of the family who is more frequently coddled and indulged and Zelda was the youngest of six. She was breast-fed till the age of four and remained strongly attached to her mother throughout childhood.

To say that Zelda was merely spoiled is to make a gross understatement. At six, she didn't want to attend school so her mother kept her at home till the age of seven. Zelda's mother made all the child's clothes and took particular pride in her daughter's attractiveness.

The maternal indulgence became, in Zelda's later development, extreme self-indulgence. Zelda did what she pleased and only what she pleased. She was without restraint or inhibition; she drank, smoked and flaunted her sexuality. The latter made her the center of local male attention and admiration, something her mother secretly admired. When Zelda's father, in an attempt to curb her adolescent wildness, forbade her to leave the house, Zelda climbed out her window with her mother's assistance.

Birth Pattern #22: Zelda Fitzgerald

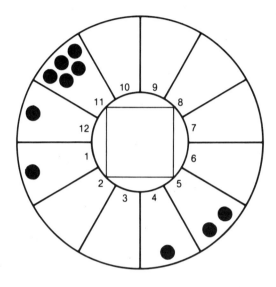

Behavior Gestalt:

Sensitivity:	7
Strength:	2
Strategy:	1

Birth Pattern #23: F. Scott Fitzgerald

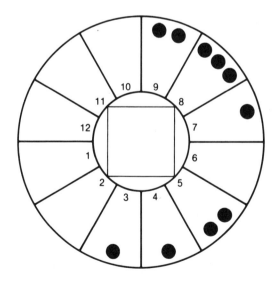

Behavior Gestalt:

Sensitivity:	5
Strength:	2
Strategy:	3

Like Zelda, F. Scott Fitzgerald was a pampered, coddled, undisciplined child. Birth Pattern #23 illustrates his Behavior Gestalt. Again, the preferred behavior is sensitivity. The Fitzgerald family had experienced the death of two previous children in infancy, so Scott's birth was a joyous occasion. He, too, was bathed in attention, indulged and pampered. He attended school only when he felt in the mood to do so. His mother, an eccentric woman, doted on Scotty and raised him with the illusion, if not the reality, of great wealth.

Scott became an egocentric youth and like Zelda was unpopular with same-sex peers. Though he was talented, he was plagued throughout his adult life with vague self-doubt. Together, Scott and Zelda simply exaggerated and fed each other's propensities for self-indulgence. Their glamorous, free-wheeling lifestyle masked their lack of maturity and made it seem unimportant. Their tragedies, however, came in part from their unpreparedness to cope for theirs was a life of flight from reality.

Birth Pattern #24 and the accompanying Behavior Gestalt illustrate the behavior pattern of Mary Baker Eddy, founder of Christian Science. The Goertzels' childhood studies note that she was a "father-smothered" child. They observe that close relationships between a child and the opposite sex parent often coincide with later difficulty in establishing mature adult relationships.

Mary Baker Eddy's father was a powerful man, rigid in his fundamentalist views. He vigorously imposed his standards on the young girl, pressured her constantly and demanded she live up to his high moral expectations. Mary Baker Eddy's health suffered continually and eventually she had bouts of rage and hysterical behavior. The latter psychological symptoms are associated with emotional tensions during the active developmental phase, according to Arthur Janov. These health problems recurred into Eddy's adult life until an apparent mystical healing that provided the impetus for her own religious development. The tenets of Christian Science actively counter fundamentalist religious doctrine. To what extent Eddy, the adult, established the autonomy of which she was deprived in childhood is uncertain. She was relieved of her physical symptoms but she remained an openly antagonistic person. To the end of her life, she was involved in power struggles and law suits.

Birth Pattern #25 and the accompanying Behavior Gestalt are those of American aviator Charles Lindbergh. Lindbergh's father was the embodiment of a Bad Father archetypal competitor. He was forceful, bold, brave, superior. He once had surgery without benefit of anesthetic. To the rather timid and submissive young Charles Lindbergh, his father presented an unmistakable challenge. How could the boy possibly gain the respect of such a father?

Birth Pattern #24: Mary Baker Eddy

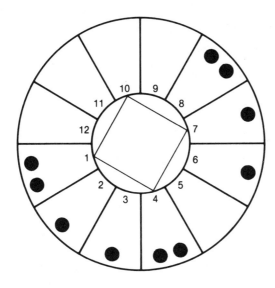

Behavior Gestalt:

Sensitivity:	3
Strength:	5
Strategy:	2

Birth Pattern #25: Charles Lindbergh

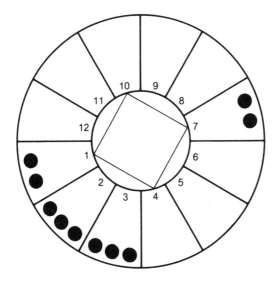

Behavior Gestalt:

Sensitivity:	3
Strength:	4
Strategy:	3

Lindbergh was a fearful child but he determined, on his own, to actively stamp out his fearfulness. Through acts of daring and risk, he gradually managed to build his strength and his self-esteem. Of the six lives studied here, Lindbergh appears to have most successfully overcome the effects of environmental pressure.

The following two birth patterns have strong strategy behavior emphases. By many analytic theories, real trauma is considered impossible once the child reaches school age. For those individuals who are vulnerable to the special pressures of this final behavior mode, this does not seem to be true. The potential for trauma lasts over a very long period of time in which the child strives to form a secure identity. The duration of this final developmental stage alone marks its greatest vulnerability. Pressures may accumulate. General stress can lead to one climactic event that so threatens the self-image it infuses behavior integration with self-doubt. For Carl Jung and Janis Joplin, one severely traumatic event was enough to leave a legacy of anxiety.

Birth Pattern #26 and the accompanying Behavior Gestalt indicate the behavior pattern of Carl Jung. Jung survived a stressful early home environment only to become more and more withdrawn during his school years. The school difficulties he experienced will be explored in the next chapter. Important to understanding Jung, however, is the fact that he had a trusted mentor, an adult family friend, who sexually molested the schoolboy, Carl Jung. Jung's biographer noted that Jung, for much of his life, harbored the fear that he might be homosexual. Perhaps he found some resolution to this critical life shock in his theory of androgeny, which postulates both male and female elements within the human psyche.

Here, again, is the birth pattern of Janis Joplin. Her Behavior Gestalt emphasizes the strategy behavior mode. Though a gifted child, she received little support during her school years and the early family support could not protect her from her own innate vulnerability. She grew increasingly unpopular with her peers and much of her extreme early behavior was obvious rebellion against the pain of peer rejection. The intensity of her social vulnerability is indicated in her behavior pattern. For Janis Joplin, the crisis event did not happen until her college years, a fact that again emphasizes the length and importance of the final developmental stage. After years of rebellious searching for a self to be, a self important enough to gain some peer tolerance if not acceptance, Janis was able to have some small successes as a singer in her college community. Then, as a prank, a fellow student nominated Janis as a candidate for Ugly Man on Campus. It was the last straw and soon after she escaped to California where her career took off but her self-esteem never recovered.

Birth Pattern #26: Carl Jung

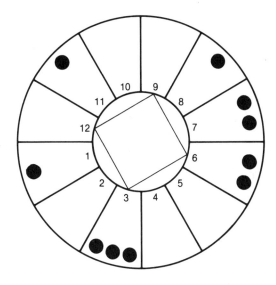

Behavior Gestalt:

Sensitivity:	2
Strength:	3
Strategy:	5

Birth Pattern #20: Janis Joplin

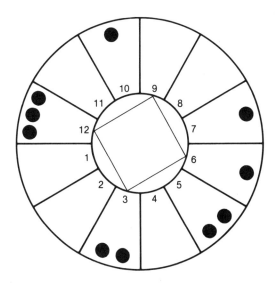

Behavior Gestalt:

Sensitivity:	2
Strength:	2
Strategy:	6

Behavior Conflict

Just as equally weighted needs produce conflicting priorities, equally weighted behaviors produce conflicting actions. Obviously, the person with a behavior conflict does not do two things at once. Instead, he or she sends conflicting behavior signals.

The sensitivity/strength conflict casts a receiver in the roles of friend/competitor. The receiver feels warm and included one moment, under fire the next. Conversation turns into a series of battles and truces. The sender wonders why the reciever is getting so defensive.

The strength/strategy conflict casts a receiver in the roles of competitor/ stranger. The receiver is vigorously involved one moment, subject to cool, detached analysis the next. The bottom drops out of the conversation yet the sender quietly asks the receiver why the receiver is so worked up and emotional.

The sensitivity/strategy conflict casts a receiver in the roles of friend/stranger. The receiver may be greeted with warmth and affection only to feel progressively distanced and shut out. The sender then asks why the receiver will not open up, share, commit.

The sender sees the receiver's conflicting behavior quite clearly yet fails to see that the receiver's conflicts respond to the sender's behavior cues. People with two behavioral alternatives equally available and equally weighted vascillate automatically. They have no sense of self-contradiction but rather see the contradiction in others. A person's behavior pattern, whatever it is, is so much a part of the person that it emerges naturally and remains largely invisible.

Undoing is another invisible habit characteristic of behavior mode conflicts. The person adapts through one behavior mode only to negate that adaptation by using the other.

In undoing, people can be very active yet never progress. They spin their wheels. The two competing behaviors succeed only in restoring the situation to its original conditions. Action plus action equals zero when things apparently done are undone.

Both undoing and sending conflicting signals are behavior habits that yield to insight. The conflict still remains but as gestalt psychologist Frederick Perls insists, the goal is never to end a conflict. The goal is to strengthen the person. Then, conflict itself invigorates the personality.

Behavior Transitions: The Conflicts of Change

The three behavior modes represent three significant developmental stages. However, no behavior emerges full-blown and no stage ends for the next stage to begin. Instead, behavior stages overlap. Major behavior phases extend, stabilize, and fulfill a single behavior potential. Transitional stages present two behavior alternatives; the certain, achieved behavior's attractiveness wanes while the new behavior's potential dawns. Every behavior transition marks a period of tension and turmoil and conflict between the familiar and the new, the easy and the difficult, the safe and the risky.

The Behavior Gestalt indicates behavior conflicts in which two equally weighted behavior modes compete to determine action. Behavior conflict may be overt. The competing behaviors carry greater psychological weight than the remaining behavior. In overt conflict, there is no preferred behavior and hence no clearly defined behavior role. Such overt conflicts appear in 16 percent of the five hundred birth patterns in the original sample.

Most behavior conflicts are covert. The conflicting behavior modes carry less psychological weight than the remaining preferred behavior. The behavior role, in such cases, can represent an active attempt to overcompensate underlying conflict through either friendliness, assertiveness, or restraint.

The sensitivity/strength behavior transition generally takes place during the second year of life. This behavior conflict accounts for much of the terrible in the "terrible two." Developmentally, the child lacks the biological readiness and self-maintenance skills to achieve greater freedom yet the child demands greater freedom all the same. At this training stage, the parents become teachers and the lessons involve basic life skills leading to biological self-sufficiency.

The training stage and the sensitivity/strength behavior transition are crucial to self-esteem in individuals whose Behavior Gestalts indicate overt sensitivity/strength conflicts:

Sensitivity	5	Sensitivity	4
Strength	5	Strength	4
Strategy	0	Strategy	2

Though three remaining patterns contain sensitivity/strength conflicts, the conflicts are covert and masked by preferred strategy behavior. These patterns are:

Sensitivity	3	Sensitivity	2	Sensitivity	1
Strength	3	Strength	2	Strength	1
Strategy	4	Strategy	6	Strategy	8

The 3–3–4 behavior pattern is by far the most significant of the three since the underlying sensitivity/strength conflict makes the preferred strategic behavior more significant than measurement weight alone suggests.

The training phase covers the famous Freudian anal stage, the point at which children's instinctual desires first meet with regulation and hence with frustration. The child learns to reward its parents by giving and punish them by withholding; here, Freudian theory reflects the conflict between sensitive cooperation and assertive competition.

Regardless of its overt or covert conflict quality, any conflict has specific characteristics at this stage. Erik Erikson's developmental theory describes the successes and failures inherent in sensitivity/strength conflict. The successful child takes the first steps toward independence and gains self-esteem through the newfound capacity for self-regulation. Self-regulation allows the child to end the dependency of the sensitive behavior stage in order to prepare for the autonomy of the strong behavior stage.

Too many failures during the sensitivity/strength transition create lingering doubt and shame, says Erikson. Conflict makes the child unable to either hold on or let go. The general feelings of being inept and unworthy lead to attempts to gain power through stubbornness, picky attention to detail, and punitiveness. This is the child's first introduction to the capacity to choose and doubt confuses choice.

The sensitivity/strength transition is the first behavior transition and the sensitivity/strength conflict the first developmental conflict. The strategic behavior mode is unique in that it is the only behavior mode to actually cover or compensate for earlier conflict. The 3–3–4 Behavior Gestalt alone among all possible behavior patterns allows for the possibility of early doubt and training conflicts to color subsequent social adjustment. Shame during the first teaching stage weakens coping during the second teaching stage, the school years when peer acceptance and social competence are crucial to self-esteem. Exaggerated shyness or rebellion, hypercaution or daring, perfectionism or crudeness can all appear as adolescent strategies to avoid inner conflict, doubt, and shame. Conflict during the first behavior transition accents the anxiety inherent in the strategic behavior stage.

The second major behavior transition, the strength/strategy transition, marks the change from the home environment to the school environment. For the first time, the child is thrust into the world outside the family's protective care, yet the child depends on both the family and the teacher to shape and structure a world he or she cannot yet fully organize or independently understand. These years demand that teacher also be mother to a great degree, thus the strength/strategy transition is a more mature version of the earliest sensitivity stage.

The quality of the home-to-school transition is crucial to coping for individuals with overt strength/strategy conflict behavior patterns:

Sensitivity	0	Sensitivity	2
Strength	5	Strength	4
Strategy	5	Strategy	4

The covert strength/strategy conflict appears in the remaining three conflict patterns of which the 4–3–3 Behavior Gestalt is by far the most significant:

Sensitivity	4	Sensitivity	6	Sensitivity	8
Strength	3	Strength	2	Strength	1
Strategy	3	Strategy	2	Strategy	1

If the environment has been too protective, sheltering, and undemanding in the early sensitive behavior stage, the child's dependence becomes abundantly clear when he or she must leave that environment. No longer is the child the center of attention and admiration. The child is suddenly just one of the group.

The strength/strategy transition introduces the child to work, industry and task completion. The child at this stage needs praise, instruction and support to feel competent. Now the child begins to solve his or her own problems. The conflicts of this transition, if unsuccessfully resolved, lead to a sense of inferiority and inadequacy. Particularly in behavior patterns where the conflict is covert, the person may continue to seek out more competent others to solve his or her problems and may be overly vulnerable to others' opinions. Fears of ridicule or rejection confine active coping in both overt and covert strength/strategy conflict patterns.

The final behavior transition occurs when the individual first forms an intimate relationship. Thus the time frame is extremely variable since it is determined more by actual experience than by biological readiness. True, puberty has set the stage for a mature relationship, but the actual experience of committing to and caring for a special other is subject to vast social pressures. Part of this final strategy/sensitivity conflict is the conflict between the adolescent's biological readiness and the culture's social restrictions.

The strategy/sensitivity conflict closes the behavioral pattern since in this final life transition the newly achieved identity and self-definition must be integrated with the identity of another through mutuality and caring. The strategy/sensitivity conflict is overt in the following behavior patterns:

Sensitivity	5	Sensitivity	4
Strength	0	Strength	2
Strategy	5	Strategy	4

First love, for individuals with either overt strategy/sensitivity conflict tests the capacity for mutuality versus self-centeredness and commitment

Birth Pattern Behavior Stage	Approximate Age	Paul D. MacLean The Triune Brain	Arthur Janov Primal Levels
Sensitivity	0–18 Months	Reptilian Brain Structures	Primal Level I Biological Suffering
Sensitivity/ Strength Transition	1–2 Years		
Strength	1–6 Years	Paleomammalian Limbic Brain Structures	Primal Level II Emotional Pain
Strength/ Strategy Transition	4–8 Years		
Strategy	4 Years through adolescence	Neomammalian Cortical Brain Structures	Primal Level III Social Pain
Strategy/ Sensitivity Transition	Post Puberty		

versus self-insistence. The conflict is covert and hidden behind strong, assertive behavior in the remaining patterns of which the 3–4–3 Behavior Gestalt is by far the most significant:

Sensitivity	3	Sensitivity	2	Sensitivity	1
Strength	4	Strength	6	Strength	8
Strategy	3	Strategy	2	Strategy	1

With the covert conflict patterns, fear of intimacy and loss of autonomy may consolidate a strong, forceful front. The aggressive person who insists on independence has the greatest difficulty resolving the conflicts between individuality and mutuality. Force only aggravates the conflict and unresolved strategy/sensitivity conflicts turn relationships into battlegrounds for control. People may actually compete with their mates or assume top dog/underdog relationship dynamics.

Erik Erikson notes that resolving the final transitional conflict between sensitivity and strategy frees the person both from parents and from parent-like institutions. The person takes the final steps toward maturity and adulthood at this time. Failure to resolve this final conflict leaves a lingering fear of intimacy that isolates the person from warm interpersonal contacts and undermines the capacity for mutual social give-and-take.

Sigmund Freud Psychoanalysis	Erik Erikson Life Stages	Gordon Allport on Individuation	Lawrence Kohlberg Moral Development
Oral Stage	Basic Trust vs. Mistrust	Bodily Self	Preconventional (1) Egocentric, Deferential
Anal Stage	Autonomy vs. Doubt Shame	Self-Identity	Preconventional (2) Naive, Instrumental
Phallic Stage	Initiative vs. Guilt	Self-Esteem	Conventional (3) Cultural Conformity
Latency	Industry vs. Inferiority	Self-Extension	Conventional (4) Authority and Social Order
Latency	Identity vs. Identity Diffusion	Self-image, Rational Coping	Postconventional (5) Social contract Commitment
Genital Stage	Intimacy vs. Isolation	Propriate Striving	Postconventional (6) Conscience, Universal ethics

The actual dynamics of behavior development involve three stages of behavior stability and extension each leading to a natural transition. The overall behavior cycle generates six significant stages. Theorists from psychobiology to clinical orientations describe these stages. The table summarizes a number of varying assessments offered by those who study human development.

6 Personality in Synthesis

We come to the birth pattern with questions. We look to the pattern for understanding. In a subject as complex as personality, the simplest questions yield the most fruitful answers. If we ask the journalist's standard Who?, What?, When?, Where?, Why? and How? of the birth pattern, we achieve a rich personality synthesis. We see the whole person. The assessment techniques thus far presented enable us to answer these questions.

Who? The who of the birth pattern is, quite obviously, the person. Simply naming the person will give us the who, but the temperament type gives us a broader feeling for the person as a whole. When we answer the who of personality with a type, we establish a theme for further birth pattern synthesis. We create a one-dimensional, impressionistic sketch of the person.

What? The what question demands a matter-energy answer. Using the Trait Hypothetic-Trait Empiric measurement dimension, we establish what is most real to the person. We answer the what of personality by placing the person on the Trait Hypothetic-Trait Empiric matter-energy continuum.

When? The when of personality asks us to examine the person's experience of time. The Trait Spontaneous-Trait Continuous measurement dimension establishes the quality of the day-to-day temporal experience. We answer the when of personality by placing the person on the Trait Spontaneous-Trait Continuous time continuum.

Where? The where of personality asks us to define the person's life space. The Trait Organic-Trait Panoramic measurement dimension establishes the scope, proportions and nature of the personal life space. We answer the where of personality by placing the person on the Trait Organic-Trait Panoramic space continuum.

The what, when and where of personality expressed by the birth pattern's three trait dimensions show us the person's unique life perspective. Our flat, one-dimensional sketch now has three psychological dimensions. At this point, our birth pattern synthesis has the proportions of reality, yet it remains static. Our assessment still must capture the dynamic quality of the living person.

Dynamics is the study of forces in motion. Personality dynamics includes both the forces within personality and the movements which express these forces. To make our birth pattern synthesis dynamic, we must describe the needs which motivate the person's actions. We must answer the motivational why and the behavioral how of personality. These are complex human questions. To answer them fully, we use the patterns of the Four-Digit Need Gestalt and the Three-Digit Behavior Gestalt. At this point, our personality synthesis comes alive and we create a framework for understanding the person in his or her own terms.

Each of us sees the world and other people through the lens of our own psychological perspective, need priorities and behavioral attitudes. Though we strive for objectivity, we cannot simply set aside our entire life perspective. Our perspectives are, for the most part, invisible. Too often, the point at which we *think* we understand another person is the very point at which we successfully reinterpret the other's views, motives, and behavior to fit our own frame of reference. Such reinterpretation reduces the other person because it omits all in the other that is not like the self. When we do not reinterpret the other's behavior in this way, we have the tendency to judge and sometimes criticize those aspects of the other that are not like the self.

The birth pattern provides us with objective measurements. It asks us to accept the other person as an individual. It invites us to explore perspectives quite unlike our own with a sense of awe rather than an urge to judge. From this point on, we will explore personality in depth. We will correlate Birth Pattern Psychology's measurements with life events to see personality in action. We will observe people in the process of being themselves.

With the exception of the temperament types, all of our measurements are whole birth pattern measurements. The traits, the Need Gestalt and the Behavior Gestalt incorporate all ten planet markers and all twelve sectors. Our holistic measurements actually do the work of synthesis for us. Since our measurements express different facets of personality as a whole, combining the type, traits, Need Gestalt and Behavior Gestalt does not lead to contradiction. Instead, we have an additive birth pattern assessment technique in which each personality factor helps us see more of the person as a whole.

The Need Gestalt is more than a simple pattern of motives. Taken as a whole, it represents the self that is actualized. It is, in the words of pioneer personality analyst, Gordon Allport, the primary organization of "psycho-physical systems" that determine an individual's "characteristic behavior and thought." Each behavior mode derives its meaning from the part it plays in the need satisfaction process. Each trait describes a distinct life attitude that represents the shared factors of its component needs. The types are simple restatements of the basic needs in general human terms. They are general answers to the who of personality.

[132]

When we meet with extreme frustration, when we have problems that we cannot seem to solve, when we experience despair or sorrow or loss, we ask a single question...Why? If we have the courage to answer this question honestly, we see the why in our own personalities. A bit of introspection will answer the question, "Who am I?" but the most profound question that each of us must face is not "Who am I?" but *"Why am I?"* This question reaches beyond the practical level of basic needs and human motives to the innermost unifying principle: the sense of one's own purpose.

We will explore the unifying sense of purpose expressed in the lives of Sigmund Freud and Carl Jung. Both men were men of intelligence and keen human insight. Both men remained intensely creative in the face of criticism and ridicule. Their creativity contributed to many of the psychological principles we have explored in the first five chapters of this book.

The who, what, when, where, why, how format organizes our personality assessment. First, we examine the who of the temperament type. Since the type is not a whole birth pattern measure, this is an *optional* step in the pattern assessment process. Next, we examine the attitudes indicated by the traits. Finally, we explore the Need Gestalt and the Behavior Gestalt to achieve dynamic synthesis.

Carl Jung

We begin our birth pattern synthesis with Jung's temperament type to develop an overall impression of his personality. Jung was a Humanist, a man of great curiosity who was willing to investigate all things human. We note particularly the emphasis on people, cultures and social structures. Jung, the Humanist, would analyze people, would involve himself with people, would want to know what made people tick. Jung's biographer describes him as a Humanist in the style of the Renaissance.

The temperament traits show us Carl Jung's particular view of the world. Trait Empiric, emphasized as it is by eight planet markers of the possible ten, indicates a person who wants the facts and who is capable of working within established social structures. We sense a naturalness, a sincerity, a love of information and a logical, enterprising perspective. Trait Spontaneous adds the time-based qualities of immediate presence, great enthusiasm, versatility and impatience. Involvement and interest would be one and the same. We look for dramatic shifts in the course of Jung's life. Trait Panoramic completes the trait portrait adding a dimension of interpersonal interest and an urge to find common themes. We sense the man who could blend many sources into a unified theory. Trait Panoramic is, as well, a self-transcending trait that can be spiritual and mystical.

Birth Pattern #26: Carl Jung

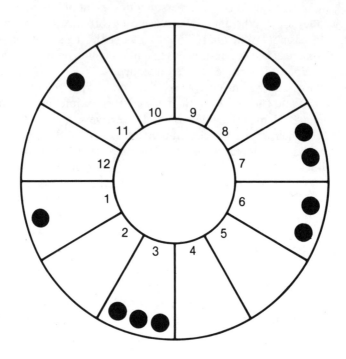

WHO?:	Humanist temperament type
WHAT?:	Trait Empiric 8
WHEN?:	Trait Spontaneous 7
WHERE?:	Trait Panoramic 7

WHY?:	Need Gestalt	
	Growth	1
	Security	2
	Stimulus	6
	Love	1

HOW?:	Behavior Gestalt	
	Sensitivity	2
	Strength	3
	Strategy	5

Jung's temperament traits help us construct his overall viewpoint, a viewpoint that would stress information about human cultural life leading to a vital, immediate feeling of unity. As a boy, Carl Jung's main interests were science and comparative religion. Later, in his early professional years, Jung spoke out against those who were trying to limit scientific inquiry and psychological research. He was particularly critical of people who rejected theories which they had not themselves tested or explored.

Carl Jung was a doctor, a careful researcher, and a man devoted to empirical methods. Science, he stated, was not a profession based upon faith. Jung was indignant when critics of his work insisted that his theories were too mystical and unscientific. The animus or masculine aspect within every woman and the anima or feminine aspect within every man were significant parts of Jung's personality theory. In *Aion,* Jung wrote that the animus and anima were discovered empirically and their existence was "either directly verifiable or at least rendered probable by the facts."

Read any account of Jung, the man, and you will find ample testimony to his Traits Spontaneous and Panoramic. He is said to have had a forceful first impact on others and to have emanated charisma. Freud spoke of the spell of Jung's personal presence. Additionally, Jung was a deeply spiritual man whose religious views might be characterized as broadly Christian. The lintel of his home bore the motto, "Called or not called, God is present."

The Stimulus Need dominates the Need Gestalt. We are struck by the one-pointedness of the six-planet emphasis on the wide, diverse, explorative curiosity. The need for stimulus is so strong that it clearly motivates most life choices. The Security Need is a very weak second while the Growth and Love Needs with one planet marker each indicate a potential conflict between identity and intimacy. Jung would need a great variety in his life before he could establish roots, pursue independent aims, or invest himself in close relationships.

The force of the Stimulus Need cues us to the importance of social factors and social acceptance. Loneliness is a threat to people with strong stimulus-affiliation needs. The Need Gestalt is a profile of a man with a sense of public, humanitarian purpose with, perhaps, little left for the nurturing, caring aspects of family life or the drive toward more personal creative ends. We have seen that the Humanist will, at times, show far more concern for new contacts than for family. It is the thrill of discovery that most motivates when the need portrait is so heavily weighted toward the single stimulus factor.

The Behavior Gestalt completes our chart synthesis and shows us Jung in action. The emphasis is on the communicative strategic behavior mode. Thus we see the freewheeling splash of high stimulus need expressed through objectification. Though basically quite sociable, Jung would want time to himself and a place to be alone and gather his thoughts. The potential is there for productive use of solitude. Jung would have to face the anxiety innate in his preferred behavior mode. The three planet-marker emphasis on strength shows us that once Jung made a decision, he would present it forcefully. The cooperative element of sensitivity is lowest, thus the whole pattern shows us a decisive man who would wait to make his move but who would depend on help from others only as a last resort. He would express as much as he chose, but something would doubtless be held in reserve. Jung would be more apt to go his own way rather than bend.

Vincent Brome's biography captures the essence of Carl Jung. The comments of those who knew Jung merge the Trait Empiric information, the Trait Panoramic democratic diversity, the Trait Spontaneous immediacy and the high stimulus demands within a framework of communicative behavior and moving away from boredom. One acquaintance comments that Jung was "capable of out-talking most people on any subject" when he chose. He could communicate with people from many different walks of life "when he put himself out to do so." Jung himself stated that when he had seen through the object of his interest, the magic was gone. He could be blunt and even rude when he was bored. Should the conversation with another run dry, Jung was inclined to make a break for he was unable to tolerate monotony. The following incident shows us the marriage of high stimulus need with strategic behavior.

An established patient of Jung's arrived late one day for his appointment. Jung had gone sailing. The angry patient hired a boat and chased after his elusive therapist. When the patient grew close, he shouted to Jung but Jung sailed rapidly away. Finally, the patient managed to corner Jung only to hear his doctor shout, "Go away—you bore me!"

This seems strange behavior for a therapist, but we are not exploring a therapist, we are exploring Carl Jung's unique temperament. We need not agree with Jung's behavior to see that his actions were very much in character.

The work of Birth Pattern Psychology begins with pattern synthesis; it does not end there. Synthesis gives us a framework. We must then apply that framework to life events to see those events in the light of individual temperament, needs, and behavior potentials. When we understand Jung's personality, we understand the lonely child who retreated to the attic of his home as an escape from bickering parents in a failing marriage. We understand the boy who carved a puppet for a friend. Because we understand strategy and its connection to anxiety, because we appreciate the importance of peer acceptance to a child with strong stimulus needs, we know the impact when Jung's teacher humiliated him before his schoolmates by insisting that Jung forged an essay. The teacher claimed that a boy of Jung's age could not have written such an excellent work. As a result, Jung developed what he called a second self, an objective self who was detached from the pressures of the young boy's life.

A colleague remarked on Jung's growing fame and his demand as a speaker and lecturer abroad. The colleague suggested that at that stage in his career, Jung could well afford to give up his private patients. In the framework of Jung's Need Gestalt, we understand his reply, "Oh, no, I need their stimulus."

Because we know Jung's temperament traits, we appreciate the naturalness of patients arriving at his home to find him dressed in old clothes, chopping wood. We know how important it was for Jung to build a special room where he could be alone, a room that was always locked with a key which he kept on his person. We understand the man who could chat with the postman as an equal but who would leave abruptly in the middle of his own dinner party if he got bored.

Three important themes ran like a thread through the fabric of Carl Jung's adult life. The first was the theme of infidelity. In 1910, Jung and his wife Emma had their third child. That same year, a young woman named Antonia Wolff came to Jung for therapy. Toni Wolff was independent and intelligent and stimulating. She was everything Emma Jung, devoted wife and mother, was not. It was Toni Wolff, not Emma, who fit the pattern of Jung's needs so perhaps it was inevitable that she would become his mistress. Both Emma Jung and Toni Wolff became analysts themselves but it was Toni who collaborated in Jung's research. She expanded Jung's concept of the man's feminine aspect or anima to include the images of the Medium, the Amazon, the Hetaira and the Mother.

Not only did Jung maintain the affair, he attempted to draw Toni within the Jung family circle. She came to Sunday dinners. The Jung children called her Aunt Toni. Emma protested but Jung would not hear of divorce. Toni protested but Jung refused to leave his family. He was caught between the demands of strict Swiss morality and his own pattern of needs. He could not give up the woman who so fit his own personality, but he refused to leave the wife and family who fulfilled other needs as well. With the logic of a man pressed by heavy inner stimulus demands, he simply stated that the prerequisite for a good marriage was "the license to be unfaithful." Toni Wolff remained Jung's mistress until her death many years later. Perhaps keeping a wife and a mistress in such close quarters influenced Jung's theory that a woman's animus manifests itself through complaining and nagging!

A second theme that crops up whenever Jung and Freud are discussed is the theme of anti-Semitism. In the first years of Hitler's rise to power, a German, Kretschmer, resigned as editor of the leading German psychological periodical. Carl Jung took his place. In the first issue under his editorship, Jung wrote an article discussing the differences between the Aryan and the Jewish unconscious. This in itself reflects Jung's interest in cultural myths and is more an expression of his diverse theories than an admission of racist feelings. The publication, like everything else in Germany at that time, came under the rule of the Nazi party. Jung was the target of criticism. Within the psychological community, some charged that he should have done the honorable thing, he should have behaved as Kretschmer had behaved. From the perspective of Birth Pattern Psychology, the real complaint was that Jung should have displayed the Hypothetic's tendency to stand on principle. But Jung was not a Hypothetic, he was a very strong Empiric. He claimed that he did what he did to maintain the psychoanalytic movement at a crucial stage in its development. This was very much in keeping with his strongest temperament trait for, as we have seen, Empirics can stay within a system as long as they can achieve their goals and Jung felt that he could further analysis in spite of, not because of, the Nazi movement.

A third and final theme is reflected in the strategy quadrangle birth pattern emphasis. We know that the strategic mode is a duplistic behavior mode that demands the coordination of two facets of the self. The clash between these elements of personality creates anxiety. We have already noted that in Jung's boyhood he developed two distinct sides of his personality in reaction to early difficulties. One side was detached and powerful, the other was vulnerable and hurt.

In 1913, Jung and Freud severed their relationship. Jung was shattered. He resigned from his long-standing job at the Burgholzli Psychiatric Hospital in Zurich. At first, he was uncertain and disoriented and he was plagued by the problem of discovering his own personal myth. He began to have deeply disturbing dreams and fantasies. He withdrew and his wife, mistress, and friends worried. He played games from his childhood, building miniature cities out of stones.

The years 1913–1916 are generally considered the years of Jung's breakdown. But what precisely was the broken psychological element? We have seen that locked-in behavior patterns take the individual away from the pattern of basic needs and that this pattern is, in a higher sense, the pattern of self and purpose. From a birth pattern perspective, the strategy and detachment broke apart to reveal the underlying needs. Jung had to confront his own motives and, in a sense, claim them for himself. As Brome notes, Jung faced the facts that he took his wife for granted, that he forced his mistress upon his own family circle and that he had little interest in his own children. He did not live by the morality that he preached. But the confrontation, through fantasy accompanied by anxiety and sometimes sheer panic, with the reality of himself led Carl Jung to a point of acceptance. He found not self, but Self. From the time of his recovery, he was a more creative person. Jung reached into his own breakdown and emerged with his now-famous work on the psychological types.

We have explored the human side of Carl Jung. Now we will apply our personality synthesis techniques to achieve an appreciation of Sigmund Freud, the man who deserves the title "father of psychology." Although he has been dead now for nearly half a century, Freud's name evokes a strong reaction in many people.

Sigmund Freud

We note immediately the type and trait similarity between Sigmund Freud and Carl Jung. Both share the Humanist temperament type and Traits Empiric and Panoramic. According to birth data from astrologer Reinhold Ebertin, the third noted psychoanalytic pioneer Alfred Adler was also a Humanist with Traits Empiric and Panoramic. Since all three men emphasized observation and scientific study to formulate the general rules of the human mind, we should not be surprised to see the great similarity in their temperaments. Both Adler and Jung shared the preferred behavior mode of strategy. Both men moved away from mainstream Freudian analysis to found their own schools of psychoanalytic thought.

Freud's Humanist temperament type clues us to the importance of social factors. He was born in Moravia at a time when Catholic authorities kept a register of Jews. Though Freud inherited his father's liberal religious attitudes rather than his mother's orthodoxy, he was sensitive to the social pressures unique to membership in a social minority. Freud lived nearly all of his life in Central Europe. The tide of anti-Semitism that crested in Nazi Germany was brewing throughout Freud's life. From the temperament type alone, we understand Freud's sensitivity to this anti-Semitism and his tendency not to seek friendships with Gentiles. Freud never accepted royalties from sales of Hebrew or Yiddish translations of his books.

Freud's strongest trait was the interpersonal, self-transcending Trait Panoramic. Freud was never one to pay much respect to those in authority and this trait saw him frequently at odds with the well-known psychological authorities of his day. The psychoanalytic movement was a grass-roots movement in which Freud concentrated on recruiting new, young analysts at the bottom of the psychological establishment rather than converting those at the top. Freud sought the spread of his ideas rather than personal power and his many letters show his constant concern for the cause of psychoanalysis.

Trait Empiric shows us Freud the scientist, the expert in neurology who hoped to find a physiological basis for psychological states. He once commented that his techniques were founded on "worldly-wise common sense" and he pleaded with psychoanalysis' detractors to pay less attention to those in intellectual authority positions and pay more attention to the facts.

Birth Pattern #27: Sigmund Freud

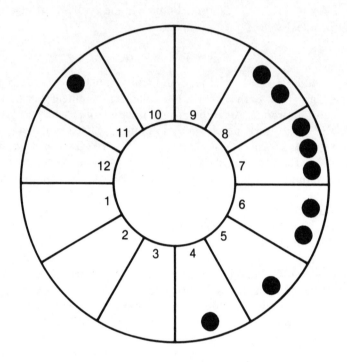

WHO?:	Humanist temperament type	
WHAT?:	Trait Empiric 6	
WHEN?:	Trait Spontaneous 5/Trait Continuous 5	
WHERE?:	Trait Panoramic 7	
WHY?:	Need Gestalt	
	Growth:	1
	Security:	2
	Stimulus:	4
	Love:	3
HOW?:	Behavior Gestalt	
	Sensitivity:	4
	Strength:	4 } Conflict
	Strategy:	2

Trait Spontaneous and Trait Continuous are equally weighted. Thus, neither can be considered wholly characteristic of Freud. We explore Freud's sense of timing to show us his unique blend of these two opposing trait factors, his merger of immediacy with continuity. Nowhere is this more evident than in Freud's relationship with his future wife Martha Bernays. For Freud it was love at first sight that led to a protracted four-year engagement. The marriage day waited for a sudden, great discovery that was to establish Freud's professional reputation. In the end, it was Martha's inheritance rather than Freud's scholarship that provided them with the essential income.

Freud's technique of psychoanalysis was a merger between the moment and the past. The patient, through a Panoramic process of free association, told the therapist Spontaneous bits of information while the therapist discovered a pattern of Continuity related to the patient's past.

We see in Freud's Need Gestalt a clear hierarchy beginning with the dominant Stimulus Need, continuing with Love, then Security and finally Growth. In contrast with Jung's Need Gestalt, no single need completely outweighs the others. The difference between the fulfillments which the two men enjoyed shows us clearly how important it is to consider the Need Gestalt as a whole pattern rather than to examine single isolated needs.

Both Freud and Jung had a two-planet emphasis on the Security Need. Security bears a close relationship to nurturance and parenting. Freud by all accounts was a concerned, attentive father whose youngest daughter Anna became a well-known psychoanalyst. Jung left the bulk of the parenting responsibilities to his wife Emma. The difference was very much a difference in the *balance* of needs that defined overall fulfillment for these two men.

Freud had a four-planet-marker emphasis on the Stimulus Need and a three-planet-marker emphasis on Love. Jung had a six-planet-marker emphasis on Stimulus and a single planet-marker emphasis on Love. Their relationship goals thus showed strong differences too. Freud and Jung began their relationship, the bulk of which was carried on through letters, as a professional sharing of information. Freud was fifty at the time and Jung in his early thirties. They shared the excitement of their research, exchanging case histories and published papers. Quite early in their correspondence, Freud expressed the wish that they would become intimate friends. He began to open his letters to Jung with a heading, "Dear friend." Throughout, Jung continued to address his letters to "Dear Professor Freud." Freud corresponded, as well, with Emma Jung while one of Freud's children later remarked that Jung remained rather distant from the Freud family.

The Love Need was Freud's second priority following closely after his Stimulus Need and he was a devoted husband. By all accounts but one, that is, for Jung insisted that Freud was emotionally involved with his wife's sister Minna Bernays. Minna lived with the Freud family. Unlike Martha Freud, who was not interested in psychoanalysis but kept her opinion of her husband's work to herself, Minna Bernays was enthusiastic about Freud's cause. Jung appears to have concluded that since Minna knew a great deal about analysis and Martha knew little at all, Freud and Minna must have had an affair. Since Freud was immensely unpopular because of his sexual theories, it seems likely that such information would have been seized upon by his detractors. Yet the only accusation of infidelity came from Jung. Here, at least, Jung appears to have looked at Freud's situation through his own subjective perception based on his personal pattern of needs and, possibly, his own infidelity.

It is Freud's Behavior Gestalt that gives us some crucial clues to aspects of his personal life and facets of his psychoanalytic theory. We note that the sensitive behavior mode and the strong behavior mode are equally weighted. This conflict is associated with cultural sexual stereotypes as we have seen from the last chapter. This behavior conflict helps us understand Freud's actions in pursuit of his personal pattern of need satisfactions.

Freud's biographer describes him as a man who could combine impassioned pleas with practical diplomacy. Freud was a sensitive father and husband but, at the same time, rigidly patriarchal. Most significant, perhaps, for the history of the psychoanalytic movement, was Freud's pattern of forming close intellectual relationships that degenerated into bitter rivalries. We have seen that the sensitivity/strength conflict puts the other person in the position of friend/competitor. We can now apply this to Freud's professional career.

Sigmund Freud began the work that led to his now-famous theories in cooperation with Josef Breuer. Breuer was well established at the time but Freud had yet to make his mark in the field of psychiatry. Together, the two men published *Studies in Hysteria* but this marked the end of their collaboration. Breuer had been Freud's mentor, sending him patients at a crucial time in his beginning therapeutic practice and often lending him money as well. Freud grew increasingly critical of Breuer's unwillingness to emphasize the sexual basis of hysteria. While Breuer backed away, Freud seized upon their work as the promise of an important new discovery. It was the chance he had been waiting for.

After the split with Breuer, Freud worked in what he called "splendid isolation." The force of his Stimulus Need and his desire for intellectual companionship makes it rather unlikely that the isolation was, indeed, splendid. He formed a relationship with a young surgeon named Wilhelm Fleiss. Their relationship and particularly Freud's seeming emotional dependence on Fleiss mystified Freud's biographers. Why was a man of Freud's intellect so involved with Fleiss whose numerological theories seemed absurd? Why did Freud openly and unquestioningly accept Fleiss as an equal?

We have explored the behavior conflict indicated in Freud's birth pattern and noted that it contains both masculine and feminine cultural behavior archetypes. Fleiss postulated two numerical cycles, a masculine 23-day cycle and a feminine 28-day cycle. His numerology eventually led Fleiss to conclude that people were basically bisexual. Fleiss's work struck a chord in Sigmund Freud. So close was their bond that when Fleiss operated on a patient of Freud's and left a length of surgical gauze in the poor woman's incision, Freud excused him from any wrongdoing. Fleiss confided the whole of his research to Freud and told Freud of his hopes to publish an important paper on bisexuality. We can imagine Fleiss's surprise when he received a letter from Freud announcing that *his* next work would be about bisexuality and would be the definitive study of the topic! It was a topic Freud never took up himself. However, Freud inadvertently leaked Fleiss's theories and another researcher rushed them into print, beating Fleiss to the punch. Fleiss felt betrayed, wrote to Freud for an explanation and received a letter telling Fleiss not to bother Freud with such trivial matters. Their relationship ended on this strained note.

The same conflict in Freud's behavior contributed to his break with Carl Jung. Freud hoped that Jung would succeed him as leader of the psychoanalytic movement. Freud held sway in Vienna while Jung kept the psychoanalytic movement growing in Zurich. Though the Viennese group was torn by dissention, Freud had great hopes for the Swiss. Together, the groups formed the core of the International Psycho-Analytic Association. Jung wrote Freud that Eugen Bleuler was a constant source of difficulty. He was increasingly critical of analysis and Jung saw in Bleuler a potentially divisive force. Freud agreed. He told Jung that they should not put up with Bleuler's abuse. What followed was a classic instance of the undoing characteristic of behavior conflict. Bleuler resigned from the Association ending the rift between himself and Jung. Freud's letters had called Bleuler a "prickly eel" and he had encouraged Jung to "really rake Bleuler over the coals." Jung's relief was short-lived for no sooner was Bleuler gone than Freud wrote that perhaps Bleuler might still come to terms and Jung should meet him halfway. Freud would "greatly welcome the news that he had rejoined (the Association)." Understandably, Jung exploded and demanded to know of Freud just who was defecting and from whom.

Ultimately, the behavioral differences between Freud and Jung contributed to the break in their relationship. Emma Jung saw the makings of the break long before it occurred. She also saw the conflict in Freud. Once, she was bold enough to ask Freud if he was attempting to offer Jung leadership of the psychoanalytic movement while wishing, in actuality, to keep the leadership for himself. Freud promptly put her in her place, but she had put her finger on the source of Freud's ambivalence. The Freud-Jung letters testify to the disintegration of their relationship.

We have seen that a person with a behavior conflict sees the conflict in others if he does not see it in himself. There was, for all Freud's self-analysis, an element of this in his association with Jung. It culminated in Jung's outburst that Freud used analysis to treat his pupils as patients, that he pointed out their symptoms while he remained "on top as the father sitting pretty."

The differences between the Behavior Gestalts of Sigmund Freud and Carl Jung emerge in their differing theories of human development. Freudian oral, anal, and phallic stages, respectively, reflect the sensitivity, sensitivity/strength transition, and strength behavior modes in his own Behavior Gestalt. Freud theorized that personality forms by the time the child enters school and the family experience alone with its inherent power struggles and conflicts accounts for psychological disturbances. Jung, by contrast, felt personality emerges at puberty, the time Jung labeled "psychic birth." Jung perceived in himself the Wise Old Man archetype, an archetype that clearly implies the Good Mentor behavior role. He was as much a teacher as a therapist, often giving his clients reading assignments as an essential part of their therapy.

Freud's behavior conflict is particularly essential to understanding his view of human nature and human life. People are perpetually in conflict in Freud's theory and, though his contemporary followers, the ego psychologists, no longer hold exclusively to this view, the Freudian theory of personal desires in constant conflict with competitive social realities still shapes many personality theories. The pattern of Freud's Behavior Gestalt raises the question of the degree to which one man's personal conflict may have shaped the way a generation of psychoanalysts viewed human nature.

Conflict, too, makes for strength and endurance and there is no doubt that Freud withstood great social pressures. His ideas were constantly under attack. The conflict shows us as well how a rather puritanical and fastidious man proposed the theory of infantile sexuality. In our freer sexual times, it is difficult to relate to the shock wave set off by Freud's discussion of childhood sexuality at the turn of this century. Sexuality, to Freud, included all "tender feelings" and it was more Freud's idea of the child's incestuous wish for the opposite-sex parent than sexuality per se that brought him such vigorous criticism.

In our discussion of the sensitivity/strength conflict we noted that people with this conflict tend to adopt a very traditional view of masculine and feminine roles. This view is clearly presented in Freud's theory of penis envy. Freud was convinced that the male sexual organ influenced the childhood sexual development of both male and female children. Freud theorized that a young girl discovering the absence of a penis would blame her mother for the lack and feel inferior. The theory of penis envy led theorist Karen Horney to retort that she knew as many men with womb envy as women with penis envy.

Freud felt, as well, that men resolve their childhood conflicts and develop strong superegos while women do not resolve their conflicts as sufficiently. Though Freud's own theories clearly reflect Freud, this is not to imply that his theories are without merit. Freud's personal conflicts generated many important psychological concepts. While he postulated the idea of penis envy, he also outlined the defense mechanisms. His theories have stimulated a vast amount of research from both his followers and his opponents. Freud made us all aware of the importance of childhood influences. This alone is enough to divide humanity's struggle to understand itself into two phases: before Freud and after Freud. Freud's love for his family, his support of Emma Jung and his concern for his many patients stand in great contrast to his personal drive and ambition to succeed. It seems clear that Freud did not attempt to suppress his personal conflicts. Instead, he turned them into a full life and a highly productive intellectual outpouring.

The fundamental contributions to analysis of both Freud and Jung are enormous. They have contributed not only to our ability to analyze ourselves, but also to our motivation to do so. Up to now, we have concentrated on the basic techniques of psychological synthesis. Before we can analyze a birth pattern, before we can look deep within personal consciousness, we must establish a context. We must get to know the person as a whole. Only then do we have a framework for a deeper exploration of personality.

Birth Pattern Psychology's synthesis techniques provide the assessment tools essential to seeing personality as a whole. We have explored two birth patterns in depth using the who, what, when, where, why and how format to organize the pattern assessment. The other twenty-five charts in this section give you an opportunity to apply these techniques and develop your skill in birth pattern synthesis. (Birth data for Birth Patterns used throughout can be found in Appendix A.) Biographies are readily available for many of the well-known individuals whose patterns you now have. If you will choose the birth pattern of a person who particularly interests you and outline that person's temperament type, trait perspective, motivational and behavioral patterns, you will establish a framework of understanding that allows you to turn to that person's biography and apply your assessment tools to actual life events. This exercise is not simply an interpretive exercise. Rather, you use the birth pattern as a means of understanding, as a bridge between you and another person. The birth pattern is not the end of the synthesis process.

Ultimately, it is not even the pattern that we want to understand; we want only a medium for objectively seeing the person, and the birth pattern is that medium. The chart liberates us for a time from the confines of our own innate viewpoints and opens our eyes to other perspectives quite as valid, as interesting and as informative as our own.

Part Two: Analysis

7 Masks People Wear

Synthesis measurements let us step outside the boundaries of our personal preferences and perspectives to see others more clearly. An individual's Need Gestalt, Behavior Gestalt, type and traits introduce us to that person. Once we meet people through birth pattern synthesis, our interest broadens to concern for their problems. If we study our own patterns, our personal problems concern us. At this point, we must move beyond assessment to helping or self-help. This is the step from synthesis to analysis.

If we want birth pattern analysis to help us or help others, we must know what help really means. Webster's defines help in these words: "to make it easier for a person to do something..." This brief definition makes two important points. First, the helper creates a climate in which the help-seeker can more easily do something. Birth pattern analysis makes it easier to examine our attitudes. Analysis defines and clarifies our life choices. It is easier to make self-actualizing choices in this climate of awareness but we, the help-seekers, must choose. The second point tells us that the help-seeker and not the helper makes the actual effort. The helper only assists. The birth pattern is a mirror in which we can see our own self-defeating attitudes *if* we make the effort to see them. If we expect the birth pattern to make the effort, to give us answers or to solve our problems, we will be gravely disappointed. The birth pattern helps because it moves us to ask ourselves important questions about our attitudes, our lives and our selves. The answers to these questions lie within us.

The problems birth pattern analysis brings to light are psychological in nature. However, these final chapters explore nothing more exotic than the basic problems of everyday psychological life, our fears, our frustrations and the self-protective tactics we use to avoid feeling bad about ourselves. Using our birth patterns as tools to look inside ourselves for the sources of our difficulties is neither to probe for our weaknesses nor to chastise ourselves for our shortcomings. It is, instead, to see how we interrupt the flow of our lives with our demands and self-imposed rules.

Birth pattern analysis can, for instance, help Robert understand why he is uncomfortable meeting new people. Birth pattern analysis will not solve Robert's discomfort by telling him the best days to make friends or accept social invitations. Birth pattern analysis can help Ann understand why she allows men to treat her like a doormat. Birth pattern analysis will not promise Ann that next year a "good man" will come along to treat her differently. When we choose to study ourselves in a psychological framework, we have to face psychological facts. Ann will never find a good man if she continues to play the doormat role and Robert will have no good days for meeting people so long as he is uncomfortable in social situations.

The word problem comes from the Greek words meaning "to throw forward." When we solve our inner problems we are, in fact, thrown forward. We progress toward better life skills and more meaningful life experiences. We gain a sense of triumph and accomplishment. We like ourselves better. Our birth patterns are mirrors that move us to ask ourselves those questions which lead us to the source of our problems.

Ultimately, the problems themselves are not the true difficulties. The difficulties are the inner barriers preventing actual problem-solving. To turn inward is to pass beyond these barriers. It is to meet the problem-solver within. It is to go beneath the appearance of self to the truth of Self.

The Persona

The basic Growth, Security, Stimulus and Love Needs organized into a distinctly personal need-hierarchy form the self gestalt. Early on, these needs are simply felt. The self senses excess or deficit. It knows the sensation of impulses seeking release or the emptiness of deficits waiting to be filled. These feelings then differentiate into more specific feelings related to each basic need.

Stimulus feelings become the excitement of discovery, the pull of curiosity, the sense of belonging as well as the dullness of boredom and the loneliness of alienation. Love Need related feelings define the sense of closeness, intimacy and pleasure and the contrasting discomforts, distance and isolation. Growth feelings become the sense of significance and importance but also the sensations of weakness, meaninglessness and insignificance. Security feelings evoke the sense of permanence, firmness and persistence contrasted with feelings of futility, incompletion or despair. Each need relates, thus, to pleasant and unpleasant feelings.

All these feelings happen time and again over the course of development. The more persistent a feeling, the more familiar it becomes. The feeling of self derives from the familiarity of repeating inner patterns. Feelings are not simply states; they are the states of a feeling person, a person who learns to say "*I* feel excitement," or "*I* feel weak," or "*I* feel important." This *I* is the ego. Analytically, it is the part of the self that is aware of its own existence.

The chain of development does not end with the transformation from needing, to feeling, to evolving the ego that feels. The process culminates in role construction. All along the way, the role develops. As the person meets and resolves the identity crises discussed in Chapter 5, and then masters the various behavior challenges, he or she eventually adopts a persona. The persona, in the words of Jungian psychologist June Singer, is the "compromise role in which we parade before the community...." The persona is the part of the self that is readily apparent. It typifies the self but it is not the whole self. We should not find this chain of events unusual since we already know that it is possible to type personalities according to their dominant needs.

June Singer describes the evolution of the persona in her book *The Boundaries of the Soul:* "The individual's typology plays an important part in determining the nature of the ego and consequently the choices the ego will make. These decisions, supported by the underlying typology, act to build up a persona...."[10]

The persona as a means of social self-identification is not harmful in and of itself. It is the personality's calling card, a psychological aid to getting a social foot in the door. But if the persona instead stands in the way of deeper interaction, the persona itself becomes a problem. No longer a mere tool of the greater self, it poses as a surrogate yet lesser image that confines the self's potential.

Persona problems do not occur overnight. They emerge during the course of personal development and maturation. They are constructed over time. In birth pattern terms, the persona involves the time perspective indicated by the birth pattern's behavior quadrangles in relation to the feelings that emerge from the birth pattern's need triangles.

June Singer continues: "Persona problems are common in all parts of society, for as people identify themselves as belonging to a certain category they begin to adopt behavior appropriate to that category and to discard what does not fit. Thus the 'identity crisis' about which Erik Erikson has written so much, tends to find a partial solution, at least, in the assumption of a persona. It may not be the best solution but it often works, until something happens to break down the persona. While the persona is functioning well, many people identify with it."[11]

The persona that dictates to the self becomes not a role but a problem. It begins to strip the whole personality of the freedom to explore a range of life choices. It locks into a single, narrow self-definition.

Birth Pattern #27: Sigmund Freud
Dominant Stimulus Need

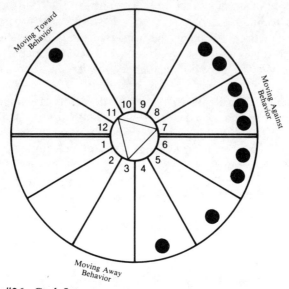

Birth Pattern #26: Carl Jung
The Dominant Stimulus Need
is Behavior Pervasive

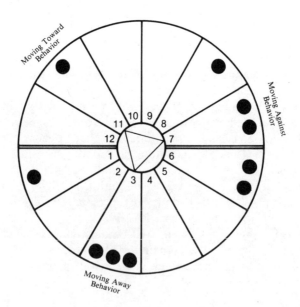

Needs define choices, personality type and thus persona type as well. The illustration depicts the birth patterns of Sigmund Freud and Carl Jung. Both men had a dominant Stimulus Need. Both were Humanist personality types. Both therefore adopted the Stimulus Persona.

Note carefully the distribution of the planet markers in Freud's birth pattern. The planets fall in the seventh and eleventh sectors only. The third sector of the birth pattern contains no planets. In terms of the behavior pattern, the third sector moving away behavior lies outside the person's scope, so in Freud's case, the persona and dominant need are one and the same. Such personae tend to be consciously chosen and acted out. Seeing the role is not the issue; the person knows perfectly well what he or she is doing. The persona is deliberately constructed, the false image knowingly adopted, the fake enthusiasm or interest, fake affection or helpfulness purposely displayed. According to analyst S.R. Maddi, this persona leads to a sense of alienation from other people if it is problematic.

Note now the distribution of the planet markers in Jung's birth pattern. Here the markers occupy *every* segment of the Stimulus Need Triangle, the third, the seventh and the eleventh sectors. Jung's Stimulus Persona touches every behavior mode. We will refer to the need that includes all three behavior modes as a *behavior pervasive need*. While both Freud and Jung felt themselves to be men of destiny, Jung often remarked that his life had been foreordained. He felt his role had been chosen for him. Such feelings often mark the personality whose persona image arises from such an all-embracing dominant need. Maddi notes that the unconscious quality of this persona alienates the person from himself/herself.

The persona that has a hold on every behavior the individual is likely to perform can take over the personality as a whole. The persona that can "move toward" or "move against" or "move away" is truly self-sufficient. It seems to require nothing from the rest of the personality since it appears to possess the means to control or respond to every situation.

In developmental terms, the behavior pervasive need recurs at every stage of identity formation. At every stage, the same crisis theme is met. At every stage, a single solution seems sufficient. As more crises are met and mastered, the familiar solution becomes more and more appealing. It gathers steam with each life transition.

"The purpose of the persona," says Salvador Maddi, "is to make a good impression, both on others and on oneself." This latter purpose makes the behavior pervasive persona doubly difficult. If it were only a mechanism for favorably impressing others, it might easily be dropped once the stage of first impression is passed. But since the persona often holds great appeal for the individual, its masquerade is as much for the self as for anyone else. The persona parades as an ideal to which the person strives to conform. The self-image keeps unacceptable feelings at bay while allowing the person to feel good about the image. Though the facade parades its humility, it conceals arrogance. Karen Horney writes extensively of the difficulty people experience in giving up such "idealized self-images." They seem to present the ego in its best, most attractive form. But an idealized image, cautions Horney, is "a treasure house loaded with dynamite."

The strong persona with access to and control over all behaviors produces *automatic* persona-oriented behavior. We can characterize this automatic role-playing as unconscious since the person rarely makes a conscious choice to act it out. This is the core difficulty. The person *must* do it, *must* play out the role in order to see it. The role is obvious only in hindsight. People who automatically act out their roles generally do, in the aftermath of difficulty, know what they have done. They later say, "I did it *again*." Hence the predictable pattern is finding oneself in difficulty, afterward seeing one's hand in the difficulty, vowing not to do what one does ever again, and then repeating precisely the same behavior when the situation next comes up.

To go from automatically acting out a role to consciously choosing behavior requires seeing the persona-related activity in process. It ceases to be a hindsight matter of "I did it again," and becomes a process matter of "I'm *doing* it again." This is a crucial realization. People cannot change what they have done but they can interrupt what they are doing. To change automatic role behavior a person must accept the self as cause and be willing at the same time to risk feeling unacceptable feelings: doubt, disappointment, anxiety, anger.

The persona bears the distinctive stamp of the need from which it is originally constructed. To some extent, then, the Individualist personality type and the Growth Persona are the same, the Realist personality type and the Security Persona are the same, etc. However, our analytic concern in these final chapters is with problem exploration and not personality typing. It is here that the type description and the persona in action part company. To the latter belong specific feelings and barriers to self-actualization, the musts, the standards, the absence of choice. Therefore, the following descriptions contain two separate elements. Each need-related persona is discussed as a general personality factor. Additionally, each role description includes questions directed to you, the reader, to help you analyze your own persona-related attitudes and behavior.

The Growth Persona:
The Behavior Pervasive Growth Need

The Growth Persona begins with the natural desires to live meaningfully, feel significant and be important. Through all the developmental crises, it is crucial for an individual to achieve the sense that his or her life makes a difference, that he or she matters. Perhaps it is even more significant for people with behavior pervasive Growth Needs since growth entails the discovery and appreciation of one's uniqueness.

To risk what one is in order to become even more demands the special kind of courage distinctive of the high Growth Need person. When all of life is an experiment, it is best to be intrepid. The road less travelled is a hard one even if it is the sole route to individualistic meaning and private purpose. The Growth image sensitizes a person to people, objects and objectives having a special singularity.

The rigid Growth Persona is only confident when it acts a part, when it plays its role on center stage. The confidence it displays comes not from the sense of ability to meet and conquer challenge but rather from a borrowed importance. Growth Personae sell their significance. They subscribe to the "If-you've-got-it, flaunt-it" theory and they do flaunt it.

The behavior pervasive Growth Need commands notice. The person cannot move toward without overwhelming, move against without overshadowing, or move away without leaving an identifying mark. The Growth mask is hooked on its own feelings of importance. In the game of life, the Growth Persona must always play the trump card. It must also get its way. It must be great. It must make an impression. The Growth Persona believes life must be lived in heroic proportions or life is simply no good at all.

The behavior pervasive Growth Need with its Growth Persona masks a set of attitudes that are almost always unconscious. It is a habit pattern that provides an automatic and unvarying response. It is a closed circuit within the otherwise open-system that the personality is meant to be. Any closed structure is apt to contain a great many feelings that cannot emerge into awareness as long as the habit structure is in place. The behaviors that bring gratification during development are generally unsuited to the demands of mature life with its constant pressures for continuing adaptation. The Growth Persona is an archaic pattern, remembering the satisfactions of the past and caught up in its own personal history. "That's just the way I am," it insists if anyone should suggest it change.

The Growth Persona cannot deal in trivia. Its realm is always heroic in scope. One behavior's expression simply leads the next behavior to take a greater step in the same direction leading finally to inflated self-significance and the feeling that anything can be accomplished. Because the Growth Persona touches every behavior mode, *any* call for action can set it off. The person is off and running and can run a very long way before the Growth Persona exhausts itself.

A Growth Persona is not a problem when the individual feels in control. The person can say yes to what interests him or her. The person can also say no to the uninteresting, the irrelevant, and the meaningless situations which offer immediate persona-gratification at the expense of real satisfaction.

The Growth Persona is composed of attitudes that individualize the private self-image. Because it is developmental and because external influences shape the expectations people have of themselves, the Growth Persona is particularly vulnerable to perpetuating roles for which it received early notice. The Growth Persona loves to mimic a childhood hero/heroine. It is self as the ego commands it to be, not as it develops through unique experiences. The identity is usurped; the role-definition confines the abilities.

A Growth Persona frequently indicates dependence on a role that once worked but has ceased to satisfy. Yet others expect the Growth Persona to continue its impressive display even though the role has long-since been stripped of the excitement of self-enhancing growth. Growth Personae mask a wealth of pent-up frustration. Every attempt at change soon becomes a variation on some already established theme.

If there is a history of doubt in the early years, the Growth Persona clings to a stereotyped image. A career or a mate may have seemed the quick solution to the pressing need for self-definition. Whether the career is medicine, teaching, the ministry or politics, the career is sure to be one offering clear-cut personal and social statements.

The problem of behavior pervasive Growth Needs comes down to an absence of real growth. There is a great deal of activity but there is very little change. The mask may originally be adopted because some significant other or society itself expresses admiration for that role. The role is little more than a caricature, however, because the real spark of inner creativity is missing.

The Growth Persona cannot be altered until the attitudes supporting the behavior pervasive Growth Need come to light. The behavior related to the persona is so automatic that the person keeps sending off behavioral cues that say "I am my persona. Respond to me as you have always responded." The person will not break out of the fraudulent identity until he or she begins to send new cues that say, "Look. I'm changing." The behavior must show clear, concrete signs of a fresh identity. This means that the person must make decisive choices that take him or her out of the familiar role. However, leaving a successful Growth Persona behind is a risky business and many habitual attitudes and behaviors must be simultaneously altered. The person must acknowledge the differences in himself or herself, display a new self-expressive pattern and verbalize new attitudes. This is a massive change. It is made even more difficult by the contrast between the comfort of past importance and the impending possibility of risk and failure.

Birth Pattern #28: Johnny Carson
A Behavior Pervasive Growth Need

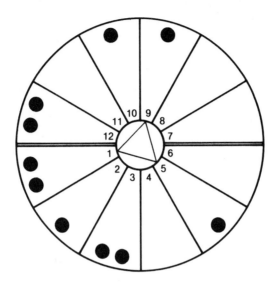

Birth Pattern #29: Jimmy Carter
A Behavior Pervasive Growth Need

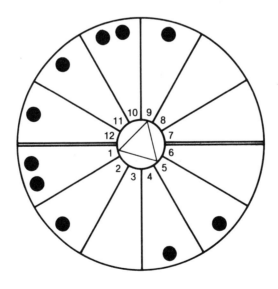

Johnny Carson's role as the perennial host of the *Tonight Show* is an example of the distinctive character of the Growth Persona. His attempts to leave the role he has made his own illustrate the difficulty inherent in altering any long-term persona pattern. He has cut down on the number of shows per week. He has shortened the length of the show itself. But he is still the *Tonight Show* host.

The behavior pervasive Growth Need pattern also shaped in the persona of former president Jimmy Carter. Carter sought the role of president, yet many of his critics feel he was not "presidential material." He was criticized for his abilities, not for his efforts during his term in public office. The danger in seeking any publicly defined role is that the public does, in fact, have its own concept of that role.

Is the Growth Persona the mask that your personality pattern wears? If you have a behavior pervasive Growth Need, it is important for you to examine your identity and the statement it makes. What about you makes you feel important? Can you make clear statements about yourself in concrete terms? Do you have a realistic sense of your personal abilities? What is unique about your personality that clearly distinguishes you from other people?

Look behind your Growth Persona and ask yourself some hard questions as well. Do you try to impress others with your abilities? Are you easily insulted? When was the last time that you blamed a personal failure on someone or something outside yourself? Do you feel that you never have time to do what you really want to do? Do you feel that something very meaningful is going to happen to you, something that will change your life? How vigorously do you defend your personal philosophy, your social or political or spiritual viewpoint?

A generalized sense of personal ability can be a great asset when you shape that ability, define it and apply it to the business of living. When you rely solely on ability, you tend to give up when the going gets rough. You are using your ability well, if you can see your failures clearly and failure does not diminish your sense of significance. You will not be easily insulted if your self-esteem has a base in reality. You will rarely use the easy-out of blaming other people. You do not invest your time and effort on projects that do not interest you, thus you have time for projects that you truly enjoy. You know who you are and you know what you like.

When you equate life change with your sense of choice, you do not wait for events to happen to you. Meaningfulness is a byproduct of self-awareness and self-awareness is the byproduct of experience vigorously sought and selected. Growing, changing, capable people wear their philosophies and their persona lightly. They are continually revising their views and testing new ideas. Those who struggle to grow are aware that the experiment of life is often painful. Personal truths are won through risk and failure and endurance, thus a personal truth need never be defended. Truth is a private affair, not a merit badge. Your Growth Persona urges you to examine yourself and your life. It asks who you are but, more significantly, it asks why you are.

The Security Persona
The Behavior Pervasive Security Need

The Security Persona springs originally from the desire for productivity, the capacity to assess and the urge for respect. The search for self-respect runs through the maturational crises faced by the person with a behavior pervasive Security Need. If respect emerges, accompanied by a continuing sense of certainty and trust, it persists in the face of daily ups and downs. It provides stability for the personality as a whole.

So long as valuing remains a feeling process, the Security Persona stays flexible. It permits rearrangement and life reorganization as they are necessary. Once significant successes are stored away like favorite pictures in an album, they can be reviewed from time to time but they do not distract from present opportunities. The subjective sense of comfort signifies the fruit of efforts rewarded and jobs well-done. The Security image sensitizes the person to those experiences, goals, inner qualities and outer conditions offering deep personal rootedness.

The rigid Security Persona is, by contrast, addicted to the sense of its own authority. It is in control of every situation, always knowing the correct thing that must be done. There is a right way and a wrong way to live and the Security Persona prides itself on its right living.

The behavior pervasive Security Need controls every action. All attempts to be more caring, more assertive and more objective simply feed the Security Persona, inflating the sense of potency and the conceit of control. These feelings, of course, remain beneath the surface. The Security mask is helpful, concerned, loyal and above all thoroughly competent. The Security Persona lays down its rules for the whole of the personality: I must be ambitious; I must get on in the world; I must prosper; I must never yield to pressure nor look intimidated. People must see that I am always cool, calm, composed.

While all personae involve dependence, the Security Persona and the Love Persona do so more noticeably. Security and Love needs are related specifically to the parents and the Security and Love Personae often signal that the parent has been more than a model for behavior patterning. The Security and Love Personae include a high degree of unconscious imitation of parental behavior as well as the projection of the parental role onto some familiar, comfortable situation. The mate, the career, a boss, an admired mentor, or political/social/religious belief system, are particularly good screens on which to project the image of a nurturing, protective parent.

When we are small, a parent is the strong one who keeps us from harm and insures our continuing safety and satisfaction. People with Security Personae often feel small, weak and vulnerable to life's slings and arrows. Once they comfortably identify themselves with an external source of security, they feel powerful and big and important. Then, their masks take on the character of the external security source. The roles reverse; the Security Persona becomes parental. Think of a child playing dress-up and you can better imagine the identification process that happens beneath the Security Persona.

Bobby is wearing his gun and holster, his chaps and his stetson. He is not playing cowboy; he *is* a cowboy. He thinks cowboy, he presents the image of a cowboy, he even feels like a cowboy. The more satisfying his cowboy image grows, the more he invests himself in that image. It is crucial to Bobby that other people treat him as a cowboy. Bobby becomes accustomed to the rights, privileges, success and authority of the cowboy role.

The problem with Bobby-the-cowboy is that "cowboy" becomes the only game he can play. If we want to play with Bobby, we must play cowboy too. Bobby must translate all of his life experiences into cowboy terms in order to understand them. The experiences that do not fit his persona are either denied or reinterpreted into cowboy terms. Thus Bobby-the-cowboy maintains and extends his prestige and his authority.

Think of the Security Persona as a pedestal supporting life experiences. The Security Persona works when the person continues to add to the pedestal, to work on the pedestal and from time to time rebuild it completely. The secure image is altered by living and under constant construction. It is never finished, never complete, and never perfect. The Security pervasive person builds a private pedestal of support and knows where repairs are most necessary. Not all of the pedestal is built during the best of times and some of it is flawed. But the person accepts the flaws and thinks, "This is how I learned."

People with Security Personae incorporating external sources of support buy their security pedestals ready-made. At the time of the purchase, the pedestal may be quite adequate. It seems, in fact, to be a gold-plated, guaranteed base on which to stack life events. But the weight of experience sits atop the borrowed security base in a most uneasy fashion. What passes for safety is not safe at all and the person is caught in a balancing act. At some point, life is sure to hand the Security oriented person the one experience that simply will not stack and the whole uneasy structure will collapse.

Breaking through the security mask is difficult. It means facing the facts of being rigid rather than flexible, demanding rather than achieving, reactionary rather than smart. The person is taking far more from a role than the role can give. Hardest of all, there are many other people with insecurities of their own who respect and admire the false face of a Security Persona.

Bringing a Security Persona into the light of full awareness means recognizing childish wishes to be taken care of, provided for and nurtured. It means trading these wishes, comfortable though they are, for face-to-face encounters with real challenges, challenges that almost certainly mean false starts and failure before realistic security is forthcoming. Some consolation can be found in self-realization. The crisis involved in willingly giving up a security-smothering persona is minimal when compared to the crisis of rebuilding the whole life structure after an unrealistic security base crumbles and falls apart. We feel psychologically naked when all our doubts and insufficiencies come to light. But we may be publicly humiliated if we cling to pseudo-security when it is strikingly clear to everyone but ourselves that our security is cut from the same cloth as the Emperor's new clothes.

Birth Pattern #30: Muhammad Ali
A Behavior Pervasive Security Need

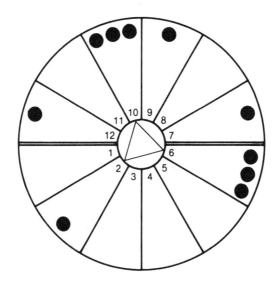

Birth Pattern #30 illustrates the behavior pervasive Security Need in the archetype of boxing great Muhammad Ali. When we appreciate the strength of a very powerful persona buoyed by the sense of personal mastery and achievement, we can better understand how difficult it is to leave a once-satisfying security role behind. It may be easier to suffer defeat at the hands of youthful opponents than to face the contents of one's own unconscious self-evaluation.

If you have a behavior pervasive Security Need it is important for you to assess your personal security base. Security is a difficult subject to discuss with others and it is often a subject that we avoid thinking about altogether. The very topic of our subjective sense of safety tends to arouse immediate, defensive feelings.

The following exercise can increase your awareness of your personal sense of security. First, list two or three themes that have remained relatively constant during the past five years of your life. The themes might be relationship- or career-centered. Now ask yourself the following questions: What would I do tomorrow if this relationship or this job were to end? How would my self-assessment change? Would my personal responsibilities increase or decrease? Could I spend an evening conversing with a stranger without talking about these life themes?

Now ask yourself some hard security-related questions. How long is the list of people whom you really trust? When was the last time you proved to someone else that you were right and they were wrong? Do you expect others to win your confidence, earn your approval, merit your concern? Do you feel that life is basically futile? Are you secretly glad to hear of other people's failures?

An internal security base shapes the persona as value-giver, not possessor of valuable objects or status positions. We invest objects and people in our lives with value, thus they are personally significant to us. Whether they are of equal value to our neighbors or strangers is irrelevant since what we value we esteem for private, not public reasons.

We cherish the enduring things in our lives because they provide us with continually fresh satisfactions. Our security in our inner strength and capability leads us to accept responsibility and our responsibilities allow us to discover our real depth.

We trust from the core of all that is best and enduring within us. We know that when we mask our trust, our real humanity cannot touch what is human in others.

You can wear your Security Persona lightly when you are realistically secure. You are realistically secure when you exchange your rights and wrongs for the right to be wrong occasionally. You leave proof to the scientists in laboratories.

You accept with grace what others give and give open-handedly of your talents to those in need. Secure, confident, successful people refuse to live life as a barter system where scores must be settled, accounts must be balanced and people can be bought, sold, or possessed. Secure people are self-possessed rather than possessive, self-respecting rather than self-seeking and fulfilled rather than futile. They want others to succeed because they know the joy of personal success.

Your Security Persona urges you to examine the threads woven deep into the fabric of your on-going experience. They ask you, the weaver, to own and interpret your creation.

The Stimulus Persona
The Behavior Pervasive Stimulus Need

The Stimulus Persona grows from the desires for inclusion, belonging, attention. It pursues the excitement of first encounter and thrives in a climate of variety. The developmental crises faced by the person with a behavior pervasive Stimulus Need center around the themes of interaction and social discovery.

A flexible Stimulus Persona is open enough to adapt to the demands of immediate, fresh encounter but stable enough to maintain poise and social competence. The Stimulus image is sensitive to ideals, situations and people offering immediate, interesting, broadening prospects.

A rigid Stimulus Persona is the mask of the know-it-all. "Never ask if you can tell" is its motto. Everything has an explanation and the person with a rigid Stimulus Persona can supply it. He or she can always be found at the planning stages of anything interesting but magically vanishes once the planning turns to actual hard work and snags and problems arise.

The Stimulus Persona presents an image designed to charm and fascinate. It is addicted to movement and change and detests the thought of doing anything a second time. To keep moving is to avoid feelings of anxiety which often underlie the behavior pervasive Stimulus Need. So long as the Stimulus Persona keeps doing something, *anything,* it masks its inner uncertainty. The Stimulus Persona has its musts as all personae do: I must never be bored; I must always be alert; I must never miss out on anything; above all, I must know and if I do not know I must find out immediately.

The Stimulus Persona, as all personae, is basically a dependent structure, prone to projecting its contents onto society and mistaking its own projections for social truth. The Stimulus Persona simultaneously fears exclusion and loneliness while demanding inclusion and social support. It is particularly active in situations where new people are met or where many people are involved. The Stimulus Persona's internal image is self as part of something greater than self. It is the self which belongs as well as the self which cannot fit in.

The behavior pervasive Stimulus Need touches every stage of social development. It includes images of the parents' relationship to each other because this is an important model for the way that equals interact. If the parents' relationship has been an unequal interchange where one parent decided while the other agreed or one parent chose while the other passively complied, then the image contained in the Stimulus Persona is the image of non-mutuality and superiority/inferiority. The unconscious conclusion is that social relationships are never democratic interchanges. They consist, instead, of an active party who lays down life rules and a passive party who agrees to play by non-self-determined standards. To agree is to belong and be included. To disagree is to risk exclusion or punishment.

The models for social interaction develop in the family and are also reinforced by sibling relationships. If the image of privilege and choice for some versus punishment and exclusion for others persists, the sense of nondemocratic relating is strengthened. This same inequality will be reinforced in peer interactions during childhood play, the school experience, and the growing consciousness of broader social themes. Adolescent experiences will simply prove what the person has suspected all along: real choice and real sharing simply are not possible.

From the standpoint of the Stimulus Persona, it makes little difference whether the formative experiences have sent a constant message of superiority, privilege and in-group or a message of inferiority, exclusion and out-group. Both lack the qualities of mutuality and free, flexible interchange that form realistic attitudes promoting realistic assessment of life experience and human relationships. The order-giver and the order-taker, the know-it-all and the know-nothing are two sides of the same coin. Neither has the ability to think things through clearly because life answers have been predetermined.

Once the contents of the Stimulus Persona are safely projected on the outer world, the person feels able to explain everything. When they feel socially superior, Stimulus Personae are adept at defining the game of life in rules that allow them to win. They have a keen sense of public expectation and an eager willingness to meet that expectation. They cannot diversify or explore or expand because they cannot transcend the group mores. They must confine themselves to social standards that permit social recognition and public reinforcement. Stimulus superiority goes for the easy win involving no real risk and lacking any real excitement.

Stimulus-inferior people feel themselves to be outcasts and all their experiences reinforce an outcast social image. Stimulus-inferior people define the world in such self-constraining terms that there is no possibility of winning. Their social inferiority insures that they will always be scapegoats, victims of prejudice, and recipients of unwarranted criticism. They are excused from participating in a society that does not appear to want them but, more importantly, they are justified in their urge to get even.

The Stimulus Persona supports the social identity when the individual is open to new social input and free to explore new relationships. A good measure of the Stimulus Persona's openness is the breadth of social relationships and the diversity of past experiences. Generalized feelings of belonging help the person overlook petty social slights.

A Stimulus Persona's unconscious attitudes emerge into awareness in the company of resentments and confusion. The narrower the mask, the more the person feels pressured and pushed and confined. Letting go of an unrewarding Stimulus Persona leaves the person temporarily out-of-place in a world where everyone else appears to know where they belong. Hanging on, however, pushes the Stimulus-masked person into a corner where a backlog of irritations and frustrations threaten to erupt. The flood of accusations pouring from a Stimulus Persona's shattered self-constraint shows how truly unrealistic the social image has become. Facing up to the inner attitudes means letting go of the excuses for social failure or the expectation of easy social success.

Birth Pattern #31 illustrates the behavior pervasive Stimulus Need in the birth chart of Manson family member Susan Atkins. When an individual for any reason feels excluded and hemmed in by social constraints, he or she is particularly attracted to a group that offers belonging and freedom. When inclusion and belonging are given unconditionally, the Stimulus Persona believes it is everything it imagines itself to be. The group can project its real frustrations en masse. Manson's far-fetched social visions illustrate the ease with which unrecognized social fears and inferiorities transmute into smug, self-righteous superiority. Atkins's total involvement is a testament to the powerful hook of belonging and group acceptance.

The visionary outcasts accuse and punish society. The superior, socially-compliant in-group purifies itself by purging undesirables. Both are extreme; neither is capable of dialogue and realistic communication. Each would destroy its uncertainty by destroying the other. What each group fails to see in the group it dislikes is the mirror image of its own unconscious projections.

A spiritual maxim states that when we kill another person we kill ourself. In the case of Susan Atkins and Sharon Tate this was strikingly true. Here are the basic personality patterns of both women:

Susan Atkins—Need Gestalt		Sharon Tate—Need Gestalt	
Growth:	2	Growth:	1
Security:	0	Security:	1
Stimulus:	6	Stimulus:	6
Love:	2	Love:	2

Birth Pattern #31: Susan Atkins
A Behavior Pervasive Stimulus Need

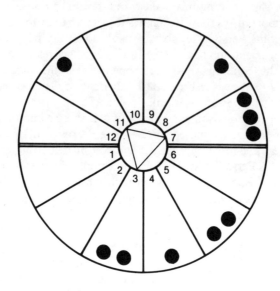

Birth Pattern #32: Sharon Tate
A Behavior Pervasive Stimulus Need

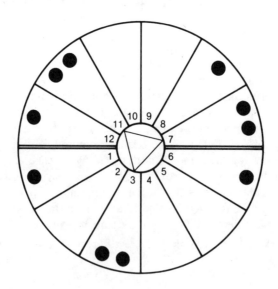

The persona emphasis in each woman's personality pattern is based on a behavior pervasive Stimulus Need.

If you have a Stimulus Persona, examine your looking-glass self, the self that you experience when you see your reflection in another. If your Stimulus Need is behavior pervasive this can be challenging. What does your first conversation with a new person tell you about yourself? Are your first impressions of others overly critical or overly generous? Is a new relationship an opportunity to see a new you or simply a chance to prove that you are what you know you are? Do your wider social affiliations reflect parts of yourself that are changing? Or do you simply join to belong without contributing?

Ask yourself some hard questions about your interpersonal attitudes. Do you expect to be recognized? To go unrecognized? Do you tell people who you are instead of allowing them to discover you? Do you say things specifically to get a reaction? Are other people jealous of your knowledge or your success or your position? Do you size people up and look for their flaws and weaknesses? Do you wonder what people will say about you when you are not around?

People who drop their social masks actively contribute in their dealings with others. They can give to an interchange and take from an interchange with equal poise. Because their first impressions are realistic, they characterize without judging. They can say yes to interesting prospects but they can say no when real interest is lacking. They do not feel so self-important that their honest "no" will devastate a total stranger.

You know that your social self-image is realistic when it is constant enough to make a personal statement yet flexible enough to change with every new encounter. You can converse without proving yourself and you can say what you mean without dramatizing for effect or mystifying for safety.

Your Stimulus image is a bridge that spans the distance between your distinctive experience and your experience with others. It is an ever-available link to all that is bright and stimulating and exciting. It is not a drawbridge to be arbitrarily lowered and raised.

If your social self is a comfortable self, you see life as a book to be read with interest, not a popularity contest to be won or lost. You feel that you belong where you are and you are where you belong. The multiplicity of human differences piques your curiosity. You explore people, you compare for the sake of contrast, you know for the sake of interest satisfied. The ins and outs, ups and downs, rewards and disappointments of social life strike you as natural, ever-shifting patterns rather than universal laws of caste. Your Stimulus Persona asks equally about your commonality and your distinction, your equality and your style. It asks what you have to say and why you want to say it. What is the message you send to the world around you?

The Love Persona
The Behavior Pervasive Love Need

The Love Persona comes from the desires for acceptance and pleasurable mutuality. Self-acceptance is a challenge that repeats through every stage of maturation. The behavior pervasive Love Need requires ongoing, intimate closeness and mirrors the Security-based stability translated into the sphere of significant, special life relationships. When the crises of identity formation are successfully met in a Love Need pervasive personality, the resulting self-acceptance insures a flexible attitude toward deep, emotional commitments.

The Love Need image sensitizes the person to those other people and those distinct experiences offering comfort or harmony or profound and feelingful satisfaction. People with self-enhancing Love Personae radiate happiness because they constantly achieve it by their own actions.

The rigid Love Persona accepts everything and everyone with equal enthusiasm. It offers the same cheery platitudes to everyone and gives the same uplifting message whatever the real circumstances. The emotions are only a foil for manipulation, however, since the Love Persona too has its dictates: I must be cheerful; I must be kind; I must accept what comes my way; and I must not be down or unhappy or uncomfortable. Since I am nice, people must treat me well and give me what I want.

The Love Persona shares with the Security Persona a tendency to perpetuate an internal parent. The internal parent is not, to any great degree, the real parent because the internalized parental image is far too perfect and far too idealistic to reflect any flesh-and-blood human being. Just as the Security Persona perpetuates the wish for nurturance and bounty, the Love Persona hopes for unquestioning approval and automatic intimate bonding. These ideal satisfactions are qualitative and escape concrete definition. The Love Persona feels an inner fullness of self when the sense of satisfaction is present and terrible emptiness when there is a lack.

The Love Persona dictates to the whole personality. Whatever the Love pervasive person's behavior, he or she will confront the overwhelming desire to be part of something deeply meaningful and special. The loved child has a sense that he or she holds a distinct place in the family. This is the sense of being important, in and of the self, of being utterly irreplaceable and completely wanted. Should the child go away, the child would be missed and should the child be lost, the loss would not go unnoticed.

The Love Persona projects outward the inward desire for total acceptance and the inner horror of rejection. When people with Love Personae establish relationships, they are often victimized by their own demands for reassurance. They say yes when they really mean no to prevent any possibility of distance because, for them, distance and estrangement are one and the same. They follow a predictable pattern in relationships beginning with easy-going agreement and fond warmth, progressing to intense mutuality and ending, eventually, with cold aloofness from the very other that it was so desperately important to please in the beginning. If the estrangement seems odd, we must explore the Love Persona's contents to see why its unhappy endings are so expectable.

Getting in touch with the real feelings masked by the Love Persona requires a willingness to feel a great deal of fear. In the warm rush of establishing a mutual relationship the Love Persona avoids feeling the natural fears we all feel. Someone is important to us and we want to be equally important to them but until we commit to each other, we feel the mixed doubt and joy of first relatings. When we form a committed relationship, we form quiet, compassionate, enduring bonds of mutual satisfaction.

The Love Persona stamps out self-doubt and eventually comes to project this doubt onto the loved one. Now, the other seems to confine because the other cannot prove to the Love Persona that he or she is special, acceptable, important. As the realization grows that the loved one is not able to provide the lacking sense of inner acceptance, the Love Persona begins to resent the loved one. Retreat, withdrawal and emotional abandonment follow. Perhaps someone more important than the current lover will satisfy the Love Persona's insatiable need for significance, will confirm the persona in its irreplaceable and significant role.

To break the pattern of intimate fusion followed by aloof withdrawal, Love pervasive people must discover that they really fear themselves. No other person and no success or achievement will give them the happiness they want until they become self-validating, self-significant, and self-accepting. They will continue to reject because they fear their own unimportance and they will be unable to accept real satisfactions until they set their own restless spirits at ease. They must face their fears on their own because reconciling oneself with oneself is a lonely task and real mutuality lies on the other side of this reconciliation.

The emotional crises of the Love Persona need not be played out on the stage of intimate relationships. The same progression from acceptance to rejection marks everything the Love pervasive person does. Unless they are willing to own the responsibility for their own happiness, they will be frustrated in work or in friendship or in personal involvements of any kind.

Birth Pattern #33: John Lennon
A Behavior Pervasive Love Need

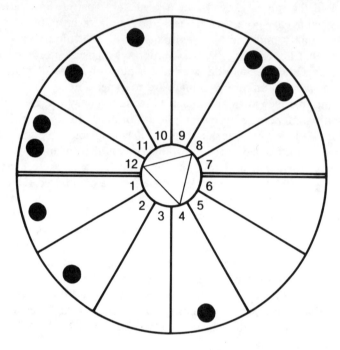

The partial birth pattern #33 illustrates the behavior pervasive Love Need in the chart of John Lennon. Lennon's relationship with his wife Yoko Ono passed through the stages that characterize the Love Persona. When their once-passionate and intense unity began to disintegrate, Yoko Ono made the difficult choice to leave Lennon alone. She did not accept the role of disappointer nor would she take responsibility for Lennon's unhappiness. She left him to hit emotional bottom alone. Far from being cruel, she allowed him the freedom to suffer all that he was bent upon suffering. Had she attempted to keep him from himself, she would not have succeeded. Lennon's ability to find within himself a capacity for commitment and sharing was a human triumph. If we measure the Lennons' post-crisis reconciliation on the yardstick of time, it seems tragically short. But if we measure in the realm of spirit where love really exists, we see that love is itself immortal.

If your personality wears a Love Persona, it is important for you to examine your most intimate expectations. This is especially true if you have a behavior pervasive Love Need. Do you find that your anticipation of an activity tends to be more satisfying than the activity itself? Do you ever pretend to be happy when in reality you are not? Is one of your personal goals to *be* happy? When was the last time that you felt misunderstood?

The greater the Love Persona emphasis, the more you need to ask yourself some hard questions as well. Do you often make demands on those who care for you? Are you critical of your loved ones? Are you easily exploited? Do you give and withdraw affection to punish others? Have you ever deliberately "put down" your mate in front of other people? Do you make promises to other people that you have no intention of keeping?

People who sincerely like themselves enjoy living. They approach what they do with an inner sense of pleasure, they do not attempt to wring pleasure out of what they do. They realize that happiness is a byproduct of living rather than some abstract state to be attained. People who accept themselves know themselves. They see the emotional highlights and the disappointments and they can show both their joys and their sorrows without shame or sham.

The presence of a person with innate self-appreciation often makes us happy. Such people do not try to lift our spirits; they simply radiate what real happiness is all about. People who truly love can say both yes and no to those they love. They realize that love says yes and no while fear only says yes to evoke the other's yes and says no to prevent the other's no.

If you are successfully expressing a Love Persona, you are a loving person. As a loving person, you feel special because you love, not because you are loved. You do not question your importance in the eyes of your loved ones because you feel important in loving. You know you would be missed and you know you cannot be replaced. You have experienced the pains of parting and the joys of reunion. You feel the completeness with which you are bound to the other and to the whole of the universe when you escape the bondage of your own doubts and fears. A behavior pervasive Love Need in your own birth pattern asks you to explore your attitudes toward your intimate sense of self. It asks whether you are able to be loved because you have the ability to love.

The most interesting persona phenomenon of all is the hidden persona that is itself masked by a stronger conscious role. A need only has to occur at the three level (three planet markers) to be behavior pervasive. At this level it may not be the dominant need. The mask itself wears a mask.

This can be a powerfully frustrating combination to the person trying to project a dominant need image, when actually in the grips of the behavior pervasive secondary need. In this case, less is more. The dominant need is a tool of the lesser need and becomes subservient to it. The person sabotages primary aims and does not realize it. The greater need and its feelings protect the behavior pervasive secondary need. The middle child of the need hierarchy runs the show, dictating to its siblings both older and younger.

Jungian psychologists describe a phenomenon called the "turntype." The turntype is a person who expresses some lesser element of personality in seeming preference to a stronger personality factor. The turntype is less self than he or she could be.

The usual explanation for the turntype is that a turntype acts out the type of a forceful parental model rather than the personal type. In the context of Birth Pattern Psychology, which at core is the psychology of being what we by nature are, this explanation does not suffice. Our needs come from our feelings and we cannot feel another person's feelings no matter how significant that other person is. If the wherewithall to become a turntype is innately a facet of the personality, it is much easier to see how the turntype evolves. Life experiences reinforce the pervasive need consistently regardless of its actual position in the hierarchy. As its theme recurs in each stage of development, the person gradually and imperceptibly brings the lesser need to a false prominence and consistently acts it out. The potential is, thus, in the person to begin with. It is not impressed on the individual from without.

The challenges and frustrations may be greater for the turntype but the solutions are the same. The behavior pervasive need and its related feelings must first be seen and acknowledged, then interrupted in process to give the person the possibility of choice in what is generally perceived as a no-choice situation. The conscious must wrest control from the automatic unconscious wherever there is a behavior pervasive need.

The goal is not, of course, to make the turntype to behave in character. It is simply to achieve free behavior and free choice in order to satisfy needs in self-enhancing, self-actualizing ways.

If the strong persona poses difficulties, the weak persona does too. The evenly distributed need patterns of the 3–3–2–2 and 3–3–3–1 hierarchies are particularly fertile soil for the weak persona if none of the needs is behavior pervasive. We have already noted the strong conflicts experienced by people who find that they want it all. These conflicts grow even stronger when the person is unable to adopt a public mask or play some introductory role. Said one man with a high conflict 3–3–2–2 need hierarchy, "I'm always overlooked. No matter how hard I work, I just never seem to get noticed. I feel invisible."

A sense of being somehow lesser or unnoticed leads to fruitless comparisons. "Why is she so successful? She's not doing anything that I don't do!" "What's he got that I haven't got?" The answer to these questions is that others may well present a more consistent self-image operating through a well-defined persona. Such consistency eludes a weaker persona precisely because the weak persona shifts with the tides of the situation attempting to be all things to all people on all possible occasions.

Janis Joplin's life illustrated several problems that challenge any person with a weak persona. Her Need Gestalt (Growth: 2, Security: 2, Stimulus: 3, and Love: 3) is a variation of the 3–3–2–2 need hierarchy. Biographer Myra Friedman describes Joplin's personality as "disordered, decentralized, diffused." During her short life, Janis often felt that nothing was good. She worried about not getting what she wanted and found it hard to deal with frustrations. She wanted so much that whatever she had always seemed to be too little.

Like all individuals with weak personae, Janis Joplin was easily threatened and quick to defend. She was constantly "defending against an attack that might not even be coming." Without the social cover of the persona, the ego is exposed and people without strong personae are often labeled egocentric. The search for a self to be is so absorbing that people who lack strong personae become highly self-involved. Defensiveness and hypersensitivity are simply the byproducts of this constant self-involvement. Since the self-involvement is more visible to a viewer than is the persona diffusion, the person appears egocentric.

When the pattern of inner needs and feeling is diffuse, people sometimes identify with their behavior. Some behavior mode starts to overcompensate for the missing persona. Behavior ceases to be the means to achieve specific satisfactions. Instead, it becomes a personal statement.

The psychological fallout for the person who identifies self with behavior is enormous. The inner message reads "I am my actions." Solving both personal and interpersonal problems demands separation between individuals and their actions. When this is not possible, the simplest disagreements turn into major battles:

Chris is waiting for her friend Eleanor. Eleanor is half an hour late for their luncheon date. Since Eleanor has been late on a number of other occasions, Chris decides to discuss the matter.

"Hi, Eleanor, I've been waiting for half an hour. Didn't we agree to meet here at noon?"

"Well, you know how I am. I had a hard time getting organized today."

"Maybe we could set later luncheon dates. On days like this when I have a lot to do we don't have much time together if you're late."

"Well, aren't you the busy one! I'm so sorry I messed up your day."

"That's not what I'm saying, Eleanor. I really enjoy our time together and I really like you. Maybe if we met at a more convenient time...."

"So! I'm an inconvenience to you. Is that it? And I thought I was your friend."

Though the issue is Eleanor's behavior, Eleanor identifies with her lateness and takes her friend's statements personally. Once Eleanor identifies with her actions, she doesn't respond to the opportunity to solve this simple problem.

When an individual identifies self with behavior, internal conflicts get externalized. The persona, for all its drawbacks, does organize inner states. Conversely, the weak persona exposes inner states. Janis Joplin, her biographer notes, could not read her own internal signals well. She relied on other people to define her inner states by responding to her actions. She "handled her conflicts by acting them out."

The behavioral overcompensation, the defensiveness, the self-involvement and demandingness of the weak persona searching for its image yield to the same solutions as the rigid persona. Both interrupt the self or the whole. Both weak and strong personae are parts attempting to substitute for the whole of personality. Both attempt to avoid necessary choices involved in the life experience. Both stop the necessary flow and change of real feelings by imposing musts.

The functional personality, no matter what its pattern and no matter what its priorities, cannot escape the demands of choice. The parts, whether they war or whether they form false alliances to exclude or avoid weaker parts of the self, do not triumph over the whole for long. As Jung said, "The experience of the Self is always a defeat for the ego."[12] It is a defeat for the persona as well.

Coping means choosing over and over again. The persona's "I must" protects the ego. The underlying themes are "I must be" and "I must have." True satisfaction is not hooked onto its satisfier; it comes from the feeling Self. The excitement, the intimacy, the discovery, the invention, the achievement belong to the self. There is simply nothing external to self that one *must* have or *must* do or *must* be because satisfaction can come from multiple satisfiers and various situations. Musts arise in specific situations. Musts are specific to their satisfiers. Both exalt the external at the expense of the internal. Thus they are false. To give up one's musts is to face a life of endless choice, but choice is far less overwhelming than the attempt to live up to self-imposed demands.

Perhaps, as you read this chapter, you find parts of it specifically relevant to you. What are your musts? Must you live up to the image your persona dictates? *Why* must you? Must you have some specific satisfier? Your attachment to the idea of getting what you want may be obscuring your real need-related feelings. Must you behave according to some general standard like "being good" or "being successful"? Counter such vague generalities with specifics. What exactly is being good? Why must you always be good? What is success? Why must you succeed?

Albert Ellis suggests that the tendency to impose musts does not give the necessary psychological freedom to live fully or freely. Musts give a false sense of absolute right where no such right in fact exists. Musts, like all dictators, are insatiable. The more we think we live up to them, the more insistent and demanding they become.

To keep our wishes in realistic perspective, Ellis suggests that we look at our choices as they truly are. If Andrew feels ready to make a commitment and wants to marry Jane, he prefers Jane to others who might also potentially satisfy his intimacy need. If he knows that he *prefers* to marry Jane and she refuses his proposal, he knows he still has other life choices. He is disappointed, but he is not devastated. If he thinks that he absolutely *must* have Jane and Jane alone can make his life complete, then he falsely believes that there is no one else in the world to whom he can make a commitment and no one else with whom he can achieve intimacy. If Jane refuses marriage when Andrew *must* have her, he feels destroyed.

Toward all possible satisfiers, our attitude is always one of preference so long as we recognize self as chooser. The ego, whether trying to uphold an inflated self-image or avoid unwanted feelings or center an unfocused self, imposes musts. To stop musting is not to undo the ego as an everchanging feeling process. It is only to undo the ego as dictator, the persona as tyrant.

Flaws in the Mask

"It is true that you may fool all the people some of the time; you can even fool some of the people all the time; but you can't fool all of the people all the time." So wrote Abraham Lincoln. He might have been writing about the masks people wear.

Regardless of the specific mask, the mask is constructed. It is a piece of psychological handiwork and the pride of the craftsman is clearly in evidence when the mask is well made. The better the mask, the more the ego likes to strut about in it. But pride, says the Bible, is one of the seven deadly sins and the Greeks caution against hubris or arrogance:

Steven is attending a dinner party. He feels he must make a good impression. There are many important people at the party, people who could help him a lot. So Steven polishes up his persona. He must be witty; he has to be interesting, polished, the equal to the others who are there. Amazingly, he sees that he is seated in a place of prominence next to his hostess.

"What a piece of luck," thinks Steven to himself. "I'll charm her."

So Steven tells his best stories, stories designed to fascinate his hostess. He looks into her eyes with serious concentration; he presents his persona with splash and verve. "She adores me," he notes with pride. He flashes her his most brilliant smile.

He flashes her the piece of spinach firmly wedged between his front teeth.

Hubris say the Greeks, invites the nemesis and the nemesis is the avenger, the evener of the scales, the bearer of just retribution, the keeper of the spinach. Pride, the Bible states, goeth before destruction.

Though a persona may be all-involving, it is never perfect. Since it is always less than the self gestalt, it is never complete. The more a person tries to convince others that he or she is persona and persona alone, the more the unaccepted remainder of personality threatens the facade. The persona can face people, but it is afraid to show its backside. It is afraid to reveal other personality aspects that are less well-formed and more uncertain.

More than anything else, the persona fears its nemesis, its downfall. The nemesis is the part of personality that can be felt but cannot be easily verbalized. Analyst Harry Stack Sullivan's theories suggest that some portions of the psyche are disowned. Sullivan calls this unclaimed territory of the self the Not Me. The persona and nemesis together signify a self divided into the owned persona image (the Me) and the disowned nemesis (the Not Me). The nemesis is a constant challenge because it brings out the worst in the person. This need not be so, but it often is. The more an individual insists on a perfect persona, the more damage the nemesis is capable of doing. The nemesis only damages the image to be sure, but to the person who relies on image alone, it appears that the nemesis threatens all hopes and plans.

The nemesis appears in the birth pattern in the form of the singleton planet. Any need triangle containing one planet and one planet only indicates a need that is felt rather than conceptualized. Furthermore, it has no emotional range and tends to operate full tilt or not at all. The persona, for all its flaws, does exhibit emotional control though this very control allows it to show the feelings it prefers to show, feelings it can deliberately fake. The persona is like a heating system with a range of settings from cold to cool to tepid to warm to hot. It has black and white but it also has grey. Not so with the nemesis. The nemesis resembles a machine that is either on or off, cold or hot, or in the realm of the emotions perfectly calm or out of control.

Persona and nemesis always work together. They play off each other and do not make much sense separately. The logic of the persona/nemesis combination is a "since-A-then-B logic." It says "Since I am my persona, I automatically deserve to have my lesser need gratified." It is a royal edict from the persona; it is a demand on life. It springs from the part of us that loves doing what we find easy and natural and dislikes doing what is hard or distasteful. The nemesis exists because none of us likes to feel bad and it is born in some situation or moment when we feel terrible and do not know why. We fear the nemesis because all in connection with it seems arbitrary and thrust upon us. So we strengthen our personae as a form of psychological insurance against the arbitrariness of the nemesis. Ironically, when we do, we give the nemesis its power.

The hierarchy of basic needs allows us to make a quick assessment of the personality structure. The dominant need with rare exceptions belongs to the persona. The middle level needs belong as a general rule to the ego, and the healthiest expressions of ego often coincide with need triangles containing three planet markers. Singletons always belong to the self.

The singleton differs significantly from the need triangle containing no planets at all. The empty need triangle adopts a *que sera, sera* attitude toward the need in question. The need and its related feelings are situational. In relevant situations the need shows itself but when the person is not in the situation the need subsides. With no planets at all in a need triangle, the individual seems content to cross that bridge when he or she comes to it. Not so with the singleton. Where there is a planet, there is a piece of the self, a piece that is at once threatening and captivating.

Are we talking about the nemesis, the bringer of defeat, the ugly step-sister to the persona's Cinderella? Is the nemesis the horror that we hope to avoid? As we have seen time and again, no personality factor is one-dimensional. The singleton planet, if it is disowned, makes the personality an incomplete gestalt. This last piece in the puzzle of personality is also the quintessence, the missing element which, if regained, turns the base metal of incompleteness into the gold of wholeness. If life has arbitrarily snatched it away, might not life magically bring it back? No...but we do not want to admit this. We ride off in our personae to find the job or the mate or the success that will complete us. When we get what we ask for, we still do not feel complete. The nemesis rises up to wave its wand of disappointment. Just as we kiss the handsome prince or the perfect princess our kiss turns the other into a toad.

Reality Therapist Glenda Allen uses Birth Pattern Psychology routinely with her clients. She finds it is often difficult to tell a very strong basic need from its singleton counterpart. The person often gives the singleton an exaggerated importance. The falseness of this emphasis is evident even though the person may be quite insistent. Behavior related to the singleton need is very artificial and contradictory, says Allen. With singletons, the person's reactions to situations involving that need are out of proportion and marked by extreme low tolerance for frustration.

Once a singleton need and its related feelings get "hooked" we often see very bad behavior. Where singletons are concerned there is no such thing as grace under pressure. The singleton need is the need that we want, no, *demand*, to have satisfied. We want all the good feelings related to its satisfaction. And we simply will not tolerate any of the bad feelings related to its frustration. The bad feelings and our terror of them form our nemesis.

The Growth Nemesis

The emotional tone of the Growth Nemesis is one of constant yet subtle frustration. The frustration is all the more difficult because it has no external source. To deal with it, people with growth singletons inevitably place themselves in frustrating circumstances or relationships, trying to get what's inside them into external form.

When Thoreau wrote that most people "lead lives of quiet desperation" he captured the inner intensity of the singleton growth planet. The source of the desperation is the Growth Nemesis itself. The nemesis feels like a trap, an invisible barrier separating the person from a core sense of firmness and direction.

The Growth Nemesis is both angry and terrified of anger. It fears its own discontent and therefore displaces its discontent onto life circumstances. To keep the persona and its image intact, the individual with a Growth Nemesis cannot directly confront the things or people in life that evoke resentment. Instead, it isolates itself and plots little revenges. The Growth Nemesis hides behind petty victories. It delights in throwing a monkey wrench into other people's plans. It is the subtle obstructor, the masked avenger, the undercover impediment to life's real progress, the perpetual devil's advocate.

"Gee, honey, I'd help you cook dinner but you know I can't even work a can opener." "Oh, I've overdrawn the checking account again? Well, you know me. I'm awful with numbers." The Growth Nemesis loves to use its supposed insufficiencies and lack of ability as grounds for self-defense. What it is really doing in these and all such instances is deliberately, if unconsciously, controlling a situation while avoiding direct action and overt confrontation.

The Growth Nemesis hides behind a persona that masks its real motives. If it can draw others out into the open, if it can force them to reveal their plans, if it can only evoke the other person's opinion first, then the Growth Nemesis feels in a position of power.

A Growth Nemesis stands up for everybody's rights but its own and tends to find socially acceptable outlets for its most aggressive feelings. This keeps the sense of resentment at bay but it is a stop-gap measure at best. It is the mate saying, "Look what you're doing to the children" when the real message is "Look what you're doing to me." The latter message cannot be spoken, however, without opening up a real hornet's nest of antagonism. To people with growth nemeses, antagonism and ill will mean nothing short of disaster. Particularly when the antagonism drives them to reveal their true demands, their desire for attention, their craving to be important and their fear of insignificance.

The Growth Nemesis is born of a fall from grace. The personality has, till the birth of its nemesis, lived in a circle of importance and felt itself significant. One common source of the Growth Nemesis is the displacement in the family's center of attention that happens with the birth of a sibling. Whatever the actual source situation, the person moves from the center of attention to the periphery, from center stage to the wings. The Growth Nemesis is the archetypal Adam or Eve cast out of Eden and wanting very much to get back.

The growth singleton craves attention yet its persona forms to counteract this craving. The Growth Nemesis is an inner anger. The loss of the central position must be avenged. People with growth singletons use charm or success or sympathy to regain a sense of importance but the importance is often shallow and unsatisfying.

More than anything else, the Growth Nemesis fears being alone. Not so much in the social sense as in the psychological sense. The Growth Nemesis perpetuates an illusion of understanding or meaningful sharing or significant exchange but these are its fantasies. Because it is a deeply resentful nemesis, it is loath to reveal its true anger and thus cannot reveal its basic identity. The Growth Nemesis gradually strips the personality of confidence and substitutes diffidence in its place. It talks a great game of integrity and high standards but avoids direct contact with its own weaknesses. The Growth Nemesis is a chip on the shoulder of the persona.

The Security Nemesis

The dominant feeling of a Security singleton is the feeling of being used. People with security singletons often become tools, allowing themselves to be manipulated to the benefit of others because they would rather feel used than feel alienated, isolated or insignificant. People with security singletons do not evaluate their personal resources well, either tangible resources, physical resources or emotional reserves. They see themselves as having so much to give that they give automatically. Giving feeds their personae. Their largesse makes them feel popular or kind or important. What they have, they squander without ever questioning whether other people really want what they are giving. People, being people, generally take what is freely offered and people with security singletons do not just offer, they insist. "Take my car, it's okay, really." "I'll work overtime if you need me."

The nemesis darkens behind the mask. All the extra effort, the overtime, the forced generosity mount up. One day, the security singleton person feels strapped, broke, tired, and drained.

"Hey, Tom, buddy. Lend me ten till payday, will you?"

"What do I look like, a damn BANK! The last time I lent you ten, you didn't pay me back for a month."

"But you kept telling me it was okay. You said you didn't need the money."

Tom's friend finds out the hard way that security singleton people feel compelled to give but they hate to be asked for anything. "If you need anything, just ask,'' they often say because it makes them feel big to say it. But they do not really mean it. They see it as an imposition when someone takes them seriously and calls them up on their offers. To be asked for something is to fail in the eyes of the security singleton person. Security singleton people feel guilty that they have not foreseen the other person's needs and fulfilled those needs unasked.

Security singleton people carry about a vague feeling of indebtedness, a sense of obligation. They owe something to life, they just sense it but they do not know what it is they owe, to whom it is owed, or just what incurred the debt in the first place. Therefore, they have to give to everyone in every situation just to cover all the bases.

The debt itself is lost somewhere in the past. The original incident may have been very trivial on the surface but it provoked in the security singleton person the sense of being selfish and grasping and self-serving. It left an aura of guilt so pervasive that the person determined never again to feel those feelings.

The Security Nemesis dogs the steps of everything the person does. Security is most relevant in the life process at points of completion and finality. Only then is any experience secured. Only then can the results of an experience be evaluated. But processes do not always end in useful products or gains. Some processes end in waste. People who are comfortable with their own sense of security take the waste with the gains and expect some chaff with the wheat. Not so people whose nemesis is security. They demand the gains for their efforts but they despise wasted effort because waste evokes in them a powerful and depressing sense of futility.

Endings have a magical quality for security singleton people. They think in terms of "after I finish this job" or "when I complete this project." Something full and wonderful and rich always awaits these magical endings, yet analyst Alfred Adler notes that most of our endings are fictional. We simply create points of finality but life goes right on. The security singleton person often fails to fully understand that he or she can terminate life circumstances that are displeasing and go on to something new. Such terminations often involve leaving behind situations and relationships about which nothing can be done and from which nothing further can be gained. Such situations stubbornly refuse to terminate themselves. If at all possible, security singleton people arrange it so that others must do the actual terminating and hence bear the guilt for it. It is their fancied association between guilt and endings that keeps security singleton people in unfulfilling circumstances trying to pay off unpayable debts and tie up imaginary loose ends.

The Stimulus Nemesis

The predominant feeling of the stimulus singleton is awkwardness coupled with resistance to and deep resentment of change. To fully understand the stimulus singleton, we must differentiate between real change and the appearance of change because the persona masking this singleton takes on the guise of Renaissance man or woman. It is more the mark of the dabbler who is afraid to get too deeply into any one thing lest he or she loose the right to choose other equally appealing alternatives. These are not real alternatives though; they are simply escape hatches.

The Stimulus Nemesis is an inner nag, constantly critical and incessantly fault-finding. Anything one says to a person with a Stimulus Nemesis is apt to be taken as a slight and is equally apt to be met with resentment. People with stimulus singletons are socially thin-skinned. Their personae are constructed to help them avoid real interpersonal contact. They hear what they want to hear and see what they prefer to see but they are often deliberately avoidant of what is really going on in their environments.

All information from the external world and the social world begins as stimulus. It is new and it is unfamiliar. The stimulus part of personality is the part most exposed to the immediate situation and most active in the moment. People with Stimulus Nemeses try to fend off the moment and avoid its impact. The moment threatens to inundate them with more information than they can handle.

Resistance to the moment and protection against it leads to odd attitudes about time. The Stimulus Nemesis appears in daily life as procrastination. Putting things off until the last possible minute allows people with stimulus singletons to perform below the level of their real capability and still feel good about what they do. Whatever they produce, they produce under duress. Therefore, no one should take their products as evidence of their true talents. Any criticism of their work is depersonalized since they always could have done much better if they had only had more time.

The Stimulus Nemesis is born in a moment of social exposure. Some event shows the person at his or her worst. It is a "No exit" situation in which the person feels cornered, trapped, embarrassed, and persecuted. Sometimes the triggering event involves the apparently arbitrary loss of a status that was originally unearned. The feelings of the Stimulus Nemesis begin with "They had no right..." and end with the determination to avoid any future exposure. The Stimulus Nemesis is a deeply angry nemesis bent not on revenge but on exclusion and escape.

The things in life that most people take for minor irritations are major hassles for people with Stimulus Nemeses. This is due to stimulus singleton people's general lack of self-discipline. For all their apparent diversity of interests, people with Stimulus Nemeses have great difficulty getting anything off the ground. They give up too frequently and too easily when faced with opposition and obstacles. The Stimulus Nemesis is the constant seeker of the easy out, the free ride, the handout and the unearned reward. People with stimulus singletons must exhaust all paths of least resistance before they tackle anything in earnest.

Because the Stimulus Nemesis is hurt and resentful, people with stimulus singletons are uncooperative. Sometimes they are deliberately cruel to punish others who appear to have caused the alienation they feel. Since they are separated from people in general by a wide gulf of angry feelings, they tend to cement this alienation by incorporation of elements of differentness, secretiveness or well-concealed superiority into their personae. Since they are angry, they are not really interested in other people at all. They tell themselves that it is just too much trouble to get acquainted or involved so they pass the entire responsibility for arousing and maintaining social interest to others. Others are supposed to involve them. Above all, others are supposed to take all the social risks.

If the Stimulus Nemesis is quick to avoid contact with the moment, it is equally quick to place demands on the moment. Of the four manifestations of the nemesis within personality, the Stimulus Nemesis has the lowest tolerance for frustration and makes the highest demands on life. The stimulus nemesis wants what it wants when it wants it. Though it uses tactics of delay for itself, it will not stand for delay when its own needs are aroused.

The message behind the Stimulus Nemesis can be summed up in one sentence: I can do as I please when I please and no one has the right to stop me.

The Love Nemesis

The prevailing emotional tone of the singleton love planet is the sense of being outcast, alone, cut off from support and separated from pleasure and happiness as though by an invisible wall. People with singleton love planets feel compelled to bridge the gap they feel toward significant others by being especially warm, winning and emotionally expressive. They are often labelled "emotional" because their feelings surface readily and are rarely concealed. They show their pleasure or their pain openly and can be carried away easily if they have any reinforcement from others. This can be particularly difficult for men since they are socially conditioned to avoid displays of feeling. The Love Nemesis often drives a man to very rigid persona-oriented behavior since it is far more acceptable for a man to appear strong and important (the Growth Persona), charming and sociable (the Stimulus Persona) or successful and capable (the Security Persona).

The emotional display of the Love Nemesis is quite deceptive. Through the persona, the Love Nemesis attempts to strike a bargain with important others, a bargain implying the love nemesis person should never feel bad or disappointed or unhappy. It is a bargain of which the partner is not aware, however, so the partner becomes the disappointer, the let down, the spoiler. The Love Nemesis begins its bargain with the familiar, "If you loved me you wouldn't..." and can complete this demand in a hundred ways.

The love singleton is the paradox of hidden dependence courting others to depend on it and masked sadness parading about as cheer, sweetness and good will.

It is the mark of instant enthusiasm or reinforcement that is, underneath, ambivalent and noncommittal. People with love singletons form relationships that feed their personae but not their real feelings; then they force themselves to continue in such relationships because they do not want to admit to living an emotional lie.

People with Love Nemeses wake up one day to find that they despise their work or they feel nothing whatsoever for their mate or they have made commitments about which they literally do not care. The shock of feeling nothing at all when they expect to feel and to feel intensely cannot be overestimated. Nothingness is a powerful emotion, a yawning hollow chasm, deep but empty.

The Love Nemesis is itself born of a situation of disappointment but it is the person with the Love Nemesis who feels that he or she has disappointed others. There is guilt and sadness over not living up to some expectation (generally quite an unreasonable expectation) and the Love Nemesis person tries ever after to achieve an overly-idealized image of self-projected happiness. The Love Nemesis is, deep inside, a sort of secret apology for some imagined wrong. The external symptoms are hyper-conscientiousness and hyper-seriousness.

Individuals with love singletons take other people's expressions of discontent or disfavor personally. If there is emotional strain, they have somehow caused it or have, at least, fallen victim to it. They have a very low tolerance for any negative display of feeling primarily because they take emotional stress in their environment as a sign of personal failure. They must be the ones to pour oil on the troubled waters; they must be the ones to soothe the hurt; they must unruffle any ruffled feathers.

The weight of the constant inner pressure to project contentment, to inspire passion, to be happy, is a burden that is simply unbearable. When the persona, whatever its guise, stops tap dancing for the rest of the world, the Love Nemesis strikes in the form of swift and sometimes shattering disillusion. What the person has and what the person thought he or she had are not one and the same. What the person is and what the person hopes to be differ. The Love Nemesis, above all else, is a hidden wedge that quietly but inevitably separates the person from perceived sources of comfort and consolation. It delights in false hope and its elusive goals are precisely that. The Love Nemesis seems bent on making the person accept pain as a part of life and suffering, particularly emotional suffering, as inevitable. It is the persona's denial of pain, however, that powers the Love Nemesis and separates the love singleton person from inner satisfaction.

Any nemesis is nothing more than the person. It is the person who constantly tries to balance the scales of life and integrate the missing element of personality. If the nemesis did not wear such a dark and threatening face, if it did not evoke such painful feelings, the integration would be simple. But the nemesis exists as a secret within. The longer one attempts to keep the secret, the darker and more damaging the secret seems to be. It is a magical secret that, once told, has the power to make friends turn their backs, lovers depart, importance vanish, and success slip through the fingers like water.

F. Scott Fitzgerald captures the essence of the nemesis in *Tender is the Night:* "One writes of scars healed, a loose parallel to the pathology of the skin, but there is no such thing in the life of an individual. There are open wounds, shrunk sometimes to the size of a pinprick, but wounds still. The marks of suffering are more comparable to the loss of a finger, or of the sight of an eye. We may not miss them, either, for one minute in a year, but if we should there is nothing to be done about it."[13]

There is nothing one can do about the nemesis directly. Doing is, in fact, the core of the problem. The more the person does to even the scales, the more the scales seem to tilt. The nemesis does not yield to action. Nor does it yield to reason. It yields only to acceptance.

The nemesis need not persist since it gets its force from the persona. To remove the mask is to cast light on the nemesis. Since the nemesis's secrets thrive in darkness, willing self-exposure deprives it of its strength. This means choosing to be vulnerable. Vulnerability and self-exposure are not easy choices. The psyche has other choices that deliberately keep the nemesis in the dark, the ego satisfied and the persona in place. We will explore these alternative self-protective measures in the next two chapters.

If we think of the personality as a journey and of living as travelling, the trip is circular. It starts with self. It ends with self. The end is in the beginning. Between the self of the beginning and the self of the ending stand the ego and the persona. We should not think of them as barriers, however. Without the ego and the persona there might be no trip at all. Nothing ventured, nothing learned. And no destination.

This trinity of being, the self, the ego and the persona, are reminiscent of a children's game:

Paper covers rock.

The ego emerges from the self. It is alive with awareness and recognition. True, it obscures the self to some degree, but it can say "I feel who I am."

Scissors cut paper. The persona emerges from the ego. Now the ego itself is obscured. But the persona can look at other people and announce, "This is who I am."

Rock smashes scissors.

The nemesis shatters the persona's illusions and the game comes full circle. The self triumphs and experiences a homecoming.

8 Divided Personalities

Henrik Ibsen's drama *Ghosts* is a psychological study of life lived on the defensive, of secrecy, of self-protection and self-defeat. Ibsen's characters personify the facets of the psyche well. The proper Reverend Manders speaks for the persona. He insists that appearances are important. "Under no circumstances have we the right to offend the public." If Manders lives in ignorance of the play's darker undercurrents, his counterpart nemesis, the lame carpenter Engstrand, does not. Engstrand is a perfect nemesis, a drunk whose penchant for setting mysterious fires brings the play's long-kept secrets to light. Fittingly, Engstrand the nemesis operates by appealing to Manders's vanity and propriety. Manders, the persona, defends Engstrand and excuses his weaknesses.

Between Manders's arrogance and Engstrand's veiled threat stands *Ghost's* central character, Helen Alving. Her mission is protection. She has sought protection from Manders but he gives her a role to play and insists that she play it. She chooses, instead, to protect Manders in his image, protect her dead husband's reputation, protect her son from the family's sordid inheritance, protect her young charge Regina from her supposed father Engstrand, and if at all possible, protect herself.

Midway through the second act, Mrs. Alving concludes that the courageous thing to do is to tell the truth and take its consequences. Manders persuades her that ideals are more important than truth, that it is kindest to continue the old falsehoods, that it would be cruel to shatter long-held illusions. Helen Alving voices much of the play's conflict. Ultimately, her protective maneuvers are for naught. At the play's conclusion, she meets with a dilemma and finds herself in a lose-lose position.

If we split our own psyches into persona and nemesis, we too develop protective mechanisms. It is not enough to choose a role, a mask, a false face. It is not enough to push the nemesis into the background of personality. We must, if we adopt a persona, protect its image and prove that the mask is real. We must, additionally, protect ourselves from the conflicts and dilemmas of real human life if we are to live in the unreal world of the persona's perfect image.

The persona's form and the nemesis's threat take their distinctive shapes from the need pattern of an individual's personality. So do self-protective tactics. A Growth Persona, for instance, masks those conflicts and dilemmas specifically involved in growth processes. A Security Persona covers a different set of life conflicts. Both conflict and dilemma are parts of life, inherent in the clash of inner needs and native to the sometimes contradictory demands of daily experience. Self-protection might be termed the art of conflict avoidance and the science of dilemma denial.

Inner psychological conflicts come from the opposing qualities of the four basic needs. Each need poses its distinct demands. The demands of one need are often at odds with the requirements of other needs. Some degree of inner conflict is thus a fact of psychological life and the self gestalt is a bundle of conflicting interests. However, self-actualization takes the conflicts inherent in the psyche and makes alternatives. Where there is conflict, there is choice. Capacity to choose and to generate alternatives keeps the personality flexible, dynamic and creative.

The six basic temperament trait measurements allow us to analyze the impact of the various need conflicts and dilemmas in a personality pattern. Each trait's strength comes from the combined weight of its two component needs. In Chapter 4, we used the traits as synthesis tools. We were concerned only with the shared qualities common to each trait's paired needs. In analysis, by contrast, we study the differences between the two needs composing each trait, differences that give rise to an innate conflict or dilemma. Conflict and dilemma in turn lead to specific self-protective tactics designed to avoid the experience of conflict or dilemma. In analysis, the pattern of temperament traits indicates the person's characteristic pattern of defenses.

Traits Hypothetic and Empiric, Traits Organic and Panoramic all indicate basic conflicts native to the clash between their component needs. Traits Hypothetic and Empiric deal with meaning, intellectual frame of reference and situational context. Their related defenses are intellectual defenses. Traits Organic and Panoramic, respectively, point out defensive attempts to strengthen the self vis-a-vis other people or to weaken other people's impact on the self. Since each of these four temperament traits and their related defensive tactics indicate attempts at conflict resolution or avoidance, we will explore them as a group in the next chapter.

In one sense, the four Traits Hypothetic, Empiric, Organic, and Panoramic might be said to have objective defenses because their dynamic, conflictful natures push them out into the world. Defenses springing from these traits are defenses against other people or against the life situation itself.

Defenses related to the remaining two Traits Spontaneous and Continuous are qualitatively different. These defenses protect the person from himself or herself. These defenses come not from conflicts but from dilemmas.

No one likes the experience of dilemma. It shows in our everyday language. People are between the devil and the deep blue sea or between a rock and a hard place. We know that dilemma means great discomfort. While a conflict produces conflict between warring parts that are usually easy to see, a dilemma is an inner tug of war between elements of the psyche that appear hidden. Dilemmas, because they are elusive, produce ambiguity.

A conflict is like a teeter-totter. One end goes up while the other goes down. Imagine, instead, a teeter-totter constructed so that both ends go up or both ends go down. Any attempt to raise one end of this machine also raises the other end. To lower one end is to see the other end sink as well. Riding on this machine is difficult because one always gets more than one bargained for and it's awfully hard to get off.

The feeling of a dilemma state is awkwardness mixed with confusion. A state of dilemma is a state of perplexity. Struggle only intensifies the dilemma.

Recent psychological researchers use the term double bind to express the damned-if-you-do, damned-if-you-don't life dilemma. The symptoms of dilemma are described by this systems theory concept: behavior vacillates, moods swing, attitudes oscillate and the whole shifts to an ever more extreme position.

Extreme is the operative word for all we are about to discuss. At times it may seem that the subject matter in this chapter is a dilemma in itself. The personality qualities related to Traits Spontaneous and Continuous represent the highs and the lows of human existence. Here are stunning feats of endurance and triumph. Here as well are the absolute depths of despair. Here are the abstract capacities that mean human progress and social advance. Here too are raw cruelty and destruction. Human beings are, after all, the only creatures who kill for their abstractions, their crosses, their flags, their philosophies.

Conflict does not appear to have the destructive power of dilemma. Neither is it so creative. Dilemmas are felt most keenly by those whose strongest trait is either Trait Spontaneous or Trait Continuous. In other words, by those whose two strongest needs combine Growth and Stimulus or combine Security and Love. These groups as a whole have a far greater incidence of self-destructive behavior, of drug use, alcoholism, hypochondria, nervous breakdown and suicide than do the remaining trait groupings. However, these traits are common in the birth patterns of artists, giving us a clue that the solution to dilemma must involve the creative act for it takes an act of creativity to perceive the dilemma at all.

Will Versus Transcendence

In the face of dilemma, there are two ways to function. We can attempt to overpower the dilemma through the act of will or we can transcend the dilemma through the act of creativity. The act of will is the commonly preferred choice because it is immediate. We can always push matters and attempt to override problems by sheer stubborn force. We get the immediate satisfaction of subduing a difficulty, not to mention a certain pride in flexing our psychological muscles. The act of will, when it is successful, raises our self-evaluation. The difficulty with any solution based on will is the difficulty involved in choosing the immediate gratification of temporary problem conquest over the real resolution of problem solving. Ultimately, things are put off till another day and there will be another test of will and another and another requiring ever more dramatic displays of what passes for inner strength.

Too often the act of will is forced bravery: the captain goes down with the ship. Though all the flags are flying, sunk is sunk. Beneath it all there is an essential split. Will is the captain, head held high, vanity preserved, bathed in an aura of self-control but will is also the self that knows it is sinking and feels that drowning is imminent. The sinking self wants very much to swim, to survive. But the captain does not allow it.

Carl Jung writes that people have an archetypal urge to dichotomize, to see things in good/bad, black/white, hot/cold terms. Jung's psychology emphasizes polarities and Jung himself states, "I see in all that happens the play of opposites." Once we make such splits in our perception of the world, of other people and of ourselves, will becomes necessary. If we see ourselves, as psychologist Harry Stack Sullivan suggests, split into a Good Me and a Bad Me then it is only through sheer willpower that we express the Good Me and override the Bad. Such splits lead to the double level behaviors and mixed signals so characteristic of both Traits Spontaneous and Continuous when they are emphasized in a personality pattern. Traits Spontaneous and Continuous grapple with the dilemmas they contain by seizing on black/white opposites. The opposites do not, however, truly state the dilemma. Opposites avoid dilemma and defend against it precisely because they give the will something to work with. The experience of real dilemma is the undoing of the will. When a Trait Spontaneous or Trait Continuous person lets go of will and the sense of self-control it provides, he or she experiences anxiety but it is only at this point that the inner problem can be solved creatively. If will meets difficulty with action, creativity meets it with acceptance. What will can only perpetuate, creativity can transcend.

Though Jung states that people are bound to think in terms of oppositions, he also says it is necessary to unite the very opposites people create. If the personality is to be actualized in any way, it must be whole. Jung terms the process of making whole transcendence. Jung is not the only writer to insist that people must resolve the opposites they make. Anthropologist Ruth Benedict notes the necessity of synchrony. Through synchrony each pole of an opposition brings out the best in its opposite. The lose/lose proposition posed by any good/evil split must be transformed into a win/win proposition that uses both elements of a dilemma to achieve a higher creative end.

People certainly do not like to think of themselves as evil. In the rush to be human, they try to forget their animal roots. Then they rush to be spiritual or ethical or religious and try to forget they are human. This split is most dangerous to the highly Spontaneous or Continuous person. When people with these traits conclude they are superhuman, they make the ultimate split between the ideal (which is good) and the mundane (which is bad). They claim the lofty heights of abstract thoughts at the expense of concrete satisfactions. They frustrate themselves in the name of self-control or spiritual evolution. They say all the right words but they cannot make their lives fit their words.

If people do not like to think of themselves as evil, they do take a special delight in thinking of themselves as good. This is the trap of the Spontaneous and Continuous elements within each of us. Good moves toward the ideal. Once people embrace the idea of the ideal then they look through the lens of their dichotomizing traits for the opposite of ideal. Unfortunately, consciously or not, they find the opposite. It is the real. This is the heart of the defenses related to Traits Continuous and Spontaneous. These defenses protect the person's image in his or her own eyes. They allow the person to see himself or herself idealistically while at the same time preventing him or her from being real, from being simply human.

Regression and the Inner Child

Traits Spontaneous and Continuous, as we noted in Chapter 4, relate to the experience of time. The time experience of these traits is itself a dichotomy. On the one hand, Traits Spontaneous and Continuous are the real age. They grow through the accumulation of actual life experiences. On the other hand, these traits know all that the person has ever been, either through the Trait Continuous process of recall or the Trait Spontaneous process of recognizing the past alive in the present. For the former, time is linear and for the latter it is circular but both Spontaneous and Continuous people are, in essence, time travelers.

Every age that a person has ever been is woven into the fabric of these traits. This includes the inner child or immature version of the self. Under pressure and during times of self-defense, the inner child is particularly likely to emerge. A defensive child-state lacks the charm of childhood. Instead, it is little in a world where everything else is big. Hence it is afraid and will do just about anything to not feel afraid.

In psychoanalytic theory, Freud proposes that people return to child states as a defense. This he terms regression. Regression is a retreat to an early stage of development and it is accompanied by childish behavior. Freud felt that people regress to stages that were, for them, times of satisfaction or freedom from pressure, anxiety, or frustration.

Each behavior mode indicated by the birth pattern is related to a specific stage of development. Self-protective actions characteristic of Traits Spontaneous and Continuous always involve a retreat to the child form of the person's preferred behavior. The childish behavioral qualities and attitudes are generally quite open. An observer cannot fail to note them. This is the irony of the Spontaneous and Continuous self-protective devices. They are both the strongest and the weakest defenses. They are strong in the sense that they prevent any other from dealing effectively with the person using a regressive, childish protective mode. They are weak in the sense that they are so visible. The other knows quite well that interaction has ceased. The other knows the Spontaneous or Continuous person is defending rather than relating. These defenses, then, serve only one purpose. They keep the person from clearly perceiving himself or herself. They fool no one else.

When a strong Trait Spontaneous or Trait Continuous appears in a birth pattern emphasizing the Strategic mode, the person regresses to the related developmental stage, the school years. Most often we would label this defensive behavior adolescent since it is marked by stubborn willfulness contrasted with giving-in tendencies. It is blindly conforming or flagrantly non-conformist. It is stuffy and prudish and self-involved one minute and, if this does not achieve the desired end, it becomes wanton and unabashedly self-promoting.

Since all defenses related to Traits Spontaneous and Continuous spring from the tendency to form opposing viewpoints, all defenses related to these traits are polar. The pole that works, i.e., that protects the person from perceiving himself/herself clearly, is the pole the person uses. Should a behavior cease to protect the person from feeling bad about the self, the person will simply switch to the other pole. Such quick-change artistry frustrates others against whom the defense is directed. The self is thus always in control in a childish sort of way because it perpetually manipulates to keep the other off balance.

The strategic type would, for instance, conform until the other "bought" the role or image of conformity and then turn, suddenly, to shock the other. The other is perpetually unsure and forced to respond in equally contradictory ways. The self grabs the lead. It is defensive but it seems to be saying the best defense is a strong offense. The strategist is particularly adept at controlling. It is not regressed so far that it cannot fake some image of relative maturity, thus it is somewhat more subtle in its manipulations than are the other two behavior modes. Though all regressive, manipulative defenses pride themselves on their will and capacity to direct the defensive interchange, the strategic type thinks itself particularly clever.

Strong defensive behaviors in the service of Trait Spontaneous or Trait Continuous are more clearly childish. They involve an odd combination of forcefulness and fantasy. Pride and vanity are clearly in evidence. A bold show of courage to the point of sheer foolhardiness might turn into timid backing away. This moving against behavior mode in the service of self-protection is self-indulgent yet begs to be indulged. When indulged by any other, its narcissistic, self-involved arrogance is clear. If the strong behavior succeeds in controlling the situation, it is frequently through the two-year-old's penchant for nay-saying. This is the back-handed win whose only goal is to delight in the frustration of other people. One wins by default, by making the other lose.

"Moving toward" defensive behavior manipulates through apparent shows of sincerity and sensitivity when in the grip of Spontaneous or Continuous defensive patterns. This sensitivity is just a fraud to put others off guard. Who could possibly hurt such a fine human being? Who could possibly doubt the word of someone so obviously caring and concerned? But all modes of self-protection related to all traits serve the purpose of avoiding some difficulty the person does not want to face. Hence protection is always self-serving and the sensitivity displayed defensively in this behavior is sensitivity toward the self masquerading as concern for the other.

Sensitive behavior in extremely defensive instances deserves the label infantile. It is grossly optimistic one minute, thoroughly pessimistic the next. It is reminiscent of the infant in the crib crying for a toy, then throwing the toy away only to beg for another. And more than any other behavior mode, the moving toward sensitive mode childishly exploits others, their resources and the situation to serve the self's immediate childish whims. In short, the individual defends in a framework that predates the awareness that other people have their own needs and wishes and desires.

When defensive and childish, the strong behavior mode does recognize desires in other people. The question is whose desires will win out, whose will be satisfied. Mutuality is out of the question. To successfully defend involves elevating the self and doing away with the other simultaneously. The strategic behavior mode recognizes desires in others and uses this awareness as a tool for defense. Other people can be manipulated precisely

[193]

because they do have needs and wishes and the strategic-behavior protective devices are subtle enough to make other people think they will actually get what they want from the strategist.

The remaining Trait Organic, Panoramic, Empiric and Hypothetic defenses all differ in their expression when displayed in actual behavior. They, too, have their strategic, strong and sensitive protective versions. What makes Traits Spontaneous and Continuous different than the remaining four traits is their clearly regressive impact on a person's overt actions.

Defensive regression brings out the childish quality in each behavior mode when serving Spontaneous or Continuous protective ends. It is destructive because defense itself is destructive of any real satisfaction. The split is complete. The person can feel safe or feel gratified and, due to fear, opts for safety. All regression, however, is not childish. All expressions of Traits Continuous and Spontaneous are not defensive. If there is a willful, spoiled, frightened child within each of us capable of turning these traits into defensive manipulations, there is also a wondrous, naive, joyful child within us whose very innocence sees all life in instinctively creative terms.

While regression in the service of self-protection makes us childish, regression in the service of self-actualization makes us childlike. The former is self-defeating; the latter is infinitely creative. Defensive regression springs from the Good Me/Bad Me split in self-perception. Creative regression, by contrast, resolves the anxiety-producing splits through providing a totally fresh appreciation of the life circumstances. If childishness makes for problems, childlikeness provides the means for their solution.

Psychoanalysis uses the term "regression in the service of the ego" to indicate the playful psychic state from which creativity springs. Traits Spontaneous and Continuous do, as already noted, appear at high levels of impact in the birth patterns of highly creative people in both the arts and the sciences. To regress in a creative way is to reverse time and use the child state to play with ideas and feelings and actions. The major difference between defensive regression, which is childish in its immediate wish to avoid discomfort and frustration, and creative regression, which is childlike for the sheer pleasure of being so, is the time element. Defense cares only for right now. Playfulness is timeless.

The Trait Spontaneous or Trait Continuous person who has ready access to the inner child-state can use this state to better explore and understand problems. Creative regression is optimistic. So much so that the solutions it presents can be good or bad and the person using the child state in problem solving can accept either result. The results are not the goal so much as the playful attempts to achieve them. A regressive review of old feelings and situations can either defensively justify self-protective acts or creatively expand the appreciation of self.

The Trait Spontaneous/Trait Continuous Duality

Every temperament trait comes from the pairing of two basic needs. Every trait emphasizes some quality which the paired needs have in common. Growth and Stimulus Needs combine to form Trait Spontaneous. Both needs share the quality of outgoing energy release. This expansive quality extends the boundaries of the personality claiming ever greater portions of the world and bringing ever greater territory into the self's domain. The Security and Love Needs combine to form Trait Continuous. Both needs share the stabilizing quality of energy accumulation, deepening the personality and giving it a profound rootedness in its own inner nature.

The shared qualities which form Trait Spontaneous and Trait Continuous differentiate these particular traits from the four remaining traits because the shared qualities characteristic of Traits Spontaneous and Continuous are more primitive, more archetypal. They are qualities symbolic of the personality's very core, hence their far greater capacity for both destruction and creation. Traits Spontaneous and Continuous are, in a sense, more instinctual or it may be more accurate to say that people with these traits feel the basic tides of instinctual need more keenly than most.

The outgoing Trait Spontaneous's instinctual equivalent is aggression if aggression is defined as Frederick Perls defines it. Perls believes that aggression is nothing more than the force within life that breaks down the barriers between the individual and potential need satisfiers. So defined, aggression is the force that overcomes life obstacles and it is the basis for constructive, expansive mastery of life problems. It is not an inherently violent force. Its destruction is simply a de-structuring, a capacity to take a thing apart and examine its elements so that only the productive parts of any experience will be incorporated into the personality's whole. Aggression, as it relates to Trait Spontaneous's primal expression, differs from annihilation or the wish to obliterate, wipe out, reduce to nothing.

The incorporative Trait Continuous's instinctual equivalent is sexual in the Freudian sense of the term. By sexual instincts, Freud means bodily pleasure in a rather broad sense and he compares the sexual instinct to hunger and the taking of nourishment. Perls opts for the hunger urge directly to define these contrasting elements in the psyche.[14] Trait Continuous symbolizes the deep longing or hunger for oneness through the assimilation of Trait Spontaneous's de-structured elements into a unified whole.

The very depth of the qualities symbolized by Traits Spontaneous and Continuous may in itself make them more difficult to express in constructive ways. The instinctual element underlying each certainly provides a firm basis for good/evil dichotomizing by modern civilizations whose attitudes toward both sex and aggression are ambivalent at best. We have inherited a moral tradition bent on denying the open expression of either and a culture that cannot wait to see mayhem on the nightly news followed by the mindless humor of sexist situation-comedies. It may be inevitable that those individuals most closely attuned to their own inner primal currents suffer most keenly the discontent and anxiety humanity builds into its own cultural dilemmas and civilized dichotomies. Trait Continuous and Trait Spontaneous people are encouraged by society to be too civilized for their own good.

These traits work to the benefit of those individuals whose intellects emerge from their deepest nature, whose abstractions evolve from what is most concrete and native. The truly destructive and self-destructive who have these traits have pitted their minds against their bodies, their heads against their hearts, their ideas against their instincts. They are forever embattled because they are split to the core.

Otto Rank, an early follower of Sigmund Freud, frames the basic distinction signified by Traits Spontaneous and Continous in terms of life urges and death urges. To Rank, life or the Spontaneous element in humanity is the force that separates, makes individual and distinguishes the self from all others. Death or the Continuous element in human nature is the urge toward union, toward fusion and dependency. Andras Angyal distinguishes autonomy or aloofness from surrender or dependency. David Bakan divides the basic human expressions into *agency* or active manipulation of life experience versus *communion* or unity with other people, the environment or ideas.

Piaget, the noted developmental psychologist, defines two processes essential to learning. Through assimilation, or taking in of information, the child incorporates ideas. Through accommodation, the mental framework expands. The combined forces of assimilation and accommodation are necessary in any coping behavior. The four traits we will explore in the next chapter, Traits Organic, Panoramic, Empiric and Hypothetic all combine assimilation with accommodation. All characterize coping functions. Traits Spontaneous and Continuous, by contrast, do not. Pure accommodation, the equivalent of Trait Spontaneous, is seen in a child's imitative, copying behaviors. Pure assimilation, the equivalent of Trait Continuous, is seen in the child's play, fantasies and dreams. Great works of art are products that copy the artist's inner childlike responses or the artist's playful dreams made visible. Destructive behaviors are, by contrast, childish last-ditch efforts by people who feel they cannot cope.

Trait Continuous, The Security/Love Dilemma, and Communion

Every defense protects the self from something. Every instance of self-defeating behavior begins in a moment of perceived threat. The traits we will examine in the next chapter all deal with sources of threat that are outside the self: the power of other people and the vagaries of the environment. For Traits Continuous and Spontaneous, however, the threat is internal and lies in the self's own impulses. External threats come and go. Powerful others are here when they are here but when they are not immediately present they are gone completely. The same is true of an environmental or situational threat. Some life incident is troubling but when the incident is over, it too is gone. Inner impulses, by contrast, are ever-present. People can move away from a troubled environment, they can avoid troubling people, but they cannot escape themselves. To defend the self from itself is to defend constantly.

Basically satisfied people do not defend regardless of their temperaments and their specific individual traits. The presence of strong Traits Continuous or Spontaneous in birth patterns are not in and of themselves indications of difficulty. They ask the question "Does this individual live creatively or destructively?" but *they do not answer it*. To confuse the symbolic with the real at this point in our discussion is to fall into the very defenses we are about to discuss.

The defenses characteristic of any trait relate directly to the challenges involved in satisfying its component needs. Trait Continuous combines the Love and Security needs and is thus symbolic of both father and mother. It signifies family and parents and the profound dependence into which we are all born. Trait Continuous defenses are, consequently, defenses *against* a pervasive inner sense of dependency. They defend against the urge for communion.

The origin of dependence anxieties lies in the fact of human biological nature. Actual physical growth brings about a series of inevitable separations. People mature through the stages of life described by Eriksen and Millon and measured by the birth pattern's behavior quadrangles. The pleasures of infancy are the pleasures of warmth, closeness, nurturance, suckling. This earliest human dependence indicated by the sensitivity quadrangle and the sensory-attachment phase of life ends when the infant, by virtue of physical growth, becomes a child. Weaning is essential but it brings with it the separation from the breast and from the pleasure of the intimate presence of the all-gratifying other.

New pleasures emerge to take the place of the old pleasures. In the strong sensorimotor-autonomy phase of life, children develop rich resources of fantasy. They can play at life precisely because they are dependent on their families. They can let loose their imaginations because they are within the circle of the family's protective care. Maturation, again, brings this stage of development to a close. The brain itself grows and changes and the freedom of fantasy and play makes way for new mental abilities. The second stage ends with the second major life separation. The child leaves the comfort and protection of the family for the unknown world of school.

In the final strategic intracortical-initiative phase of development, the child depends on the culture to a great degree. Caring involves a great many others, both teachers and peers. The school environment is also a protective environment. The child gradually learns the life skills essential for independent adult life but these skills are learned and practiced in a protective environment that does not actually thrust the child into the adult world. Throughout the school years, the child is practicing adult skills outside the realm of the real pressures of true independence and individual responsibility. The strategic phase ends gradually but dramatically and again by the sheer inevitability of biological growth. Puberty brings with it the beginnings of adult biology and the dawning of the capacity to be a parent on whom others depend rather than a child who depends on others. Puberty not only casts the child out of the Eden of childhood dependence, it casts the child out of the once-familiar body on which the child could depend.

The birth pattern's preferred behavior mode indicates the separation that was most threatening to the individual as well as the nature of the dependency satisfaction which was lost. Loss of closeness, of protection or of innocence, each is painful in its own distinct way. In an adult, specific perceptions can evoke a similar sense of loss and separation from the sources of satisfaction and the comfort of union. Trait Continuous defenses defend against these perceptions. Perception of a gap between achieved successes and higher aspirations, a distance between actuality and expectation, or a chasm between available resources and goals all arouse fear of dependence in Continuous people.

The core anxiety-producing split is between the wish and the reality coupled with a perceived lack of means to bridge the experienced distance. Trait Continuous anxiety emerges when people feel split apart from where they very much want to be *and* feel lacking in the ability to reach their destination. "You can't get there from here" is just a funny old adage when the farmer says these words to the traveller who is hopelessly lost. The "you can't get there from here" experience in not funny; it is terrifying.

Trait Continuous emphasizes the ends at the expense of the means. Therefore, the means easily appear too weak or ineffective to reach desired ends. The defensive solution to Trait Continuous anxiety sets a process in motion, a process which splits the person's self-perception in his or her own mind. The Trait Continuous defense protects the person from experiencing the anxiety of basic dependence in order to inflate the perception of personal agency. If the person successfully denies the urge to depend, then the available means to satisfy the desired goals seem magically to inflate.

The process begins with a repression of the dependency, shoving it into the ground of consciousness. Next the agency or sense of independence is elevated to a perceived new importance. The split is no longer real to the person whose new focus is the figure of his or her own independence.

The abstract/concrete split characteristic of both Traits Continuous and Spontaneous is a split between the verbal and the behavioral. Continuous people are verbally independent and constantly interpret their experience to enhance this abstract sense of agency. The dependence and the urge for union show in Continuous people's behavior, however. As a result, they send mixed signals. Their behavior says they need communion, sharing, union, comfort, yet their words insist they are independent free spirits, alone and happy to be alone.

Defensive manipulation is essential if Trait Continuous people are to avoid dependence anxiety while maintaining the illusion of self-sufficiency. This is especially clear in the troubled person who uses drugs to stamp out the feelings of inner discomfort. In this case, the independent me is the Bad Me. Agency and the image of separateness mean playing out a Bad Me role. The drug user's drugs are a symbol of independence yet the addict's drug use inevitably puts the family in the position of rescuer. A family gets a phone call. Their son has been arrested for drug possession. They arrive at the jail and bail out their son. "I didn't ask you to come," he says, preserving his image of independence and avoiding the realization that his real behavior left his family no acceptable alternative.

Every defensive Trait Continuous attitude plays at this same game. Verbal independence goes hand in hand with behavior that says "I am helpless and needy." Any other person faced with this double level message is also faced with a quandary. To respond to the verbal message and take the Trait Continuous defender at his or her word is game playing. To respond to the clear behavioral cues of dependency is to be manipulated. The Trait Continuous defense never asks for help or comfort or care so if the other gives it the Continuous person feels no personal responsibility for the interchange. Covertly, the dependency is gratified. Overtly, the successful manipulation shores up the weak sense of agency.

Both Traits Spontaneous and Continuous complete their chains of defense with a reaction formation. This is the denial of true feelings through the mechanism of adopting an opposing posture. Reaction formation reverses a person's perception of his or her own feelings.

Continuous people's defenses push the urge for communion into the ground to make the figure of independence stronger. Their abstract verbal independent language denies their covert, dependent behavioral cues. By reaction formation, they come to believe everyone else is dependent on them. Everyone else is so demanding, so clinging, so smothering. Though defensive Continuous people can no longer find the intense feeling of dependency and longing for communion within themselves, it seems stunningly visible in other people. So they shove others away because another's open desire for communion evokes their own unconscious dependency urge and its accompanying anxiety. Continuous people, when defending, verbalize their resentment at what they perceive to be other people's unfair demands on their time, resources, emotions and attention. What they truly, though unconsciously, resent is the thought that someone else's urge for communion might be satisfied while their own deepest longing for merger remains frustrated.

Because Trait Continuous people deny their own intense urges for communion, they suffer what psychoanalyst Otto Rank calls death-fear. Ironically, they come to fear what they need most, the merger with something beyond themselves. They perceive that through merger, they would be swallowed up by another person's apparently stronger personality.

People do not successfully escape their own deepest inner currents. The currents reappear as impulses. In the case of Trait Continuous people who can no longer overtly seek the satisfaction of their Security and Love needs, the impulses are self-indulgent, hedonistic and often sexual. The sexual conquest inflates the perception of agency and independence; the mate, by contrast, evokes anxiety. Defensive Trait Continuous men can feel much greater attraction to a shallow, vain, self-involved and rejecting female than to one who is stable, open and consistent. Trait Continuous women who defend against their own dependency urges seek out fickle, attractive losers and ignore dependable, sincere males. The more unstable the attraction, the better since such relationships avoid the issue of merger and dependency altogether.

Once the urge for communion is repressed it appears in the psyche in the form of an archetype. For the Continuous person it is the archetype of the other, hopelessly idealized and therefore impossible to achieve. It is the illusion of the soul mate, the magical perfect man or flawless woman whose presence will fill the void left by the loss of the self's own deepest possibilities. The archetypal other is an abstraction of the self's wishes and not the wishes themselves; it is flat and one-dimensional. It effectively strips any other on whom it is projected of all human qualities, demands perfection from the other and, eventually, excuses the Trait Continuous person's rejection of the other when the other turns out to be simply human.

Society appears to permit dependence in women and even to encourage it, hence it might be supposed that a man would find it more difficult to deal with an extreme urge for communion than would a woman. This is not, in fact, true. Our social conventions do perpetuate some illusions that make dependence in men appear different from dependence in women. Consider, for instance, the woman in the role of wife and mother married to the man who works on an assembly line in automobile manufacturing. If the woman has no job outside the home, society labels her dependent on her husband. Society labels the husband, by contrast, independent since he has a job.

However, the husband/worker is as dependent on his employer's capacity to provide him with a job as the wife/mother is dependent on her husband's capacity to provide the family with its income. If the automobile plant closes and the husband loses his job his anxiety will not differ from the anxiety his wife would suffer should he abandon his family.

Society does adopt different views of the man and woman in the above situation, views that split apart each person's role, views that are in and of themselves double level messages. In society's eyes, the husband/worker is independent and agentic but his agency exists in name only. He has the illusion of independence but not its substance. The wife, on the other hand, hears the constant social message that she is dependent while she lives every day in the role of wife and mother, a role in which everyone else in the family is heavily dependent on her. She has been culturally conditioned from childhood to satisfy other people's dependency needs and to forgo her own. Society's collective double-level messages exaggerate the dichotomies in both men and women.

Any human being, male or female, who denies the urge for communion is like a plant which tears its roots out of the soil. Both wilt; neither blossoms or bears fruit. Analyst Eric Fromm writes extensively of the profound loneliness of the human being cut off from nature because he or she is cut off from self. The loneliness and rootlessness of modern societies only reflect the private sadnesses of their individual members.

Societies, too, martial the collective aggression denied by their members. Routinely, societies direct this aggression against those individuals who refuse to conform to social archetypes. Periodically, societies direct collective aggression against each other in a Good Society/Bad Society interchange fueled by millions of individual Good Me/Bad Me dichotomies. The rootless loneliness of modern life has its parallel in the faceless anonymity of the masses. If there is death fear, there is life fear. If people do not struggle with their dependence, they struggle with their independence. The frustrations and fears of a dominant Trait Continuous have a mirror opposite in the frustrations and fears of a dominant Trait Spontaneous.

Trait Spontaneous, The Growth/Stimulus Dilemma and Agency

The defenses characteristic of Trait Spontaneous mirror the defenses related to Trait Continuous. At core, they have many similarities. Trait Spontaneous is rooted in human biological nature. It, too, makes the abstract/concrete split. The highly Trait Spontaneous person is as much at war with his or her own deepest impulses as the highly Continuous person. If the battlegrounds are different, the battles are the same.

The aggressive impulses which Trait Spontaneous symbolizes provide the instinct for survival so essential to individuation. The survival urge counters the power of the environment, its complexity, its diversity and its sheer size. The survival urge counters fear.

If human beings are born to dependence, they are born to independence as well. The urge for communion is no more biologically rooted than the urge for agency. Both change through the essential stages of development characteristic of all human growth. The infant, sensitive, life phase with its heavy demand for nurturance is clearly dependent. Infants, however, come prepared to actively take part in their own survival. They cry to signal their hunger; they instinctively nurse when given the breast. The more researchers study infants, the more their studies conclude that infants, though obviously dependent, have a large repertoire of survival skills which they actively use.

The strong phase of childhood sees the onset of more survival skills. The most dramatic of all is the child's ability to talk. Learning to talk quite effectively changes the child's entire world and the way the child interacts with the family. Walking and moving about freely in the world are clear signs that biological agency is increasing.

The strategic school years pose no challenges which the growing youngster is unready to meet with further biological growth. The brain continues to develop and afford the necessary physical means to deal with new, social ends. The brain's growth gives the child the capacity to think in more sophisticated ways.

Clearly, agency changes with the demands of each developmental stage. The survival urge and the biological survival equipment grow up together. Each developmental stage has its fears as well and the capacity to fear may well be a necessary survival tool in and of itself. The infant's fears are inborn. Babies fear the very things that in a primitive environment threaten their existence. Humans are born fearing animals, open spaces, falling, strangers. The baby's cry is the baby's active, agentic counter to these fears for the cry brings help and help means survival.

The fantasy phase of childhood that sees the child's playful imagination enhance its growth also sees the dawn of imaginary fears. Most children go through a stage of having nightmares. This is the age of the boogyman or the fear of going down the drain with the bathwater. These fears move the child to ask questions and the child's growing language capacity gives it the means to counter these new fears. In countering imaginary fears, the child comes to actively know the world in a new way.

The fears of the final developmental phase might be termed social fears or psychological fears. On the one hand, there are the personal fears of differentness, or ineptness or being left out, cut off from one's peers. There are fears borrowed from the culture as well, fear of nuclear war or prejudice or anxiety over career choice, dating, the future. Language skills, social skills, capacity for planning and understanding help to counter these fears.

At every developmental step agency keeps pace with the demand for change in its own deep-rooted biological wisdom. The infant's cry breaks down the barriers of the infant's fear and bridges the gap between its hunger and the other who gives satisfaction. The child's physical growth helps it actively (sometimes literally) break down new barriers in the way of independence. The conceptual mental growth breaks down barriers of complexity and leads toward the acceptance of adult responsibility as the natural culmination of maturation. To Perls, all these changes would be aggressive and the overcoming of these natural barriers would involve aggressive, agentic action. Since aggression in all these forms is natural, why is it so often repressed? Cultural forces and parenting practices seem bent upon doing away with aggressive instincts. The enraged infant is left to scream alone; the child's aggression gets punished; the student's questions, if they are too numerous, elicit only annoyance. The aggressive urges are labeled bad and become part of the Bad Me. Since natural aggression is the natural counterforce to the innate fears of each developmental stage, repressing the means of survival and individuation strips away the sense of agency and leaves only the fear. Hence, Trait Spontaneous people tend, for all their overt lightheartedness, to be deeply fearful people.

Parents and cultures unable to deal effectively with their own aggressive urges will not shape new generations in whom aggression is a positive, useful force. Adults who repress their aggression feel successful when they manage to stamp out aggressive behavior in their children. To stamp it out is easy. To shape it, to mold it effectively into a tool for social survival is difficult and requires the very patience that is lost with the loss of aggressive persistence. The display of Trait Spontaneous's natural aggression in the child who enthusiastically tries over and over again to solve some simple learning problem like tying shoes or getting dressed stands in stark contrast to the behavior of the Trait Spontaneous adult whose repressed aggression does not permit persistence in the face of failure.

Trait Spontaneous defenses evolve in a manner similar to the defenses typical of Trait Continuous. Once the personality is stripped of its aggressive urge to survive, it is dependent on others to keep the fearful world at bay. It is socialized to be sure, but in the worst possible way. The dependency of the Trait Continuous person related to the circle of close relationships does not differ from the dependency of the Trait Spontaneous person upon the collective. The repressed survival urge perpetuates the illusion that the collective is something more than a group of individuals, that the collective has a life of its own quite apart from the lives of its individual members.

The Trait Continuous person struggles against dependency and defends against merger. The Trait Spontaneous person, by contrast, embraces union, fusion and dependence because he or she has given up the means to individuate and to survive alone.

When Trait Spontaneous people repress their aggressive urges and deny their own individuation, they too face anxiety. Their anxiety is aroused in the distance between the components of their dominant trait. The gap between Growth and Stimulus is the gap between the private and the public self-images. The self-concept is shaped from personal assessment of actions combined with the feedback received from other people. A significant gap between self-perceptions and social feedback causes extreme anxiety. In one classic study of social influence, classmates conspired to make an individual feel ill. "How do you feel?" one classmate asked. "I feel fine," the guinea pig replied. "Gee, you look a little pale. Are you sure you're all right?" said another person to the guinea pig. "You really don't look well." The experiment had the predictable results. The person reinforced in the role of sickness eventually began to feel ill. Though there are strong individual differences in the degree of suggestibility, no person is geared to resist social feedback completely.

The aggressive forces of real individuation, once repressed, elevate the ends or goal objectives. Fame, success, awards, honors, acclaim all go to those who achieve goals the collective deems important. Once the elements of individuation are repressed, these are the things most deeply craved because they appear to signify communion. If one is famous or successful, one will be loved and one will be respected. One will rest easy in the protective bosom of the collective.

The defensive solution to Trait Spontaneous anxiety splits the individual's perceptions exactly as the Trait Continuous perceptions are split. Now, however, it is the aggressive urge essential to agency that is repressed, thereby elevating the perception of communion, union and freedom from fear. If the Trait Spontaneous person successfully denies aloneness and agency, then the magical goals he or she seemed unable to reach alone appear close at hand. The boon of society conferred on the hero or heroine is bought with the currency of compliance.

So the Trait Spontaneous person fails to see the link between his or her ideals and actions. The ideals, goals, drives, ends exist on the abstract or verbal level. The capacity to plan and outline the map of progress is often highly developed. The Trait Spontaneous person has big dreams and appears for all the world to have the enthusiasm to get there. When one looks closely, however, the enthusiasm for the final state or the ideal goal is not accompanied by an equal enthusiasm for the concrete work required to reach the goal. Instead, there is a naive expectation of maximal reward for minimal effort.

Trait Spontaneous, too, is manipulative in its defensive manifestation. It offers love, respect, support and concern to others with all the overt sincerity it can muster. Others, in return, are supposed to act as the agents by which the Spontaneous person approaches the desired goals. At the appropriate moment (when the hard work is over and the obstacles have been removed) the other should step aside and allow the Spontaneous person to bask in the glory of ideal satisfaction.

Trait Spontaneous people's defenses distort their perception of their own actions. They feel that they are doing much more than they actually do and they interpret their actions as causing effects they have not really caused. They may, in fact, be quite active but sheer activity and agency have nothing in common. Agency is doing something to solve the problems barring oneself from one's goals. Activity for activity's sake is little more than keeping the anxiety accompanying one's repressed aggression at bay. Contrast the person who attends church every Sunday and reads the Bible daily and labels himself or herself spiritual with the person who participates and organizes church activities, leads discussion groups creatively exploring alternative interpretations of Biblical passages and lives by the Bible's wisdom. The former will preach and quote passages for every possible life experience but the latter will understand and therefore practice Christian living.

Jungian analyst and astrologer Liz Greene presents a thorough case study of a woman she names Margaret. Margaret's birth pattern indicates that she is a tenth level Trait Spontaneous. Greene relates how Margaret, through a series of relationships with creative, successful men, tries to realize her own longings for achievement and importance. Margaret, writes Greene, "had a fascination for successful men in roles of authority. While involved with a partner of this kind, her work output was excellent and she always managed to attain positions of responsibility. She also, at these times, felt that her life held some meaning. But unless such an involvement existed, she did not enjoy her work, and found it and her life meaningless. In short, her only object seemed to be one of fulfilling a fantasy of a powerful, successful father-lover who could bring the best out of her through his approval and need of her support. Left to her own devices, she had not yet begun to even remotely tap her own creative potential."[15]

This is a perfect description of the defensive Trait Spontaneous in action. Trait Spontaneous women often feel that their companionship causes the creativity in the already successful and creative men with whom they live. Though society appears to condone more aggressive, forceful behavior in men, men with strong Traits Spontaneous can be equally as defensive as women with this trait. The Trait Spontaneous man who defends against his own agency is the perfect corporation man, loyal, hard-working and possibly driven, who expects his loyalty to win him automatic promotions up the corporate ladder even though he makes no creative contribution to his job. Or it is the scientist who falsifies his data to obtain the experimental results supportive of his theory.

The defensive Trait Spontaneous is there in any statement that begins "I gave up my life for my...." Complete this with the words children or mate or career or parents. Trait Spontaneous people give up their lives easily because they suffer what Otto Rank calls life-fear, the companion anxiety to the Continuous person's fear of death. Spontaneous people fear life because they have stripped themselves of the means to live effectively. So they pride themselves on what they give up and on what they do not do. The protective philosophy of a religion often shields Trait Spontaneous people from their fear of life; religions must be the only human institutions that create words for *not* doing something, words like fasting or celibacy or temperence.

Trait Spontaneous defenders are no more successful in totally disowning their deep inner forces than are Trait Continuous defenders. The repressed Trait Spontaneous aggression erupts in impulsive, temperamental outbursts, or the spite and envy which the Gestaltists term "the aggressiveness of the powerless and the eros of the frustrated." Generally, the most available outlets for the Trait Spontaneous defender's aggressive impulses are verbal. They are rarely without a crusade.

Repressed aggression forms the archetypal inner enemy. The projection of the inner enemy onto another individual or group strips them of their human fullness by reducing them to flat, one-dimensional, thoroughly evil, animal images. Since the other is so completely bad, the badness justifies aggression. If the other is somehow different and unique, and particularly if the other is active and agentic, he or she is a perfect hook for the projected inner enemy...the best hook of all is the other who can be reduced to one word, generally a demeaning word, like Spick, Pig or Satanist.

The collective fares no better when it unleashes its combined aggressive impulses. Though the collective would never allow itself to murder human beings, it easily justifies killing gooks or commies or reds. It is impossible to know just how much of our science, our religion and our culture has arisen in the void left by the repression of the individual's natural aggression. Stripped of the deepest survival urge, a person willingly accepts social solutions to what are essentially individual dilemmas. To give people any freedom at all is to give them the fear of life as well. Institutions ostensibly devoted to human progress, salvation and welfare thrive on the part of each individual adult still fearful of "ghoulies and ghosties and long-leggety beasties and things that go bump in the night."

The Battle of Wills

When two people interact defensively through Traits Spontaneous and Continuous, it is the classic battle of wills. Perhaps interaction is the wrong word. There are two people in the disagreement, to be sure, but each person is locked within the frame of his or her own defensive posture. The other person is simply a foil, an obstacle, a problem, an irritation.

The essence of the battle of wills can be reduced to a single interchange. One screams "Yes you will." The other screams, "No I won't." The irresistible force of Trait Spontaneous meets the immovable object of Trait Continuous. Like two second-rate boxers in the ring, their only goal is to deliver a knock-out punch. A draw is unacceptable.

As the battle of wills progresses, the behavior of the antagonists regresses and becomes steadily more childish. Since these defenses spring from the time-traits Spontaneous and Continuous, they can involve all that the people are and ever have been. Spontaneous and Continuous people bring out of each other the tendency to want to finish all unfinished business on the spot. This is fertile soil for the accusations and complaints of "you always" or "you never." Imagine a disagreement between two people that can, if heated enough, tap the fears and frustrations stored over the course of their lifetimes. Imagine as well that the self-concepts of both individuals are on the line. Perhaps you can sense the intensity of the exchange. Between any two people, the level of the drama equates to the level of unfinished business within their individual psyches.

Each person involved in the Spontaneous-Continuous defensive interchange comes from the good/bad split in his or her own personality. The objective on each side is to prove that the self (Good Me) has been injured by the other (the Bad You). Each sees the other's bad self quite clearly. Each sees itself good by comparison. Thus each person feels too good to have been so unfairly wronged by the childishness of the other.

One particularly destructive form of the battle of wills is characteristic of troubled interaction in troubled families. Here, the person defensively adopts not the Good Me but the Bad Me. The message is, roughly, "I am bad and helpless but you are good and giving." This is, of course, a manipulative posture that allows the person to behave irresponsibly. If the other is hooked on his or her own Good Me, he or she is easily exploited. The message from the Good Me of the helpful other is, "You are behaving as the Bad You but I (because I am Good and Helpful) see the Good You and intend to bring out your good side." Here the helper attempts to do the impossible, that is, protect another person from himself/herself.

Psychoanalyst Howard Wishnie's book *The Impulsive Personality*[16] thoroughly explores difficulties and personality qualities characteristic of Traits Spontaneous and Continuous in their most extreme expressions. Wishnie feels that these individuals' problems are often the product of home environments in which Good Me/Bad Me roles are clearly defined during childhood. He describes a progression of development from compliant living out of the Good Me role as defined by the family during childhood to rebellious adoption of the Bad Me role at about the age of twelve or thirteen. The Bad Me role is the only alternative through which the young person can state some identity and independence.

An additional view of the Trait Spontaneous/Trait Continuous dilemma comes from Reality Therapist Glenda Allen. Ms. Allen feels that the tendency in strongly Spontaneous or Continuous people to see things in good/bad dichotomies is so pronounced that people with these traits may well define black/white roles for themselves even though their actual backgrounds offer them shades of grey. They will construct Good Me and Bad Me self-images even though their families do not. The troubled environment that itself imposes a good/bad role on the highly Spontaneous or Continuous person simply exaggerates and makes extreme the person's own natural tendencies. In this case, it is perhaps the most harmful meeting of nature with nurture if harm can be measured by the degree of inner pain experienced by the individual.

Allen's observations restate Jung's contention that the urge to dichotomize is innate. If this is true, is suffering inevitable? And are people with strong Traits Continuous and Spontaneous destined to suffer more than others? Clearly, this cannot be true since it does not follow that splitting the perceptions into black/white pairs automatically leads to pain. A basic dichotomy like day/night is essential since the contrast between day and night is necessary to the experience of both. Erase one and you erase the other as well.

The difficulty faced most keenly by Trait Continuous and Trait Spontaneous people emerges not so much from the pronounced split in their self-perceptions as from the value judgment implied in the split. When they divide themselves into Good Me and Bad Me, they force themselves to disown much of their own personalities. Removing the Good/Bad labels from the Good Me/Bad Me split leaves only Me/Me. Stripped of the value judgment, there is no split.

Few of us easily let go of the Good Me. Nor will the troubled, rebellious person let go of the Bad Me. It is a difficulty akin to taking off the Persona (the Me) in order to integrate the Nemesis (the Not Me).

In the grips of a Good Me/Bad Me split, we have no real interaction with either our environment or other people. We have no real contact with things outside the self. Perls, together with Ralph Hefferline and Paul Goodman offer the following suggestions for exploring your own dichotomies and tendencies to form opposites:

"Consider some everyday life-situations, objects or activities as if they were *precisely the opposite* of what you customarily take them to be. Imagine yourself in a situation the reverse of your own, where you have inclinations and wishes exactly contrary to your usual ones. Observe objects, images and thoughts as if their function or meaning were the antithesis of what you habitually take them to be. Furthermore, confronting them thus, hold in abeyance your standard evaluations of good or bad, desirable or repugnant, sensible or silly, possible or impossible. Be satisfied to stand between them— or, rather, above them—at the zero point, interested in both sides of the opposition but not siding with either."[17]

This exercise is useful because it appeals to the inner child. If our tendency to split apart our perceptions leads us to lose contact with what is real, the ability to play with opposites invites us to appreciate our experience in fresh ways, enhancing our contact with the real. If you have a particularly strong Trait Spontaneous or Trait Continuous, you will find the discussion and exercises in *Gestalt Therapy*'s[18] Chapter 2, "Contacting the Environment" helpful. The first section of this book is dedicated entirely to the exploration of awareness in ways designed to heal the splits between Persona and Nemesis, Good Me and Bad Me.

The pain and suffering, enmity and bitterness, envy and spite, hopelessness and futility so evident in modern life have their roots in every individual. They are the overt symptoms of the private fragmentation of single personalities into warring elements. Individuals at war with themselves are like the characters in Ibsen's play. They are haunted by their own inner currents. Their ideals make them unreal; their abstractions turn them into ghosts. And ghosts, as every child knows, live in darkness.

Ibsen, through his character Helen Alving concludes: "I almost think we are all ghosts...It isn't just what we've inherited from our parents that walks again in us. It's all sorts of lifeless old ideas and dead faiths and things like that. They're not alive in us, but they cling to us all the same, and we can't shake them off. Even just reading the paper, I can see ghosts between the lines. The whole country must be full of them, numberless, like grains of sand. And all of us are so miserably afraid of the light."[19]

9 Communication Failures

Do you recall the last words of Donn Pearce's prisoner antihero? "What we've got here," smiles Cool Hand Luke, "is a failure to communicate." For Luke, that failure is tragic.

Everyday communication failures rarely have such immediate or disastrous consequences, yet the accumulation of small misunderstandings is the stuff of which our private tragedies are made. Each of us is, to some extent, the prisoner of our own point of view. Our ability to communicate our views honestly and directly keeps us from feeling isolated, alone, and misunderstood. Family therapist Virginia Satir calls honest communication "leveling." We level when we say what we mean. We do not level when we protect our images, defend ourselves, avoid exposing our weaknesses or justify our behaviors. Not leveling sabotages our satisfaction since its short-run avoidance tactics prevent us from approaching others with what we really need.

Virginia Satir identifies four self-protective communication modes: blaming, placating, computing, and distracting. These self-protective strategies typify Traits Organic, Panoramic, Empiric and Hypothetic respectively. We adopt the communication mode characteristic of our strongest trait since the best protection is the most forceful self-projection.

We interpret events through the lens of our traits. Since our traits spring, in turn, from our needs, we see events in terms of our own inner requirements. An event that feels threatening to one individual may seem quite harmless to another if they require different things of the situation. To understand our own self-protective tendencies, we must understand the dynamics of defense. We must identify both the immediate concerns in the situation or interaction and the anticipated harm or loss.

Since it is to our advantage to level with other people, why don't we? Satir believes we stop leveling if two things happen simultaneously: we are under stress *and* doubt our own worth. This combination of strain and vulnerability feels threatening. When we feel threatened, we stop responding to the situation and react to the harm we anticipate. Since the harm we anticipate depends on the way we see the situation, it reflects our strongest traits. Our traits determine both the nature of the stress and the challenge to esteem.

Carl Rogers, father of client-centered therapy, notes that both positive regard and positive self-regard are important. We want others to esteem us and we want to esteem ourselves. Because esteem has these two distinct aspects, people can differ in the relative importance they give to positive regard and positive self-regard.

The Stimulus Need reflects an interpersonal focus and makes social esteem both meaningful and valuable. The stronger the Stimulus Need, the more significant positive regard becomes. The Growth Need, by contrast, is self-focused and indicates the importance of esteeming oneself. The stronger the Growth Need, the more significant positive self-regard becomes. Every birth pattern indicates the relative weight of the Stimulus and Growth Needs within the individual and shows us the relative balance of social esteem/self-esteem essential to that person.

The Security Need represents the achieving, goal-oriented side of the personality. It is the part of the person that feels responsible. From the Security perspective, the person has something, be it an ability, a possession, or a concept, and does not want to lose it. The Love Need represents, conversely, the pleasure-oriented, wish-fulfilling side of personality. It is the part of the person that risks vulnerability to make commitments. From the Love Need perspective, the person wants something and can fear that he or she will not get it.

Every self-protective communication mode is a distinct attempt to protect esteem by controlling a situation or communication. Every instance of self-protection guards the social-esteem/self-esteem, saves the possibility of getting something desirable, or avoids losing something of value. Some combination of these basic elements underlies every interchange in which two people do not level with each other.

Trait Organic symbolizes the combined attributes of the Growth and Security Needs. This personality trait indicates a person whose self-esteem includes a sense of success, achievement, and goal-fulfillment. This is the mark of a highly developed sense of personal responsibility. Blaming is the related self-protective communicative mode. In blaming, the individual protects his or her good opinion of self by shifting the responsibility for undesirable outcomes and consequences onto other people or circumstances.

Trait Panoramic symbolizes the combined attributes of the Stimulus and Love Needs. This personality trait indicates individuals whose social esteem includes the wish for commitment and sharing. This is the sign of highly developed inter-personal commitments. Placating is the related self-protective communication mode. In placating, the individual keeps on other people's good sides, often by appeasement. Placating keeps the person from feeling that he or she has done something unacceptable to someone else.

Trait Empiric symbolizes the combination of the Stimulus and Security Needs. This personality trait indicates a person whose social esteem derives from the knowledge that others see him or her as an achiever, a success, a responsible person. This is the sign of interpersonal responsibility and social consciousness. Computing is the related self-protective mode. In computing, the person impresses others with his or her store of information. The Computer can logically explain his or her actions, thereby avoiding embarrassment and public failure.

Trait Hypothetic symbolizes the combination of the Love and Growth Needs. This personality trait indicates someone whose self-esteem mirrors his or her private involvement. This is the mark of deep personal commitment. Distracting is the related self-protective communication mode. Distracting is the attempt to simultaneously maintain self-regard while avoiding real commitment. Distracters prevent feelings of unacceptability by changing the subject or redirecting attention away from the self, its vulnerability, or weaknesses.

Traits do not exist in isolation. They form continuums with opposing poles. Because this is true, the self-protective tactics of one trait tend to evoke and often deliberately provoke the self-protective tactics of its opposite trait. It frequently happens that two people who do not level with one another attempt to exploit each other's characteristic weaknesses.

Since opposing traits share a common theme, they symbolize two different approaches to a single problem. Both Trait Organic and its opposite Trait Panoramic deal in power. When a Trait Organic person and a Trait Panoramic person do not level, their interchange can get quite heated. By contrast, both Trait Hypothetic and Trait Empiric deal more directly with observation and information. When a Trait Hypothetic person and a Trait Empiric person do not level, they play mental games ranging from simple withholding of relevant information all the way to deliberate lies, deception and what the courts call "mental cruelty."

Every person has a characteristic pattern of self-protection involving one or more of these self-protective communication modes. People differ in the lengths to which they will go to protect themselves and it is important to note that basically happy, fulfilled people rarely waste their energy on self-protection. The birth pattern indicates the way a person defends *if threatened or vulnerable*. The birth pattern says nothing about how defensive a person actually is since this depends more on the person's actual experience than on temperament.

The four self-protective communication modes we are about to explore represent ways to avoid potentially damaging situations and encounters. The situational factors, the threat to esteem and the possibility of hurt do not tell the whole story. Self-protection begins in the person and habitual self-protection indicates inner conflict. Inner conflict in turn sensitizes the person to outer pressures. The more vigorously an individual resists inner demands the more frequently he or she must retreat into self-protection. In birth pattern analysis we want to understand both the inner and outer dynamics of self-protection. If you are using your own birth pattern for self-analysis, exploring the inner dimension of your typical self-protective communication mode can help you increase your ability to level with other people.

Power Struggles

Traits Organic and Panoramic represent the opposite ends of a single trait continuum and you can, as noted in Chapter 4, place every individual somewhere on this trait continuum. The Organic end of the trait continuum reflects a highly personal orientation while the Panoramic end is social. The former is self-oriented, the latter is other-oriented. Both traits, however, share a certain forcefulness, a directness of effect. Either trait is the mark of a person who is wholeheartedly involved in what he or she does.

Communication failure along the Trait Organic-Trait Panoramic continuum is the sign of a power struggle. The Organic tries to assert authority; the Panoramic tries to influence.

The Organic/Panoramic stuggle has a moral undertone involving respect, rights and values. It also involves a good deal of guilt and resentment. Both people involved have an idea of how things *should* be. A Freudian would characterize such an interchange as a battle between two Superegos; a transactional analyst would term this a parent-parent transaction. A Jungian would say the Organic's dominant sensation function conflicts with the Panoramic's dominant intuition and would, further, point out that the exchange is an irrational one. A witness to the Trait Organic/Trait Panoramic self-protective battle would probably agree since the witness would undoubtedly hear a great many opinions and very few factual observations. Regardless of the psychological labels, this is a forceful, energetic exchange between two people bent on controlling a situation and its impact.

Perhaps it is an overstatement to call this interchange irrational simply because it springs from the belief systems of the people involved. The capacity to believe wholeheartedly in oneself and one's values is essential and hardly makes an individual irrational. It is submitting to what analyst

Karen Horney called the "tyranny of the should" that makes both the Organic and the Panoramic so certain of the ways that people ought to behave. Both tend to become furious when people do what they just should not do.

Trait Organic used to be the political trait par excellence when politics was an exercise in individual power and one person through the force of his or her conviction would sway a great many votes. Today, it is more the mark of the rebel with a cause and the feeling that it is essential to speak up for one's personal values. The difference between sincerely protecting one's rights and dictatorially imposing one's opinions on other people is the difference between leveling and blaming in Trait Organic terms.

Trait Panoramic merits the label "the contemporary American political trait" since influence and cooperation and coalition have outstripped sheer force of individual will in modern politics. Also the mark of the cult leader (Hitler, Jim Jones, and Charles Manson all have this trait), Trait Panoramic exercises a magnetic, subtle appeal. The difference between openly identifying shared beliefs and underhandedly manipulating others through appealing to their desires for positive regard differentiates leveling from placating in Trait Panoramic terms.

To see each trait in the fullest perspective, we will explore both the self-enhancing and self-defeating sides of the trait itself. We will examine the relevant formative factors which give the trait its distinctive character, account for the individual emotional content of the trait and differentiate between the masculine and feminine experience of the trait. The self-protective communication mode related to any trait is an attempt to avoid conflict inherent in the trait itself. By accepting our trait's natural conflicts, we realize that we have choices. The knowledge that we do indeed have alternatives enhances our ability to level.

Trait Organic, Growth/Security Conflicts, and Blaming

Trait Organic symbolizes those personality factors common to Growth and Security Needs. Its power comes, however, from the differences between the expansive and stabilizing elements in personality. To actualize Trait Organic, the individual must express both the Growth and the Security elements of self, elements which are inherently opposed in many ways. The ability to distinguish the new and exciting from the stable and dependable is imperative. So is the option to choose either pole. Only when both alternatives are available choices can the Trait Organic person define the scope of personal responsibility appropriate to any situation. The individual is thus not over- or under-extended.

If Trait Organics can temporarily set aside demands for safety and security, they can experiment, take risks, and meet challenges. Conversely, Trait Organics who are confident in their independent, inventive personal images can forgo change or experiment in order to secure, maintain and nurture abilities and responsibilities they have already accepted.

At heart is the necessity of distinguishing the personal, immediate satisfactions from ongoing duties and obligations. The dual capacities to persist and to explore thus gain vigor because of the Security and Growth tension that is inherently Trait Organic. Self-enhancing life choices viewed through the lens of Trait Organic demand both alternatives because tomorrow's security can only come from today's growth.

Trait Organic's self-defeating side manifests in those people who, quite humanly, wish to grow without taking any risks or to expand without really putting their individuality on the line. Tired, outworn past achievements get trotted out again and again to prop up a faltering sense of self-esteem. If Betty was a cheerleader back in '42 but at forty-two has not invested herself in more current satisfactions, she may still be sporting her adolescent image.

Every daring challenge, once it is met, becomes a secure achievement. Dwelling in the achieved, however, is certain to strip the new of its potential excitement. Organics who sidestep the contrasting demands of Growth and Security often pride themselves on behaving responsibly while privately resenting the responsibilities they have taken on and secretly envying others whose courage wins respect.

The surest sign of failure to confront the demands of actualizing Trait Organic can be seen in those people who demand respect not for what they do but for what they do not do. Look what they have given up for their children. Listen to how they have sacrificed for their mates. They have stayed loyal to the corporation while others deserted.

The developmental influence related to Trait Organic involves the mother's impact on the private identity. The way the person feels about himself or herself may still retain the self-image reflected in the maternal mirror. The life role the person adopts might be either a concession to or a rebellion against the mother's values. Either way, the role is not freely chosen and cannot be played with any degree of genuineness and self-respect.

So often we associate mother with mother-love but support is a far more accurate description. The Goertzel childhood studies of eminent achievers reveal striving, hard-working, success-oriented mothers behind many men and women whose accomplishments transcend the limits of their environments. Rona Barrett once interviewed four wealthy, successful individuals whose hard work and outstanding efforts led to their self-made millions. Black, white, male and female, all credited their mothers as the driving force behind their personal success.

The my-mother-myself implications of Trait Organic clearly differentiate this trait's feminine and masculine expressions. A woman with Trait Organic must face the challenge of both identifying with her mother through their shared femininity while differentiating herself from her mother in order to express her own personal identity. If she completely rejects her mother's values, she rejects her own feminine model. She may achieve her sense of self but it is tinged with guilt and cannot be enjoyed. If, on the other hand, she blindly follows in her mother's role, she diffuses her own separate, private identity and in time feels constricted and resentful.

Though it is difficult enough for the Trait Organic woman to struggle to find her separate identity, she faces an additional challenge inherent in the trait itself. Trait Organic is a power trait and Trait Organic women discover that femininity in general and sexuality in particular can be a source of power and control in relationships. If the Trait Organic woman uses sexuality as a power source allowing her sexual identity to control the matrix of her personality as a whole, she faces an additional conflict. In the words of one Trait Organic woman, "When a man comes on to me sexually, I feel insulted. I think he only wants me for my body, not myself. But if a man is friendly and doesn't make any advances, I wonder what's wrong with me. I wonder why he doesn't find me attractive." This conflict cannot be resolved until the Trait Organic woman sees her femininity as only one facet of her identity as a whole.

Developmental studies suggest that mothers tend to be demanding of their daughters but more lenient with their sons. Trait Organic does seem somewhat more difficult for women and adolescent Trait Organic girls often rebel in order to establish a separate sense of self. Psychological evidence indicates that women with firm, secure identities emerge from families that encourage open discussion and allow clash of opinion. The Trait Organic woman who grows up in an environment that encourages her to speak for herself may be better able to actualize herself than her Trait Organic sisters who were confined to more demure, "ladylike" roles.

In a man, Trait Organic carries the emotional tone of the mother-son relationship. Since mother is the first female in the male Trait Organic's life, his interaction with her shapes his expectations of the way women will treat him.

Sons demand more attention from their mothers than do daughters. Boys are more self-centered in their demands and attempt to control or dominate their mothers. The mother's response influences her Trait Organic son's attitude toward male-female relationships. This interaction shows the son a female role pattern which he generalizes to females as a whole.

The mother-child relationship focuses on discipline for both sexes. Mother is the major source of training and teaching in the pre-school years.

[217]

Mother, through her instrumental training role, helps her children gradually assume responsibility for themselves. By the sheer fact that she is there, a mother lets her children know time and again that their actions have consequences.

The link between actions and consequences is a crucial element in the self-protective communication mode blaming. Trait Organic people are strivers by temperament. They take an onward-and-upward view toward life. The difference between those Trait Organics who blame and those who do not lies in their sense of self-esteem. Trait Organics believe that it is better to achieve than fail. Those who realize it is not essential to successfully reach *every* goal they set leave room in their philosophy for inevitable failures. Trait Organics who blame with regularity put their whole being on the line whenever they identify a goal and want to reach it. They esteem themselves not for their ability to maximize success while minimizing failure but for their ability to succeed at absolutely everything. Hence, they cannot take responsibility for a failure, no matter how trivial it may be.

When people are unable to accept private responsibilities or individual accountability, they protect their private esteem by blaming. It is difficult to fail at any time, but if self-regard is low to begin with, failure is especially hurtful. People with unresolved Growth-Security conflicts protect themselves from mistakes by blaming circumstances or other people when things go wrong.

Virginia Satir depicts the blamer with feet firmly planted and arm outstretched, one finger pointing accusingly. The blamer's face is red; the blamer's voice is raised; the blamer's gaze shoots the proverbial daggers.

The vocal, verbal blamer is most often a "moving against" type with preferred strong behavior. They like to throw their weight around and win by intimidation. Sensitive behavior types, because they must reconcile blaming with their desire to maintain relationships, cannot risk this open, forceful blaming style. Instead, they perfect the sigh or the tsk-tsk or the disapproving dirty look. The spouse of a sensitive blamer probably invented the phrase "if looks could kill." Strategic types are the fault-finders who pick and poke and prod other people with their accusations. Since strategists see themselves as perfect, making mistakes is not something they can easily accept. A well-developed capacity to shift the burden of responsibility onto others is the blamer's infallibility insurance.

Blamers never put their private selves to the test nor explore their own abilities to the full because they simply cannot stand the thought of error. The blamer's sense of responsibility confuses accountability with fault. Mistakes mean the loss of private esteem, they are not simply mistakes as a natural part of life. Because blamers see failure as unnatural, they are quick to assume that someone must be at fault. That someone is not, of course, the blamer.

Blamers blame for one main reason: misplaced pride. The blamer does not esteem self; the blamer esteems performance. Since the blamer's whole self is invested in doing something rather than in being something, the blamer must do what he or she does very well. The blamer *must* do things *right*. This overworked right-wrong scheme does not allow any room for honest error so error is just too much for the blamer to face. The worst part of all is that blamers, by not claiming their mistakes, never learn.

A blamer's private self runs in circles around a narrow racetrack labelled "the one right way." Blamers can't fix the things that go wrong in their lives because they simply do not see their own hand in their problems. From the outsider's point of view, blamers are difficult to deal with because they tend to moralize. A blamer's behavior is not simply right, it is righteous. Blame frequently hides behind the mask of high moral principle and the courage of one's convictions.

Leveling in Trait Organic terms enhances private self-esteem. When we follow our private path through life, we define our own individual goals. When we focus on our personal efforts, we set unique standards for achievement. The line between our private successes and failures defines the scope of our own abilities at any point in time. This line is the growing edge of self. Near the center, all is secure and we can rely on what we do well. The things we freely choose to bring close to us we accept the responsibility for gladly. Near the growing boundary of the self, all is exciting and as yet unsecured and unformed. The effort symbolized by Trait Organic is the effort we expend whenever we bring a new, unformed talent toward the center of our working skills and capabilities.

We do not blame ourselves for the raw, unformed character of the new since this is the essence of private exploration. Necessary mistakes and failure show us our inherent limits and these limits define our private selves. All motion toward the center demands acceptance of responsibility; all motion toward the boundary meets the challenge of freedom. Secure, self-esteeming Trait Organics live at the boundary where they frequently err *and* at the center where they capably succeed. Only the weak and the uncentered must avoid the ups and downs at life's growing edge.

Trait Panoramic, Love/Stimulus Conflicts, and Placating

Trait Panoramic symbolizes those personality factors common to both Stimulus and Love. The outgoing orientation of Stimulus contrasts with the deepening pleasure of Love and the difference between these two personality factors gives Trait Panoramic a dynamic quality. Both factors are available choices to individuals who express this trait in self-enhancing ways. Every Stimulus/Love choice involves differentiating between the excitement or interest of the moment and the familiarity of commitments already made. The ability to form lasting relationships demands the capacity to separate the ephemeral from the important in human interactions.

Every relationship is inherently a distance problem in which the individual must set the boundary between self and other appropriately. Through Trait Panoramic and the choices inherent in it, individuals keep involvement at a comfortable level.

Trait Panoramic's self-defeating expression stems from attempts to avoid the necessary clash between the Love and Stimulus Needs. Neither need is fully or appropriately expressed, and the social skills suffer. Forming or committing to relationships brings inner turmoil and social anxiety. Stimulus Need related skills are skills which intitiate new relationships. Love related skills bring the self-revelation so important to intimacy and sharing. The vigorous contrast between these two facets of personality helps the individual determine just how much a relationship really matters to him or her.

Trait Panoramics who refuse to express both poles of their trait often cannot separate the relationships that matter from the relationships that do not. They over-commit to relative strangers in a false attempt to fortify their social esteem and eventually feel resentful, over-extended and put-upon. Their over-booked social schedules do not leave them sufficient time for deeper moments, keeping them distant from important others and leaving them feeling guilty.

The Stimulus Need and its related social identity determine the ease a person feels in integrating self with others. It sets the tone for feeling equal, inferior, or superior in human interaction. Democratic attitudes allow the person flexibility to approach the broadest range of others with openness and interest while reserving the right to limit association according to the experienced quality of sharing.

Trait Panoramic's feeling tone is shaped by the generalization of the feeling tone of the father-child interaction. The child expects people in general to perceive and relate to him or her as the father once related. Father is an important social symbol because a family's social influence or status most often derives from his profession. His career and income determine, to a major degree, the location, neighborhood and social influences his children will experience.

Psychologists studying very young children indicate that the father influences a child's ability to cope in situations involving strangers. When the young child of a warm, involved, attentive father is left alone with a stranger, that child displays little anxiety. The father's contribution to Trait Panoramic may, at least in part, determine the social competence and interpersonal ease.

For both girls and boys, the father's attitudes about people in general condition their social expectations. If father thinks that people are basically good-hearted, the child can anticipate rewards for social effort. If father thinks that people are bad and untrustworthy, the child senses a need for social self-protective mechanisms.

Sexual roles, unlike sexual identity, are culturally based and reflect the social definitions of masculinity and femininity. Though we may lament the differences, the differences are very real and slow to change. A person's sex role determines his or her rights and duties within society, particularly those rights and duties that society believes the person should have. Sex roles define options.

For young children, play in general and toys in particular offer stimulating avenues of discovery. Fathers, far more than mothers, discourage their children from playing in non-gender-specific ways. Some fathers can be lenient with daughters who are tomboyish, but fathers generally disapprove, actively interfere and punish when their sons play with dolls or dress up in girls' clothing.

The social Stimulus attitudes reflect peer influences. Trait Panoramic links peer influence with self-acceptance. Girls rarely object when other girls play with boys' toys but boys actively discourage their peers from playing in non-gender-specific ways. Trait Panoramic tends, because of social and paternal pressures, to be more difficult for men than for women.

For either sex, Stimulus-Love attitudes reflect the father's attitude toward the child in relationship to other family members. A final source of conflict is the possibility that the child feels inferior to a more praised, more successful brother or sister. The child may, conversely, bear the brunt of the father's expectations for social success and public notice. Trait Panoramic attitudes shape the social self-esteem either supporting esteem through democratic role actualization or undermining it with social doubts and demands.

When either men or women lack social self-esteem, they protect their public selves by placating. They say what they think other people want to hear; they do not communicate their real feelings. Socially self-protective people put on pleasing public faces, faces that say very little about their real interpersonal goals or desires.

Virginia Satir depicts the placater in a kneeling position. One arm is uplifted as if to beg for acceptance, the neck is craned upward, the face wears a forced smile. The image is designed to appeal and the placater seems to say that he or she wants nothing for self alone.

Placaters have favorite phrases. They say "excuse me" a lot. They are also fond of "now promise you won't get mad" and "well what do *you* want to do?"

[221]

The placating style depends on the individual's preferred behavior. Sensitive behavior "moving toward" placaters are sickeningly sweet. Since love lurks just around every corner, they cannot afford not to be endearing to everyone. They think they cannot enjoy themselves if they are alone and they will do whatever anyone else wants for companionship.

Strong moving against placaters raise flattery to a fine art. They want social acceptance to be sure, but they want more. They have an instinct for appealing to the social weaknesses of other people, for buttering up others by telling them what they want to hear. Think of Adolph Hitler appealing to the wounded national pride of the German people and weaving tales of Teutonic glory. This is placating in the service of runaway craving for strength and social glory but it is placating all the same. The readiness to appease seems such a harmless thing until we see it in its wider social scope.

Strategic moving away placaters want peace and will pay just about any price to get it. They will buy the magazines (Girl Scout cookies, newspaper subscriptions, religious tracts) if the salesperson will just take the money and leave, and like them, of course.

Regardless of their behavior preferences, all placaters want social acceptance to such a degree that they cannot discriminate between significant interactions and insignificant ones. They just cannot let any human contact pass them by without making an impression. They want to know that the other person acknowledges them, likes them, is interested in them. It does not matter if the other person is the plumber, the sales clerk or the cab driver. No human interaction is too trivial to interest the placater and no human interaction is so brief that the placater can risk rejection.

Why do placaters placate? Why must they be so agreeable? Placaters justify their acceptance-seeking under the banner of peace, calm and friendship. For women, placating is even encouraged as socially desirable. Placaters' lives do appear to roll along merrily. They are generally found around people and that should be our first clue that something is amiss. Since a placater's social self must be flexible enough to appeal to any other person, that self makes no statement and offers no possibility of real discovery or deep encounter. Placaters resemble the Beatles' Nowhere Man whose point in every direction turns out to be no point at all. Their relationships are precisely this, pointless. Placating does not make a relationship because in a relationship there must be two people involved. The placater is simply a mirror for the other adding nothing of self to the social encounter. Placating makes for odd associations, shallow encounters and strange bedfellows. Placating does not provide the necessary commitment for real togetherness.

Every social encounter is a choice and every social encounter demands effort. On the one hand, there is the excitement and stimulus of someone fresh, new, inviting. On the other hand is the self's own deeper sense of need, involvement, willingness to commit or forgo commitment. The effort of relating involves setting limits on each encounter, limits that reflect the level of real social feeling. John may, for instance, get along with Mary very well if he sees her for an hour once a month. To see her every week might drive him to distraction. If he takes into account his real involvement and interest in Mary, he does not commit more time to her than his feelings for her allow. Thus, he is free from the frustration of getting too close for his own comfort. Though he thinks it might placate Mary to accept her invitations, to do so would rob *her* of the chance to relate to someone else, someone who would find her fascinating.

Leveling in Trait Panoramic terms enhances our social esteem since we do not promise others an involvement which we cannot offer. To level is to make a statement of our social aims, our relationship goals, our interpersonal interests. All relationships begin with the Stimulus Need and the fresh, exciting first encounter. The Stimulus-Love effort lies in determining which relationships will progress to become intimate and which relationships will remain distant and peripheral. Only by discriminating between the important and the superficial encounters in our lives do our commitments match our feelings. When our level of commitment in each encounter reflects our honest social interest, our social selves thrive. We do not rob ourselves of the necessary time to follow through on promising encounters and we allow others the freedom to form relationships appropriate to themselves. Social self-esteem grows when we return interest for interest in the mutual encounter that excites important shared discovery.

Mental Games

Traits Hypothetic and Empiric represent the opposite poles of a single trait continuum just as Traits Organic and Panoramic are opposites. Trait Hypothetic is the personal end of its trait continuum and high self-esteem or positive self-regard is essential to the self-enhancing expression of Trait Hypothetic. Trait Empiric includes the social Stimulus Need. Thus, social esteem or positive regard is linked with this trait. The dominance of either Trait Hypothetic or Trait Empiric in the birth pattern indicates a person who delights in information and in knowing about things, often for the sake of knowledge itself.

While politicians, religious leaders and musicians tend to operate through the power Traits Organic and Panoramic, writers, reporters, and psychologists tend toward the intellectual Traits Empiric and Hypothetic. The former often communicate much through gestures or signals. Words, when they are necessary, are used more for the images and passions they evoke than for their literal meanings. Hypothetics and Empirics, by contrast, depend on words and on straightforward verbal communication. Both want to define things, to be precise and to be accurate.

The intellectual traits rarely carry the force and flash inherent in Traits Organic and Panoramic. The traits of criminals reflect the crimes they commit and crimes against persons are more apt to be committed by people with Traits Organic and Panoramic. Traits Hypothetic and Empiric characterize the swindler, the embezzler, the cheat and the con whose goal is to outsmart the victim.

Communication failure, along the Trait Hypothetic–Trait Empiric continuum, is a subtle, mental cat-and-mouse game for both have a pronounced ability to dig, prod and poke while feigning innocence. This is the battle of wits in which making one's point becomes more important than the point one is making.

The Hypothetic/Empiric struggle comes down to who is right not in the moral terms of Organic/Panoramic but rather in terms of the facts and their interpretation. These two square off like lawyers in court or detectives on a case. The ultimate objective is to prove beyond any doubt that the error is the result of the other's stupidity, lack of foresight or planning.

Jung discussed the opposing personality functions of thinking and feeling, both of which he termed rational functions. To Jung, thinking and feeling represented opposing ways that people organize their observations and experiences. Freud noted that the ego, in addition to coping with the superego and its shoulds, faced the challenge of coping with reality. The reality principle was Freud's term for reason as it applied to a person's ability to manipulate his or her environment. Contemporary transactional analysis identifies one part of the personality as the adult or factual observer. The correspondance to TA's adult is much looser, however, because Traits Hypothetic and Empiric though concerned with assessment, logic and observation, are as capable as any of the other personality traits to run amok, be self-defeating and lead to self-protection.

Trait Hypothetic is more philosophical than strictly factual. It shares with Trait Organic both the demand for self-esteem and the penchant for protecting the individual's view of himself or herself. The difference between honest observation and deliberate self-misrepresentation is the difference between leveling and distracting in Trait Hypothetic terms.

Trait Empiric is a keen observer and rarely fails to notice the details of life events. Trait Empiric shares with Trait Panoramic the desire for positive regard and social esteem. The difference between perceptive, incisive self-report and vacuous, endless explanation differentiates leveling from computing in Trait Empiric terms.

Trait Hypothetic, Growth/Love Conflicts, and Distracting

Trait Hypothetic indicates those personality factors common to Growth and Love Needs. The dynamism of this trait arises from the effort necessary to express the trait at both its self-esteeming and self-committing poles. To actualize Trait Hypothetic, Growth/Love conflicts must emerge. Such conflicts involve independence, experiment, risk taking, and self-esteem on the one hand and intimacy, sharing, mutuality, and self-acceptance on the other.

Trait Hypothetic, when fully self-enhancing, permits independence to fade into the ground of attention in intimate encounters while letting mutuality come to the fore. Hypothetics with self-esteem and a clear sense of identity have no difficulty in doing this. The self can recede into the ground without a sense of loss or resentment because firm self-definition need not guard, protect, or watch a private side of which it is confident.

Conversely, in times of change, risk-taking and experiment, established intimacy fades into the ground. This is possible when honest acceptance supports spontaneous growth. The distinction between private, highly individual satisfaction and mutual shared satisfaction allows the Trait Hypothetic person the capacity to make and maintain commitments while staying equally committed to self. People who express Trait Hypothetic in self-enhancing ways know they do not have to sacrifice having an identity in order to gain another's acceptance. They know as well that they must strike their own, distinctly personal balance between their demands for freedom and their commitments and promises.

Self-defeating expressions of Trait Hypothetic come from the attempt to pacify the conflict between the Growth and Love Needs. If neither need is freely expressed, both are frustrated. The individual is faced with a sense of threat instead of tempted by two appealing alternatives. People who sidestep the essential clash between the Growth and Love Needs find themselves resenting even simple commitments which seem to encroach on their freedom while the independent, self-asserting alternatives they pursue leave them feeling guilty.

The theme of father-love and support for a growing, changing individuality is a theme of archetypal significance. To be fatherless is to be denied one's birthright. To be claimed and recognized by one's father is to have a name, to be someone, to feel important. The formative influences of Trait Hypothetic in a man's chart are equivalent to the challenges faced by the Trait Organic woman for here, the forces of identification and the demand for self-differentiation pose an equivalent masculine challenge.

Fathers who are warm, appreciative, available and accepting while valuing their children as separate, distinct individuals insure maximum effort with minimum Growth-Love conflict. The most important single formative factor is the child's ability to have the private, individual successes that bolster esteem and private self-confidence. The father is not so authoritarian that he subdues and defeats his child nor so permissive as to appear indifferent to the child's accomplishments. The term "fathering one" is appropriate here because father can be any supportive, available male.

Trait Hypothetic in a man's chart requires that he identify self with father lest he retain a "little boy" self-concept. Fathers tend to be more demanding of sons than daughters so the possibility for conflict and rebellion tends to be greater for high Trait Hypothetic men. In a man's chart, Trait Hypothetic symbolizes his attitudes about what it means to be a man. The son whose father invalidates his identity at every opportunity feels a constant urge to prove himself, to be psychologically potent, to be important.

In a woman's chart, Trait Hypothetic does not have the same meaning since her ability to differentiate self from father is rarely in question. Father is the first man in a woman's life, however, and his attitude toward her colors her expectation of how men in general will treat her. The father who appreciates and supports his daughter gives her a clear message that she is an attractive, acceptable person worthy of respect and consideration. Critical, indifferent or rejecting fathers send a very different message. Their daughters learn to feel unacceptable, unlovable, unworthy of esteem. Their poor self-estimates affect their adult relationships, relationships in which the low self-esteem woman cannot ask for commitment or consideration. Her poor self-concept and self-defeating attitudes tell her she does not deserve real intimacy and her later relationships confirm her lack of esteem. Equally low self-esteem can result from a doting father. Though father may see daughter as perfect, it is very doubtful that the rest of the world will be so lavish with its affection. Smothering love can be a set-up for severe, later disappointment with consequent loss of esteem.

When either men or women feel unacceptable, when they do not esteem their private selves, they protect themselves by distracting. They talk without disclosing the private aspect of their personalities. They say things designed to direct attention *away* from the private self and real personal concerns toward safe, irrelevant topics.

Virginia Satir draws a graphic portrait of the distracter. Picture the distracter in busy motion, arms and legs going in all directions, one hand pouring coffee, the other hand picking lint and the voice singsonging up and down without relation to the words. Think of the distracter as a "lopsided top" says Satir, spinning dizzily but going nowhere.

Distracters tell stories, philosophize, joke, spin yarns but they do not communicate. When distracters are pressed for a personal statement, they say what they are not: "I'm not angry." "I didn't lose my cool." By saying what they are not or what they do not or did not do, distracters can appear to show their private selves without saying anything personal at all. Distracters do not confront the issues in their lives squarely so they cannot say what they mean and they do not mean what they say.

Janet has dated Bob (a distracter) for a year. They have had vague discussions about marriage and now Janet wants to know how Bob really feels. She levels with him:

Janet: Bob, we've talked about marriage before and I think it's time to really look at how we feel. I'm ready to make a firm commitment. Are you?

Bob: Marriage! Do you know *anyone* who's happily married? Boy, I don't! Look at Martha and Joe. They were really happy until they got married, but now they fight like cats and dogs.

Janet: We're not Martha and Joe, we're us. I care about *you* Bob and I want to know how you feel about *our* relationship.

Bob: I'm not looking around for anyone else, am I? Besides, when two people care about each other....

Bob will go on talking about other people or marriage in general or what he is not going to do until Janet agrees to change the subject.

Distracting is an outgrowth of self-defeating Growth-Love attitudes and self-defeating attitudes encourage self-defeating behavior as well. Distracters with sensitive "moving toward" behavior patterns think distracting will get them love. They keep things fun, light, and above all uncommitted. Distracters with strong "moving against" behavior use distracting to achieve success. They tap their competitor on one shoulder and grab his job while his back is turned. Distracters with strategic "moving away" behavior use distracting to remain uninvolved. They send people off on tangents that lead as far away from their private lives as possible. Regardless of the distraction style, all distracters expect, ultimately, to get the same thing: private gain without personal commitment.

Why do distracters distract? They distract because they think they get something by distracting. Distracting works on two levels. An unreal level where it makes "sense" and a real level where it avoids effort and conflict.

Distracters think they get freedom by distracting. They think they live by important principles. Their lives just do not contain all those obstructions and conditions that seem to plague other people. So long as distracters believe they are upholding such meaningful and important principles, they will continue to distract. It is the unreal justification for distracting that makes distracting such a tricky business. It appears that the distracter will lose something (freedom, principles) if he or she stops distracting and levels with people.

Think of the distracter as standing in the middle of a circle. The distracter looks at the circle and it says "meaning, independence, freedom." From the outside, we look at the circle and see a wall of self-isolation that says "private, keep out, no trespassers allowed past this point." The sadness of distracting is that everything inside the distracter's circle is lonely and purposeless. Distracters do not live life without conditions because non-involvement is a condition of everything they do. They do not escape obstruction because they have, as Fromm would say, freedom from but not freedom to. The distracter's lack of commitment and involvement is not freedom, it is exile.

Leveling in Growth-Love terms enhances self-esteem. When we state our personal opinions, reveal our inner feelings and disclose our private identities, we let other people respond to our private selves. Some people will agree with us, support us, like us. With these people we achieve the honest understanding that is the first point of possible intimacy. Other people will disagree with us, giving us the chance to see another point of view. Some people will dislike us, letting us know immediately that there is no possibility for understanding. It is only when we level, when we say who we really are, that we can tell if people like us for ourselves. When people do not like us for who we are and what we stand for, we are in the company of Lincoln and Roosevelt and Jesus. Hardly a blow to our self-esteem.

Trait Empiric, Stimulus/Security Conflicts, and Computing

Trait Empiric symbolizes those personality factors common to the Stimulus and Security Needs but its incisiveness derives from the clash between these two separate personality factors. In its self-enhancing form, Trait Empiric demands the free expression of both interest and assurance. People who express Trait Empiric with great effectiveness are people who can differentiate between the interesting, exciting, inviting possibilities of the moment and the secure, capable, responsible goals they have already set. The distinction between discovery and mastery is essential as is the line between what has been achieved and what is yet to be explored.

Trait Empiric, in self-actualizing people, is generally the mark of an achiever because Empirics find in the moment the best practical possibility to come one step closer to the ends they desire. They have the enviable knack of breaking down large projects into component parts and reaching major goals through a series of minor successes. They do not rest in what they already know but seize appropriate situations in which to learn relevant new skills.

Self-defeating expressions of Trait Empiric dodge the essential conflicts between Stimulus and Security, between the moment and the past. Though life offers them the same chance to expand through revision of existing skills, self-defeating Trait Empirics rebel against what they see as the unreasonable demands of the moment. They expect the possibilities of the moment to magically manifest themselves without the necessity of their assuming any added responsibilities.

We have familiar adages to express the inherent clash of the Stimulus and Security facets of life experience. We know that if you want to play, you have to pay and, of course, there is no free lunch. Trait Empirics who deny the demands of making choices often harbor the illusion that they are clever enough to play without paying or crafty enough to walk out with the check.

Individuals who freely function through Trait Empiric rarely make self-defeating choices because they know their limits. They weigh the prospective benefits against the added duties involved before they take on any responsibility. What there is to be explored is tempered by what the Empiric knows he or she can handle. Not so with self-defeating Empirics who cannot stand the thought that opportunity might pass them by. They grab every new thing as though it were just what they needed, take on extra obligations and find themselves inundated by unforeseen pressures and responsibilities. Too proud to let others think that they have taken on too much, they take on even more. When they simply cannot go on under the weight they have taken on, they feel guilty. Yet the more their duties increase, the more resentment they feel.

Behind every intellectual trait lies the great "what if." It is the parallel to a power trait's should. "What if I pass up this chance," says the Empiric, "and I never have another opportunity like this one?" The self-defeating expression of either Trait Empiric or Trait Hypothetic is rife with these fruitless what ifs, with worry, and with hyper-analysis.

The formative factors related to Trait Empiric reflect the mother's influence on the child's social self-image and sense of social esteem. Her own social attitudes and anxieties are often a part of the Trait Empiric's worrisome, self-defensive "what if-ing."

Mother's role as disciplinarian and her contribution to day-by-day training in social skills determines whether her Trait Empiric child will feel socially confident and competent or socially inferior and inept. Interestingly, mothers with socially superior attitudes raise children who have poor social adjustment. Erik Erikson observes that troubled children have mothers who encourage them to maintain appearances and to assume a false, socially superior front.

A mother's status concerns need not differ substantially for her daughters than her sons. Popularity, in the sense of having the right friends, succeeding in the status activities or belonging to the best organizations, channels the efforts toward achieving the most socially enviable goals. Should the child's efforts succeed, the resulting attitudes take a smug, superior turn. Failure, by contrast,is a prime source of inferiority. If the child fails where his or her siblings have succeeded it is a double blow to the social identity and social esteem.

Children who are allowed to define their own social goals and interests and whose mothers give them support and training are able to discriminate between worthwhile pursuits and hollow status victories. Their ability to work toward important goals sets a precendent for adult achievement.

Mothers, like fathers, sometimes show favoritism. Since mother is the day-in-day-out mediator of sibling disputes, she is generally the child's court of appeal. Thus her ability to be egalitarian or her penchant for showing favoritism will not escape the child's notice. Sigmund Freud is an example of a child whose parents had high expectations for his eventual success. Freud was the favored child and received special privileges and attention. Freud spoke of his mother's favoritism saying, "A man who has been the indisputable favorite of his mother keeps for life the feeling of a conqueror, that confidence of success that often induces real success." Despite this, he was jealous of his five younger siblings. The fruits of favoritism gained are not entirely sweet.

When people's social esteem is low and they are unable to resolve inner Stimulus-Security conflicts, they protect themselves by computing. Like the Blamer, the Computer is concerned with the scope of his or her personal responsibility, but in computing the responsibilities are to other people. These are the social accountabilities and to fail in Stimulus-Security terms is to fail before an audience, to fail where it shows, to fail publicly and openly. Computing protects from the sting of embarrassment and saves social face. The Computer simply explains away his or her mistakes. It may look to us as though the Computer has just erred but the error *must* be ours. The Computer carefully explains to us that *we* have misperceived the situation, *we* have misunderstood the Computer's motives, *we* have not clearly grasped what the Computer actually meant. Had *we* been more careful, we would certainly have seen that the Computer was, in fact, warning us all along to be more cautious, more clear-headed, more rational.

Virginia Satir depicts the Computer sitting back in a chair, body rigid, neck stiff, gaze looking down the nose just a bit. Nothing obvious you understand because a good Computer must be subtle. Above all, the Computer must appear all-knowing because every good Computer knows the facts and the facts say that the Computer is always right.

Computers live a social existence that lies somewhere between the barter system and a computer program. Social exchange and business exchange look a great deal the same from the self-protective stance of a Computer. Everything must be carefully weighed and measured, every thought, every gesture, every interaction. The effect the Computer makes on other people is a calculated effect. The Computer cannot just be with another person, the Computer has to have a reason to be with the other person. A good, solid, rational reason.

Computing, like every other self-protective device, changes with the preferred behavior: Ruth, a Computer, uses computing to avoid real social exchange. It is Ruth's birthday and her friend Helen has given her a present. It is a bottle of perfume, Midnight, the rage right now. The day after her birthday, Ruth goes to the store to price the bottle of Midnight her friend Helen gave her. Now, Ruth computes what she will do for Helen's birthday. The bottle of Midnight cost thirty dollars and we can tell Ruth's preferred behavior from the cost of her gift. If Ruth is a strategic, moving away type she will buy Helen a present that costs exactly thirty dollars. This keeps the relationship even, but more important, it keeps Ruth uninvolved. She is not in Helen's debt nor is Helen in hers and this is the way the strategic type wants it. By contrast, if Ruth is a strong behavior type, the price of her gift sends a message to Helen. If the gift is more expensive, Ruth is calling attention to her greater financial success. Should Ruth wish, instead, to send a subtle message that hers is the superior position in the relationship, she can always buy Helen a present just a bit cheaper than the one Helen gave her. If Ruth is a sensitive, moving toward person, her computing is gauged to make Helen feel obligated toward her, to make Helen realize how much Ruth likes her. Ruth's gift to Helen has to be more expensive than the gift Helen gave to Ruth.

The same kind of interchange marks all forms of computing. Computers protect themselves from any real sense of social responsibility or any real accountability to others. They simply perform for their audience and carefully weigh and measure the impact of all they say or do. Computers think other people admire or envy them for their adroit skill in managing people. That is, in fact, what Computers do. They manage; they intellectualize; they figure people out. They know everyone's abilities and have a useful purpose for every human encounter. They do not know how to show real, warm, honest interest in other people. They do not know how to say "I don't know" and this inability to learn as they move along from one relationship to the next seriously impairs their life information. They simply reaffirm their social attitudes at every turn.

Everything Computers experience just goes to show them they were right in the first place. Computers live in a world devoid of surprises (which they hate) and devoid of real social enthusiasm. They are busy people and their time is so valuable that if they invest themselves in real sharing they are afraid they will not make an adequate return. They are too afraid to find something they do not already know to look closely at anything new. Computers dispute anything substantially different or unexpected or challenging.

Leveling in Trait Empiric terms is much like leveling in Trait Organic terms in that each potential conflict is resolved at the growing edge of the self. Here it is the social self, the stimulus-loving public self that is always on the threshold of new human discovery. In this exposure at the self's ever-expanding social boundary lies the possibility that all the information, the knowledge and the skill with which the self feels safe and comfortable will be overturned in the moment. There is always the possibility of surprise, discovery, and intellectual challenge in the moment. All new information and the fresh stimulation that frees the self at its social boundary changes to security as it integrates with core, established knowledge.

The Stimulus self-aspect is just as invigorated by change as the Growth self-aspect. The responsibility that the self must take is the responsibility for its own social information base, the accountability for the rightness of its assumptions and the wrongness of its presumptions. But this is life at the changing social boundary of self. One side of the boundary is within the self, what the self knows with certainty at any point in time. Outside the boundary is new and ever-stimulating information that feeds the social self, opens new paths to new interests and relates ever-more responsibly and capably. The effort involved in Trait Empiric leveling is the effort of taking the new and using it to rework the very core of what was assumed safe and enduring. Yesterday's discovery emerges as today's insight. Today's insight reaches toward tomorrow's wisdom.

Leveling in terms of any trait demands effort. Traits Organic, Panoramic, Hypothetic and Empiric all require us to maintain a personally appropriate balance between the old and the new, the achieved and the possible. Self-defeating expressions of these four traits always involve an attempt to dodge the clash between the forces of continuity and the forces of change. Each self-protective tactic clings to the illusion of the one right choice or the only sensible alternative, not realizing that this philosophy makes choice impossible and offers no alternatives. If giving in to our shoulds, our oughts and our correctness truly put our inner conflicts to rest, we would not employ the self-protective communication modes to bolster our esteem. When self-protection succeeds at all, it succeeds only in changing the internal conflict into an external one, disrupting our relationships with other people and with our environment.

The formative factors and gender differences related to the traits and self-protective attitudes aid in self-analysis *if* we use these clues to help us examine and unearth the *content* of our shoulds and oughts and what ifs. The events that once created our attitudes, however difficult or depressing they may have been, do not excuse or explain our current behavior. The me of today with its "shoulding" and "what ifing" is always the present source of the self-defeating messages underlying the self-protective measures. If today's me chooses to communicate protectively rather than level, the me of today must accept the responsibility for that choice.

Leveling is an ongoing process involving constant choices. The effort involved in discovering, defining and making life choices is a life constant. Though we rely most on the self-protective mode that works best for us, all of us at some time resort to blaming, placating, distracting, and computing. When we meet with sudden, unexpected failure we are apt to blame it on circumstances or explain it away. If we meet with disapproval, we offer excuses or try to sweet talk our way out of the difficulty. Fearing rejection, we try to avoid the issue and make ourselves more pleasing and fun for the other to be with. Or we get angry at ourselves when we do something foolish and call our loss bad luck or try to laugh it off as though it were not so important. Flesh-and-blood human beings will continue to do all these things from time to time. Insight offers us choices; it seldom makes us perfect.

Virginia Satir expresses the value of insight. She writes: "To be able to apologize without placating, to disagree without blaming, to be reasonable without being inhuman and boring, to be able to change the subject without distracting gives me greater personal satisfaction, less internal pain, and more opportunities for growth and for more satisfactory relationships with others, to say nothing about increased competence. On the other hand, if I choose to do any of the others I can take responsibility for the consequences and accept what pain comes from that."[20]

Your birth pattern stimulates self-analysis and self-examination. If you have Trait Organic it does not tell you that you blame. It says, listen to yourself when you talk to others. Do you blame? The power traits ask if you "should" yourself and others. The intellectual traits Hypothetic and Empiric ask you if your mind is working overtime creating needless "what ifs" and worry.

To study birth patterns is to choose. Birth patterns can be convenient labels, excuses, and justifications that close our minds. Our own birth patterns can be one more thing to blame for our failures, distract from our problems, placate our relationships and compute our fates. If we level with ourselves, we expect nothing more from our birth patterns than the impetus toward self-discovery that encourages us to help ourselves.

Epilogue

We live in times of tremendous change. We are confronted with big government, big business, big deficits and big spending daily. Stardom is now so common that we have invented superstardom. Never before has the individual seemed quite so small; never before has the scope and impact of the single human life appeared so insignificant. Yet each of us wants to feel important. Each of us needs the dignity inherent in our own uniqueness. Birth Pattern Psychology speaks to the heart of this achingly human dilemma. It is impossible to study the patterns of individual personalities without feeling awe for the utter distinctiveness, the precious and unparalleled originality and the total irreplaceability of each human being.

If ever people needed to appreciate their own singularity, they need to do so now. We send astronauts to walk on the moon but we still kill each other daily. We perform delicate surgical operations to extend life but we still brutalize our own children. We live in the first age when we human beings possess the means to destroy not only our own species but every other living thing on the face of this planet. Clearly our most pressing problems and our greatest challenges lie within the sphere of ourselves.

Our private birth patterns mirror our uniqueness. They show us that our lives have meaning but they do not tell us the meaning of life. That would cripple our growth. Our birth patterns do not tell us who will love us. Instead, they encourage self-acceptance, which in turn encourages us to love. When we study our own birth patterns, we learn to trust in the wisdom of our own beings. There can be no greater security than this. When we extend our interest in personality patterns to include the birth patterns of others, we find the endless stimulation of our shared humanity and the excitement of ever-fresh human discovery.

If birth pattern study teaches us anything, it teaches us tolerance for those unlike ourselves. It helps us realize that each person's self-actualization benefits us all. We need the Continuous people who guard our heritage. Their sense of history keeps us from repeating our mistakes. We need the

Spontaneous people, the keepers of the moment whose enthusiasm brightens our todays. We need the Organics and their willingness to accept responsibilities gladly. Their power elevates us beyond anarchy and chaos. We need the Panoramics, the peace-makers. Their democratic spirits feed our sense of community and spiritual unity. We need the Hypothetics whose dreams and innovative insights challenge us. We need the Empirics who seize innovation and use it to solve real problems in a real world.

Every day, as I sit at my typewriter, an elderly man and woman walk past my study window. They always walk arm in arm. Their individual steps are precisely attuned yet their pace is clearly without effort or intent. They simply walk with that unconscious harmony bred from years of familiarity. Neither leads and neither follows. Both dress in the dark, unpretentious colors worn by people who have nothing to prove. They are content simply to be and to be together. If I could have one wish for this book, I would wish that it has in some way brought you nearer to the inner harmony this couple represents to me.

Appendix A: Birth Data

Chapter 1: Measuring Basic Needs

Birth Pattern #1 (pp. 14, 15). Alan Alda: January 28, 1936. 5:07 A.M., EST. New York, New York, 73W57, 40N45. Source: Lois Rodden, *The American Book of Charts* (San Diego, Calif.: Astro Computing Services, 1980), data from a personal friend.

Birth Pattern #2 (pp. 16, 17). John Dillinger: June 22, 1903. 7:05 A.M., CST. Mooresville, Indiana, 86W09, 39N46. Source: Lois Rodden, *The American Book of Charts,* cites Llewellyn George.

Birth Pattern #3 (p. 23). Ralph Nader: February 27, 1934. 4:52 A.M., EST. Winsted, Connecticut, 73W04, 41N55. Source: Marc Penfield, *2001: The Penfield Collection* (Seattle, Washington: Vulcan Books, 1979), cites birth certificate. Biographical reference: Victor, Mildred and Ted George Goertzel, *300 Eminent Personalities* (San Francisco: Jossey-Bass, Inc., Publishers, 1978).

Birth Pattern #4 (p. 23). J. Edgar Hoover: January 1, 1895. 7:00 A.M., EST. Washington, D.C., 77W02, 38N54. Source: Lois Rodden, *The American Book of Charts,* data from him in a letter. Biographical reference: Jay Robert Nash, *Citizen Hoover* (Chicago: Nelson-Hall, 1972).

Birth Pattern #5 (p. 25). Adelle Davis: February 25, 1904. 3:00 A.M., CST. Union Township, Indiana, 87W31, 39N54. Data and biographical reference from Lois Rodden, *Profiles of Women* (Tempe, Arizona: AFA, Inc., 1979), cites data from Davis in a 1971 *Life* magazine interview. Additional matter from Davis's introduction to *Let's Eat Right to Keep Fit* (New York: Harcourt Brace Jovanovich, Inc., 1970).

Birth Pattern #6 (p. 25). Angela Davis: January 26, 1944. 12:30 P.M., CDT. Goodwater, Alabama, 86W03, 33N04. Source: Lois Rodden, *Profiles of Women,* cites birth certificate. Biographical reference: Victor, Mildred and Ted George Goertzel, *300 Eminent Personalities.*

Birth Pattern #7 (p. 28). Farrah Fawcett: February 2, 1947. 3:10 P.M., CST. Corpus Christi, Texas, 97W24, 27N47. Source: Lois Rodden, *Profiles of Women,* cites birth certificate. Biographical reference: *Current Biography,* 1978.

Birth Pattern #8 (p.28). Colette: January 28, 1873. 10:00 P.M., LMT. St. Sauveur-en-Puisaye, France, 3E10, 47N35. Source: Lois Rodden, *Profiles of Women,* cites Gauquelin's data from birth records. Biographical reference: Victor and Mildred George Goertzel, *Cradles of Eminence* (Toronto: Little, Brown and Co., 1962).

Birth Pattern #9 (p. 31). Sam Peckinpah: February 21, 1925. 2:15 P.M., PST. Fresno, California, 119W47, 36N44. Source: *Contemporary Sidereal Horoscopes* compiled by Katherine Clark, et al. (Sidereal Research Publications, 1976), birth certificate. Biographical reference: *Current Biography,* 1973.

Birth Pattern #10 (p. 31). John F. Kennedy: May 29, 1917. 3:15 P.M., EST. Brookline, Massachusetts, 71W08, 42N20. Source: Marc Penfield, *2001: The Penfield Collection.* Biographical reference: Victor, Mildred and Ted George Goertzel, *300 Eminent Personalities.* Marcia Moore and Mark Douglas, *Astrology in Action* (York Harbor, Maine: Arcane Publications, 1970).

Birth Pattern #11 (p. 34). Anais Nin: February 21, 1903. 8:30 P.M., Paris Time. Paris, France, 2E20, 48N52. Source: Lois Rodden, *Profiles of Women,* cites her friend Henry Miller. Biographical reference: Victor, Mildred and Ted George Goertzel, *300 Eminent Personalities..*

Birth Pattern #12 (p. 34). Ethel Skakel Kennedy: April 11, 1928. 3:30 A.M., CST. Chicago, Illinois, 87W39, 41N50. Source: Marc Penfield, *2001: The Penfield Collection,* cites birth certificate. Biographical reference: Victor, Mildred and Ted George Goertzel, *300 Eminent Personalities.*

Birth Pattern #13 (p. 36). John Anderson: February 15, 1922. 8:55 P.M., CST. Rockford, Illinois, 89W06, 42N16. Source: Michel and Francoise Gauquelin, *The Gauquelin Book of American Charts* (San Diego, Calif.: Astro Computing Services, 1982) cites birth records. Biographical reference: Peter Goldman, et al., "John Anderson: The Wild Card," *Newsweek,* June 9, 1980: 28–38.

Birth Pattern #14 (pp. 36, 48). George Herman "Babe" Ruth: February 6, 1895. 1:45 P.M., EST. Baltimore, Maryland, 76W37, 39N19. Source: Marc Penfield, *2001: The Penfield Collection,* cites birth certificate. Biographical reference: *Current Biography,* 1944.

Birth Pattern #15 (p. 39). Edward Kennedy: February 22, 1932. 3:58 A.M., EST. Boston, Massachusetts, 71W04, 42N22. Source: Marc Penfield, *2001: The Penfield Collection,* cites birth certificate. Biographical reference: Victor, Mildred and Ted George Goertzel, *300 Eminent Personalities.*

Birth Pattern #16 (p. 39). Billy Carter: March 29, 1937. 12:30 A.M., CST. Americus, Georgia, 84W13, 32N03. Source: Lois Rodden, *The American Book of Charts,* cites birth certificate. Biographical reference: Ruth Carter Stapleton, *Brother Billy* (New York: Harper and Row, Publishers, 1978).

Birth Pattern #17 (p. 41). Barbara Stanwyck: July 16, 1907. 8:55 A.M., EST. Brooklyn, New York, 73W56, 40N38. Source: Lois Rodden, *Profiles of Women,* cites Church of Light data files. Biographical reference: Ella Smith, *Starring Miss Barbara Stanwyck* (New York: Crown Publishers, Inc., 1974).

Birth Pattern #18 (p. 41). Eva Braun: February 6, 1912. 12:30 A.M., MET. Munich, Germany, 11E33, 48N09. Source: Lois Rodden, *Profiles of Women,* cites birth records. Biographical reference: Glenn B. Infield, *The Private Lives of Eva and Adolf* (New York: Grosset and Dunlap, 1974).

Chapter 2: The Hierarchy of Needs

Birth Pattern #19 (p. 51). Charles "Tex" Watson: December 2, 1945. 9:15 P.M., CST. McKinney, Texas, 96W36, 33N11. Source: Marc Penfield, *2001: The Penfield Collection,* cites birth certificate. Biographical reference: Charles Watson and Ray Hoekstra, *Will You Die For Me?* (New Jersey: Fleming H. Revell Company, 1978).

Birth Pattern #20 (pp. 52, 123). Janis Joplin: January 19, 1943. 9:45 A.M., CWT, Port Arthur, Texas, 93W56, 29N54. Source: Lois Rodden, *Profiles of Women,* cites birth certificate. Biographical reference: Victor, Mildred and Ted George Goertzel, *300 Eminent Personalities.* Myra Friedman, *Buried Alive, The Biography of Janis Joplin.* (New York: William Morrow and Co., 1973).

Chapter 3: Measuring Temperament Types
and
Chapter 4: Measuring Temperament Traits

Barbra Streisand (pp. 58, 72): April 24, 1942. 5:04 A.M., EWT. Brooklyn, New York, 73W56, 40N38. Source: Lois Rodden, *Profiles of Women.* Biographical reference: *Playboy* interview, October 1977. David Dachs, *Encyclopedia of Pop/Rock,* (New York: Scholastic Book Services, 1972).

Judy Garland (pp. 58, 73): June 10, 1922. 6:00 A.M., CST. Grand Rapids, Mn., 93W31, 47N14. Source: Lois Rodden, *Profiles of Women,* cites birth certificate. Biographical reference: Mel Torme, *The Other Side of the Rainbow,* (New York: William Morrow and Co., 1970).

Martin Luther (pp. 58, 74): November 19, 1483 NS. 11:00 P.M., LMT. Eisleben, Germany, 11E32, 51N32. Source: Lois Rodden, *The American Book of Charts*. Biographical reference: Hans J. Hillerbrand, ed., *The Reformation* (New York: Harper and Row, Publishers, 1964).

Johann Wolfgang von Goethe (pp. 58, 75): August 28, 1749 NS. 12:00 N. (Noon) LMT. Frankfort-am-Main, Germany, 8E41, 50N07. Source: Lois Rodden, *The American Book of Charts,* cites Goethe's autobiography: "born mid-day when the clock struck 12:00." Biographical reference: Rodden and J.O. Thorne, editor, *Chambers Biographical Dictionary,* New Edition, (New York: St. Martin's Press, 1961).

Chapter 5: Measuring Behavior

Birth Pattern #21 (pp. 105, 106). Jim Jones: May 13, 1931. 10:00 P.M., CST. Lynn, Indiana, 84W56, 40N03. Source: Rodden, *The American Book of Charts,* same data in *Horoscope* which cites birth certificate. Biographical reference: Tim Reiterman, *Raven,* (New York: E.P. Dutton, Inc., 1982).

Birth Pattern #22 (p. 119). Zelda Sayre Fitzgerald: July 24, 1900. 5:40 A.M., CST. Montgomery, Alabama, 86W19, 32N23. Source: Lois Rodden, *Profiles of Women,* cites the family Bible. Biographical reference: Howard Greenfield, *F. Scott Fitzgerald,* (New York: Crown Publishers, Inc., 1977).

Birth Pattern #23 (p. 119). F. Scott Fitzgerald: September 24, 1896. 3:30 P.M., LMT. St. Paul, Minn., 93W06, 44N57. Source: Lois Rodden, *The American Book of Charts*. Same data cited in Greenfield's biography: *F. Scott Fitzgerald.*

Birth Pattern #24 (p. 121). Mary Baker Eddy: July 16, 1821. 5:38 P.M., LMT. Bow, N.H., 71W19, 44N21. Source: Lois Rodden, *Profiles of Women*. Alternative data are offered for this birth. Biographical reference: Victor and Mildred George Goertzel, *Cradles of Eminence.*

Birth Pattern #25 (p. 121). Charles Lindbergh: February 4, 1902. 2:30 A.M., CST. Detroit, Mich., 83W03, 42N20. Source: Lois Rodden, *The American Book of Charts*. Alternative data are offered for this birth. Biographical reference: Victor and Mildred George Goertzel, *Cradles of Eminence.*

Birth Pattern #26 (p. 123, 134, 152). Carl Jung: see References, Chapter 6.

Chapter 6: Personality in Synthesis

Birth Pattern #27 (p. 140, 152). Sigmund Freud: see References, Chapter 6.

Chapter 7: Masks People Wear

Birth Pattern #28 (p. 157). Johnny Carson: October 23, 1925. 7:15 A.M., CST. Corning, Iowa, 94W44, 40N59. Source: Lois Rodden, *The American Book of Charts,* cites birth certificate. Biographical reference: Media.

Birth Pattern #29 (p. 157). Jimmy Carter: October 1, 1924. 7:00 A.M., CST. Plains, Ga., 84W24, 32N02. Source: Marc Penfield, *2001: The Penfield Collection.* Biographical reference: G. Barry Golson, editor, *The Playboy Interview,* (New York: Playboy Press, 1981).

Birth Pattern #30 (p. 161). Muhammad Ali: January 17, 1942. 6:35 P.M., CST. Louisville, Ky., 85W46, 38N15. Source: Lois Rodden, *The American Book of Charts,* cites birth certificate. Biographical reference: G. Barry Golson, editor, *The Playboy Interview.*

Birth Pattern #31 (pp. 165, 166). Susan Atkins: May 7, 1948. 1:03 A.M., PDT. San Gabriel, Calif., 118W06, 34N06. Source: Marc Penfield, *2001: The Penfield Collection,* cites birth certificate. Biographical reference: Vincent Bugliosi, *Helter Skelter* (New York: W.W. Norton Co., Inc., 1974).

Birth Pattern #32 (pp. 165, 166). Sharon Tate: January 24, 1943. 5:45 P.M., CWT. Dallas, Texas, 96W49, 32N47. Source: Marc Penfield, *2001: The Penfield Collection.* Biographical reference: Vincent Bugliosi, *Helter Skelter.*

Birth Pattern #33 (p. 170). John Lennon: October 9, 1940. 7:00 A.M., GWT. Liverpool, England, 2W58, 53N25. Source: Robert Jansky, *Horoscopes: Here and Now,* (Van Nuys, Calif.: Astro-Analytics Publications, 1975). Lennon's chart is much in dispute. Biographical reference: G. Barry Golson, editor, *The Playboy Interviews with John Lennon and Yoko Ono,* (New York: Playboy Press, 1981).

Appendix B: How to Order a Birth Chart

Natal calculations for preparing Birth Pattern charts may be ordered by telephone or by mail from Para Research, Inc. The fee is $3.00 per chart. Order forms are available upon request. Charts will be done using the Placidus system appropriate to the techniques in this book.

Para Research, Inc.
Department BP
Gloucester, MA 01930
617-283-3438

You must include the following information for each birth chart ordered:

1. Date of birth. Month, day and year.

2. Place of birth. City, county and state. As many states include more than one city of the same name, it is best to include the county of birth.

3. Time of birth. Hour, minutes, A.M. or P.M.. Time presents the most difficulty yet an accurate birth time is essential. Without it, the birth chart is meaningless. The hospital record or baby book is the best record. At the time of birth, at least in more recent decades, a card is filled out with the baby's length, weight, sex and time of birth. The card is given to the family. Many people put this card in the baby book or register the information in the baby book.

The birth certificate is also a good source for the birth time providing that it is the long form birth certificate. A short form birth certificate is often used for passport purposes and other purposes of identification. If you do not have your birth certificate, you can get it from the department of vital statistics in the state of your birth. You must specifically request that the birth certificate include the time of birth to insure that you will, in fact, get the birth time.

All other sources of birth time are questionable. Mother's memory tends to be a very poor source and should be resorted to only if other avenues prove fruitless. Family documents such as the family Bible sometimes contain birth times.

Notes

Introduction
1. Philadelphia: W. B. Saunders Company, *Theories of Psychopathology and Personality, Essays and Critiques,* Second Edition, 1973, p. 495.

Chapter 1
2. Two biographical works provided much of the basic research background for this volume. The Goertzel childhood studies focus on parent/child interactions in the development of achieving adults. *Cradles of Eminence* by Victor and Mildred George Goertzel (Toronto: Little, Brown and Co., 1961) and *300 Eminent Personalities,* coauthored by Ted George Goertzel, (San Francisco: Jossey-Bass, Inc., Publishers, 1978) assess the impact of various parenting attitudes. The specific biographical references and birth data for each example birth pattern appear in Appendix A.
3. New York: W.W. Norton and Co., *Childhood and Society,* Second Edition, 1963, p. 70.

Chapter 2
4. From *Will You Die For Me?* by Charles Watson, copyright © 1978 by Ray Hoekstra. Published by Fleming H. Revell Company. Used by permission, p. 50.

Chapter 3
5. New York: Holt, Rinehart and Winston, *Pattern and Growth in Personality,* 1961, p. 34.

Chapter 4
6. *Ibid.,* p. 347.
7. New York: Steckert, 1928.
8. New York: Pocket Books, *The Four-Color Person,* 1977.
9. New York: E.P. Dutton and Co., Inc., 1977.

Chapter 7
10. New York: Anchor Books, 1973, p. 210.
11. *Ibid.*

12. *Mysterium Coniunctionis,* CW 14, par. 778.

13. New York: Charles Scribner's Sons, Book III, Chapter 13, 1933.

Chapter 8

14. New York: Vintage Books, *Ego, Hunger and Aggression,* 1969.

15. New York: Samuel Weiser, Inc., *Relating,* 1978, pp. 141–154.

16. New York: Plenum Press, 1977.

17. From *Gestalt Therapy* by Frederick Perls, M.D., Ph.D.; Ralph F. Hefferline, Ph.D.; Paul Goodman, Ph.D. Copyright © 1951, 1979 by Frederick Perls, Ralph F. Hefferline, Paul Goodman. Used by permission of Julian Press, a division of Crown Publishers, Inc.

18. *Ibid.*

19. New York: Avon Books, *Ghosts* by Henrik Ibsen, authoritative text edition, translated by Kai Jurgensen and Robert Schenkkan, 1965, pp. 67–68.

Chapter 9

20. Palo Alto, Calif.: Science and Behavior Books, Inc., *Peoplemaking,* Virginia Satir, 1972, p. 89. Reprinted by permission of the author and publisher.

References

Introduction

Agresti, Alan and Barbara Finlay Agresti. *Statistical Methods for the Social Sciences*. San Francisco: Dellen Publishing Company, 1979.

Holt, Robert R. *Assessing Personality*. New York: Harcourt Brace Jovanovich, Inc., 1969.

Millon, Theodore, ed. *Theories of Psychopathology and Personality, Essays and Critiques,* Second Edition. Philadelphia: W. B. Saunders Company, 1973.

Wilhelm, Richard. Cary F. Baynes, trans. *The I Ching, or Book of Changes,* Third Edition. Bollingen Series XIX. Princeton, N.J.: Princeton University Press, 1967.

Zukav, Gary. *The Dancing Wu Li Masters, An Overview of the New Physics.* New York: William Morrow and Company, Inc., 1979.

Part One: General References

Allport, Gordon. *Pattern and Growth in Personality*. New York: Holt, Rinehart and Winston, 1961.

Hampden-Turner, Charles. *Maps of the Mind*. New York: Macmillan Publishing Co., Inc., 1981.

Maddi, Salvatore R. *Personality Theories, A Comparative Analysis,* Revised Edition. Homewood, Ill.: The Dorsey Press, 1972.

Sahakian, William S., ed. *Psychology of Personality: Readings in Theory,* Third Edition. Chicago: Rand McNally College Publishing Company, 1977.

Schultz, Duane. *Theories of Personality*. Monterey, Calif.: Brooks/Cole Publishing Company, 1976.

Chapter 1

Biehler, Robert F. *Child Development: An Introduction*. Boston: Houghton Mifflin Co., 1976.

Deci, Edward L. *Intrinsic Motivation*. New York: Plenum Press, 1975.

Erikson, Erik H. *Childhood and Society,* Second Edition. New York: W.W. Norton and Co., 1963.

———*Identity, Youth and Crisis.* New York: W.W. Norton and Co., 1968.

Gesell, Arnold, et al. *Infant and Child in the Culture of Today,* revised edition. New York: Harper and Row, 1974.

Janov, Arthur. *The Primal Scream.* New York: G.P. Putnam's Sons, 1970.

Lamb, Michael E., ed. *The Role of the Father in Child Development.* New York: John Wiley and Sons, 1976.

Lorenz, Konrad and Paul Leyhausen. *Motivation of Human and Animal Behavior, An Ethological View,* translated by B.A. Tonkin. New York: Van Nostrand Reinhold Co., 1973.

Montagu, Ashley, ed. *The Practice of Love.* New York: Prentice Hall, Inc., 1975.

Perls, Frederick with Ralph F. Hefferline and Paul Goodman. *Gestalt Therapy.* New York: Dell Publishing Co., 1951.

Pringle, Mia Kellmer. *The Needs of Children.* New York: Schocken Books, 1975.

Sebald, Hans. *Momism, The Silent Disease of America.* Chicago: Nelson Hall, 1976.

Snyder, C.R. and Howard L. Fromkin. *Uniqueness, The Human Pursuit of Difference.* New York: Plenum Press, 1980.

Stern, Daniel. *The First Relationship.* Cambridge, Mass.: The Harvard University Press, 1977.

Webster, Murray Jr. and Barbara Sobieszek. *Sources of Self-Evaluation, a formal theory of significant others and social influence.* New York: John Wiley and Sons, 1974.

White, Robert W. *The Enterprise of Living, Growth and Organization in Personality.* New York: Holt, Rinehart and Winston, Inc., 1972.

Chapter 2

Maslow, Abraham. *Motivation and Personality.* New York: Harper and Row, 1954.

Phares, E. Jerry. *Locus of Control.* Morristown, N.J.: General Learning Press, 1976.

Chapter 4

Cattell, Raymond B. *Description and Measurement of Personality.* New York: World Book Company, 1946.

Edwards, Paul, ed. *The Encyclopedia of Philosophy,* in eight volumes. New York: Macmillan Publishing Co., Inc., and The Free Press, 1967.

Eysenck, Hans Jurgen, Sybil B.G. Eysenck, et al. *Personality Structure and Measurement,* first edition. San Diego, Calif.: R.R. Knapp, 1969.

Grey, William, Frederick J. Duhl and Nicolas D. Rizzo, eds. *General Systems Theory and Psychiatry.* Boston: Little, Brown and Company, 1969.

Guilford, Joan S., Wayne S. Zimmerman and J.P. Guilford. *The Guilford-Zimmerman Temperament Survey Handbook.* San Diego, Calif.: EdITS publishers, 1976.

Luscher, Max. *The Four-Color Person.* New York: Pocket Books, 1977.

Malone, Michael. *Psychetypes, A New Way of Exploring Personality.* New York: E.P. Dutton and Co., Inc., 1977.

Millon, Theodore, ed. *Theories of Psychopathology and Personality, Essays and Critiques,* Second Edition. Philadelphia: W.B. Saunders Company, 1973.

———*Disorders of Personality, DSM III: AXIS II.* New York: John Wiley and Sons, 1981.

Chapter 5

Berger, Peter L. and Thomas Luckmann. *The Social Construction of Reality.* Garden City, N.Y.: Doubleday and Co., 1969.

Erikson, Erik H. *Childhood and Society,* Second Edition. New York: W.W. Norton and Co., 1963.

———*Identity, Youth and Crisis.* New York: W.W. Norton and Co., 1968.

Guilford, Joan S., Wayne S. Zimmerman and J.P. Guilford. *The Guilford-Zimmerman Temperament Survey Handbook.* San Diego, Calif.: EdITS publishers, 1976.

Horney, Karen. *Our Inner Conflicts.* New York: W.W. Norton and Co., 1945.

Janov, Arthur. *The Anatomy of Mental Illness.* New York: Berkley Medallion Books, 1971.

———with E. Michael Holden, *Primal Man, The New Consciousness.* New York: Thomas Y. Crowell Co., 1975.

Koffka, Kurt. *Principles of Gestalt Psychology,* revised edition. New York: Harbinger Books, 1963.

Sagan, Carl. *The Dragons of Eden.* New York: Ballantine Books, 1977.

Selye, Hans. *Stress without Distress.* New York: Signet, 1975.

Chapter 6

Carl Jung: Data and References

Birth Pattern #26. Carl Gustav Jung. July 26, 1875. 7:20 P.M., Berne Local Time. Kesswil, Switzerland, 9E19, 47N36. Source: Jung's daughter, cited by Rodden, *The American Book of Charts.* Jung's exact birth data is very much in dispute.

Brome, Vincent. *Jung.* New York: Atheneum, 1978.

Campbell, Joseph, ed. *The Portable Jung.* New York: The Viking Press, Inc., 1971.

Jung, Carl. *Aion,* Vol. 9 of the Collected Works, second edition, Bollingen Series XX. Princeton, N.J.: Princeton University Press, 1959.

Sahakian, William S., ed. *Psychology of Personality,* third edition, Chapter 2, "Carl Jung, Personality Theory from the Standpoint of Analytical Psychology," Chicago: Rand McNally College Publishing Company, 1977.

Schultz, Duane. *Theories of Personality.* Ch. 7, "Carl Jung: Analytical Psychology." Monterey, Calif: Brooks/Cole Publishing Company, 1976.

Sigmund Freud: Data and References

Birth Pattern #27. Sigmund Freud. May 6, 1856. 6:30 P.M. LMT. Frieberg, Moravia, 18E09, 49N38. Frieberg is now Pribor, Czechoslovakia. Jacob Freud's diary reads: "My son, Shlomo Sigismund, may he live, was born on Tuesday, Rosh Hodesh Iyar (5)616, 6:30 PM on May 6, (1)856...."

Brome, Vincent. *Freud and his Early Circle.* New York: William Morrow and Company, Inc., 1968.

Clark, Ronald W. *Freud, The Man and the Cause.* New York: Random House, Inc., 1980.

Fodor, Nandor and Frank Gaynor, eds. *Freud, Dictionary of Psychoanalysis.* Greenwich, Conn.: Fawcett Publications, Inc., 1963.

Freud, Sigmund. *A General Introduction to Psychoanalysis.* New York: Permabooks, 1953.

McGuire, William, ed. *The Freud/Jung Letters,* Bollingen series XCIV. Princeton, N.J.: Princeton University Press, 1974.

Sahakian. (*op. cit.*) Ch. 1 "Sigmund Freud, Psychoanalytic Theory of Personality."

Schultz. (*op. cit.*) Ch. 2 "Sigmund Freud, Psychoanalysis."

Chapter 7

Campbell, Joseph, ed. *The Portable Jung.* New York: The Viking Press, Inc., 1971.

Horney, Karen. *Our Inner Conflicts.* New York: W.W. Norton and Co., 1945.

———*Self-Analysis.* New York: W.W. Norton and Co., 1942.

Maddi, Salvatore R. *Personality Theories, A Comparative Analysis,* revised edition. Homewood, Ill.: The Dorsey Press, 1972.

Sahakian, William S., ed. *Psychology of Personality: Readings in Theory.* Ch. 6 "Harry Stack Sullivan. The Interpersonal Theory." Chicago: Rand McNally College Publishing Co., 1976.

Singer, June. *Boundaries of the Soul.* New York: Anchor Books, 1973.

Chapter 8

Bowlby, John. *Attachment and Loss,* two volumes. New York: Basic Books, 1969.

References

Brehm, Sharon S. and Jack W. Brehm. *Psychological Reactance, A Theory of Freedom and Control.* New York: Academic Press, 1981.

Greene, Liz. *Relating.* New York: Samuel Weiser, Inc., 1977.

Janis, Irving L. *Stress and Frustration.* New York: Harcourt, Brace, Jovanovich, Inc., 1971.

Maddi, Salvatore R. *Personality Theories, A Comparative Analysis,* revised edition. Homewood, Ill.: The Dorsey Press, 1972.

Mahl, George I. *Psychological Conflict and Defense,* second edition. New York: Harcourt, Brace, Jovanovich, Inc., 1971.

Neimark, Maria. *Personality Orientation,* translators: Jean Ispa, Alice Stone, Alexander Nahimovsky. Englewood Cliffs, N.J.: Educational Technology Publications, 1976.

Perls, Frederick. *Ego, Hunger and Aggression,* revised edition. New York: Vintage Books, 1969.

——— with Ralph F. Hefferline and Paul Goodman. *Gestalt Therapy.* New York: Dell Publishing Co., 1951.

Schultz, Duane. *Theories of Personality.* Ch. 6 "Harry Stack Sullivan: The Interpersonal Theory" and Ch. 7 "Carl Jung: Analytical Psychology." Monterey, Calif.: Brooks/Cole Publishing Company, 1976.

Wishnie, Howard. *The Impulsive Personality.* New York: Plenum Press, 1977.

Chapter 9

Maccoby, Eleanor E. *Social Development: psychological growth and the parent-child relationship.* New York: Harcourt, Brace, Jovanovich, 1980.

———with Carol Nagy Jacklin. *The Psychology of Sex Differences.* Stanford, Calif.: Stanford University Press, 1975.

Rogers, Carl. *Client-Centered Therapy.* Boston: Houghton Mifflin, 1951.

Satir, Virginia. *Peoplemaking.* Palo Alto, Calif.: Science and Behavior Books, Inc., 1972.

The following pages feature more fine titles from:

PARA RESEARCH, INC.

Do write or give us a call to receive our FREE catalog listing of all
our titles.

To Order Books: Send purchase price plus seventy-five cents postage and
handling for each book to: Para Research, Inc., Dept. BPP, 85 Eastern Avenue,
Gloucester, MA 01930.

If you have MasterCard or Visa you may order directly by telephone.
Call us at (617) 283-3438 between 8:30 and 5:00 Eastern time, Monday
through Friday.

Prices are subject to change without notice.

Books from Para Research

PLANETS IN ASPECT: Understanding Your Inner Dynamics
by Robert Pelletier

Explores aspects, the planetary relationships that describe our individual energy patterns, and how we can integrate them into our lives. Undoubtedly the most thorough in-depth study of planetary aspects ever published. Every major aspect—conjunction, sextile, square, trine, opposition and inconjunct—is covered: 314 aspects in all. Paper, $16.95

PLANETS IN HOUSES: Experiencing Your Environment
by Robert Pelletier

Brings the ancient art of natal horoscope interpretation into a new era of accuracy, concreteness and richness of detail. Pelletier delineates the meaning of each planet as derived by counting from each of the twelve houses and in relation to the other houses with which it forms trines, sextiles, squares and oppositions, inconjuncts and semisextiles. Seventeen different house relationships delineated for each planet in each house, 2184 delineations in all. Paper, $16.95

PLANETS IN LOVE: Exploring Your Emotional and Sexual Needs
by John Townley

The first astrology book to take an unabashed look at human sexuality and the different kinds of relationships that people form to meet their various emotional and sexual needs. An intimate astrological analysis of sex and love, with 550 interpretations of each planet in every possible sign, house and aspect. Discusses sexual behavior according to mental, emotional and spiritual areas of development. Paper, $16.95

PLANETS IN TRANSIT: Life Cycles for Living
by Robert Hand

A psychological approach to astrological prediction. Delineations of the Sun, Moon and each planet transiting each natal house and forming each aspect to the natal Sun, Moon, planets, Ascendant and Midheaven. The definitive book on transits. Includes introductory chapters on the theory and applications of transits. Paper, $22.95

PLANETS IN YOUTH: Patterns of Early Development
by Robert Hand

A major astrological thinker looks at children and childhood. Parents can use it to help their children cope with the complexities of growing up, and readers of all ages can use it to understand themselves and their own patterns of early development. Introductory chapters discuss parent-child relationships and planetary energies in children's charts. All important horoscope factors delineated stressing possibilities rather than certainties. Paper, $16.95

PLANETS IN COMPOSITE: Analyzing Human Relationships
by Robert Hand

The definitive work on the astrology of human relationships. Explains the technique of the composite chart, combining two individuals' charts to create a third chart of the relationship itself, and how to interpret it. Case studies plus twelve chapters of delineations of composite Sun, Moon and planets in all houses and major aspects. Paper, $16.95

HOROSCOPE SYMBOLS
by Robert Hand

This book, representing four years of writing and twenty years of research, presents an in-depth reexamination of astrology's basic symbols. Core meanings are analyzed in detail so that the astrologer can see why traditional meaning and significance have been attributed to each astrological symbol. In many cases, these core meanings also establish new interpretations as the author develops the substance and symbolism of images which astrologers have employed for centuries. Paper, $16.95

DEVELOP YOUR PSYCHIC SKILLS
by Enid Hoffman

The author's long experience with psychic phenomena is integrated with the practical implications of recent brain research showing how we all have psychic abilities waiting to be developed. The book includes exercises for training both perceptive and projective skills, for clearing obstructing beliefs, for past life recall and many more experiences now available to all who would develop their potential psychic powers. The author says, 'I have always felt it important for my students to understand how natural and human a process it is to develop one's psychic skills." She also makes it a lot of fun. Paper, $8.95

HUNA: A BEGINNER'S GUIDE
Revised Edition
by Enid Hoffman

Centuries ago, the Kahuna, the ancient Hawaiian miracle workers, discovered the fundamental pattern of energy-flow in the universe. Their secrets of psychic and intra-psychic communication, refined and enriched by modern scientific research, are now revealed in this practical, readable book. 220 pages, paper, $9.95

NUMEROLOGY AND THE DIVINE TRIANGLE
by Faith Javane & Dusty Bunker

At last a truly comprehensive and authoritative text on numerology! Part I is a complete introduction to esoteric numerology and includes a section on the life of Edgar Cayce as a case study of numerology in action. Part II includes extensive delineations of each of the numbers 1 to 78 and, for the first time in book form, a synthesis of numerology, astrology and the Tarot. Each of the Tarot cards is illustrated. *Numerology and the Divine Triangle* is number one in its field, the book to which all books on the subject will be compared from now on. Paper, $11.95